Configuration Management

TRENDS IN SOFTWARE

User Interface Software
ed. Len Bass and Prasun Dewan

Configuration Management
ed. Walter Tichy

In Preparation:

Software Fault Tolerance
ed. Michael Lyu

Configuration Management

Edited by

Walter F Tichy
University of Karlsruhe, Germany

JOHN WILEY & SONS
Chichester · New York · Brisbane · Toronto · Singapore

Baffins Lane, Chichester
West Sussex PO19 1UD, England

Telephone: **National** Chichester (01243) 779777
International +44 1243 779777

Reprinted June 1995

Other Wiley Editorial Offices

John Wiley & Sons, Inc., 605 Third Avenue,
New York, NY 10158-0012, USA

Jacaranda Wiley Ltd, 33 Park Road, Milton,
Queensland 4064, Australia

John Wiley & Sons (Canada) Ltd, 22 Worcester Road,
Rexdale, Ontario M9W 1L1, Canada

John Wiley & Sons (SEA) Pte Ltd, 37 Jalan Pemimpin #05-04,
Block B, Union Industrial Building, Singapore 2057

Library of Congress Cataloging-in-Publication Data

Configuration management / edited by Walter F. Tichy.
p. cm.—(Trends in software)
Includes bibliographical references.
ISBN 0-471-94245-6
1. Software configuration management. I. Tichy, Walter F.
II. Series.
QA76.76.C69C67 1994
005.1–dc20 94–23211
CIP

British Library Cataloguing in Publication Data

A catalogue record for this book is available from the British Library

ISBN 0 471 94245-6

Produced from camera-ready copy supplied by the author
Printed and bound in Great Britain by Redwood Books, Trowbridge, Wilts

Contents

Series Editor's Preface vii

Preface ix

List of Authors xi

1 The CM Challenge: Configuration Management that Works 1
D. B. Leblang

1.1 The CM Challenge 2
1.2 SCM Fundamentals 3
1.3 Repository Access 5
1.4 A Closer Look At ClearCase Transparency Access 7
1.5 Repositories in a Distributed Environment 9
1.6 Version Control 13
1.7 Environment Management 20
1.8 A Closer Look at ClearCase Environment Management 24
1.9 Build Management 29
1.10 A Closer Look at ClearCase Build Management 30
1.11 Process Control and Project Management 34
1.12 Conclusions 36
Acknowledgements 37
References 37

2 A Bi-Level Language for Software Process Modeling 39
G. E. Kaiser, S. Popovich and I. Z. Ben-Shaul

2.1 Introduction 39
2.2 Motivation 41
2.3 Background 43
2.4 ASL Syntax and Semantics 47
2.5 ASL Enaction Model 51
2.6 Implementation Details 57
2.7 ASL Example 59
2.8 Related Work 62

2.9 Contributions 68
Acknowledgements 69
References 69

3 Variants: Keeping Things Together and Telling Them Apart **73**
A. Mohler

3.1 Introduction 73
3.2 Representation of Software Variants 76
3.3 The State of the Art and Practice in Variant Management 82
3.4 Variant Management with Shape 88
3.5 Conclusion 93
3.6 Shapetools Status 95
Acknowledgement 95
References

4 The Adele Configuration Manager **99**
J. Estublier and R. Casallas

4.1 Introduction 99
4.2 Modeling Products and Configurations 100
4.3 Complex Objects and Configurations Models 102
4.4 Work Space Control 111
4.5 Process Support 121
4.6 Evaluation 128
4.7 Conclusion 130
References 130

5 n-DFS: The Multiple Dimensional File System **135**
G. Fowler, D. Korn and H. Rao

5.1 Introduction 135
5.2 n-DFS's Services 138
5.3 Architecture 143
5.4 Implementation 145
5.5 Evaluation 148
5.6 Discussion 151
5.7 Conclusion 152
References 152
Trademarks 154

Index **155**

Series Editor's Preface

During 1990, the twentieth anniversary of *Software Practice and Experience*, two special issues (one on UNIX Tools and the other on the X Window System) were published. Each issue contained a set of refereed papers related to a single topic; the issues appeared a short time (roughly nine months) after the authors were invited to submit them. The positive experience with the special issues resulted in *Trends in Software*, a fast turn-around serial that devotes each issue to a specific topic in the software field. As with the special issues of SPE, each *Trend* will be edited by an authority in the area.

By collecting together a comprehensive set of papers on a single topic, *Trends* makes it easy for readers to find a definitive overview of a given topic. By ensuring timely publication, *Trends* guarantees readers that the information presented captures the state of the art. The collection of papers will be of practical value to software designers, researchers, practitioners and users in that field.

Papers in each *Trend* are solicited by a guest editor who is responsible for soliciting them and ensuring that the selected papers span the topic. The guest editor then subjects each paper to the rigorous peer review expected in any archival journal. As much as possible, electronic communication (e.g. electronic mail) is used as the primary means of communication between the series editor, members of the editorial board, guest editor, authors, and referees. A style document and macro package is available to reduce the turn-around time by enabling authors to submit papers in camera-ready form. During the editorial process, papers are exchanged electronically in an immediately printable format.

We aim to produce three *Trends* each year. Topics to be covered in forthcoming issues include computer graphics, and configuration management.

The editorial board encourages readers to submit suggestions and comments. You may send them via electronic mail to bala@research.att.com or by postal mail to the address given below. Please clarify if a communication is intended for publication or not.

I would like to thank the editorial advisory board as well as the staff at John Wiley for their help in making *Trends* a reality.

Balachander Krishnamurthy
Room H2B-140
AT&T Bell Laboratories
600 Mountain Avenue
Murray Hill, NJ 07974
USA

Preface

Configuration management (CM) is the discipline of organizing and controlling evolving systems. For hardware systems, CM has been an established field since the 1950s. It was initially developed in the aerospace industry as an approach for guaranteeing reproducibility of spacecraft. The problem was that spacecraft underwent numerous, inadequately documented engineering changes during development. Moreover, the prototypes embodying the changes were usually expended during flight test. Consequently, neither accurate plans nor prototypes were available for replicating successful designs. Configuration management was thus born out of the need to track what designers and engineers developed during the course of a project.

Software Configuration Management (SCM) is the specialization of CM for software systems. Software systems, too, undergo numerous, usually inadequately documented changes. Though software prototypes are not necessarily expended, they nevertheless are an insufficient basis for further development, because of severe information loss during development and maintenance.

To prevent information loss, traditional CM mandates strict procedures for identification of parts and assemblies, for control and auditing of changes, and for status accounting. SCM goes beyond these procedures in several ways. First, since all software items are under computer control, many of the identification and control tasks can be automated and perfected. Furthermore, since software development tools run under computer control, they can be integrated directly with automatic SCM procedures. We are now beginning to see the results of this integration in terms of automated SCM systems that take away much of the tedium of traditional configuration management procedures, provide better and faster services, and reduce errors. As CAD/CAM and robotics bring manufacturing more and more under computer control, similar improvements can be expected in this area as well.

This issue of *Software Trends* provides a snapshot of the state-of-the-art of SCM. The first article, "Configuration Management That Works" by Leblang, presents ClearCase, a configuration management system integrated with software development tools. After discussing the major requirements for such systems, the author explains the technical ideas behind ClearCase and shows how it interacts with overall software development and maintenance processes.

While most work on SCM takes a product-centered view, the paper "A Bi-Level Language for Software Process Modeling" by Kaiser, Popovich, and Ben-Shaul approaches the problem from the process side. The process view is more encompassing than the product view, because it brings out dependencies among process steps, even if these dependencies do not directly manifest themselves in software components. The paper explores ways to specify software processes on two levels: the first and higher one for describing the "topology" of processes, i.e., the control flow and synchronization among steps, and the second one for describing constraints on the data and tools employed in individual process steps.

The third paper, "Variants: Keeping Things Together and Telling Them Apart" by Mahler, deals with variant control, an issue inadequately addressed by many current SCM tools. Variants are "small" variations in components and configurations of software systems, but become unwieldy if there is a large number of them. Mahler identifies the major reasons why variants arise and suggests a blend of mechanisms dealing with them through variant segregation, single source variation, aggregate variation, and derivation.

The next article by Estublier and Casallas, "The Adele Configuration Manager", presents a highly customizable and extensible SCM system that is based on three major components: a repository space manager, a work space manager, and a process manager. Software objects and their versions are stored in repository space; changes are performed on copies of software objects in work spaces; and the process manager controls the activities in all spaces. The article carefully discusses version and configuration modeling and the relationships between repository and work spaces.

A set of mechanisms that make SCM tools (and others) easier to build are discussed in the last paper, "n-DFS: The Multiple Dimensional File System" by Fowler, Korn, and Rao. The basic idea is to overload Unix file system operations. For instance, if n-DFS intercepts a request to open a file which is actually a version archive, it will regenerate a default version from data in the archive and present it to the application rather than the version archive. A number of additional services create the infrastructure for modeling SCM repository and work spaces.

In summary, the set of articles in this issue are an excellent sample of present work in SCM, spanning the entire spectrum from data to process modeling. They provide thorough reviews of present work, a good starting point for workers joining the field, and an outlook of what is to come.

Today, Software Configuration Management is an established sub-field of software engineering, and one that provides recognized benefits to software developers and managers. SCM tools have been in widespread use for decades, there is a SCM workshop series, a number of textbooks are available, and dozens of commercial tools are on the market. We can expect further progress in this field as the demand for quality software, and in particular, for quality changes of software, increases.

Walter F. Tichy
School of Informatics
University of Karlsruhe
D-76128 Karlsruhe
Germany

List of Authors

Israel Z Ben-Shaul
Department of Computer Science
Columbia University
New York
NY 10027
USA

David Korn
2B-102
AT & T Bell Laboratories
600 Mountain Avenue
Murray Hill
NJ 07974
USA
dgk@research.att.com

Jacky Estublier
L.G.I.
B.P. 53
38041 Grenoble Cedex 09
France
jacky@imag.fr

David Leblang
Atria Software
24 Prime Park Way
Natick
MA 01760
USA
leblang@atria.com

Glenn Fowler
2B-134
AT & T Bell Laboratories
600 Mountain Avenue
Murray Hill
NJ 07974
USA
gsf@research.att.com

Axel Mahler
Lampen & Mahler Software
Engineering GmbH
PO Box 100509
D-10565 Berlin
Germany
axel@avalanche.cs.tu-berlin.de

Gail E Kaiser
Department of Computer Science
Columbia University
New York
NY 10027
USA

Steven S Popovich
Department of Computer Science
Columbia University
New York
NY 10027
USA

Herman Chung-wa Rao
2B-105
AT & T Bell Laboratories
600 Mountain Avenue
Murray Hill
NJ 07974
USA
herman@research.att.com

Walter F Tichy
School of Informatics
University of Karlsruhe
D-76128 Karlsruhe
Germany
tichy@info.uni-karlsruhe.de

1

The CM Challenge: Configuration Management that Works

David B. Leblang
Atria Software, Inc.

ABSTRACT

"Configuration Management" (CM) is a widely used term, with an equally wide range of meanings. To some, it conjures images of formal, complex policies and procedures, with strict approval and reporting mechanisms. To others, it is merely the name given to an ad hoc layer of scripts over a basic version control facility.

The development process, whether it is formal, informal, or somewhere in-between, is supposed to help an organization obtain specific business goals. If the organization fails to meet these goals, the process is a failure. A CM system can either help to achieve these goals or it can be a bureaucratic obstacle.

This paper discusses some of the CM challenges faced by large software enterprises and explains why many CM systems fail to meet these challenges. It also discusses how the ClearCase® [Cle93] version control and configuration management system addresses these problems. ClearCase is specifically targeted at the needs of large commercial software producers — typically with 50-150 programmers working on many million lines of code.

Configuration Management, Edited by Tichy

1.1 THE CM CHALLENGE

The SEI CMM framework [Pau93] lists configuration management (CM) as one of the fundamental capabilities required to move an organization from "immaturity" to various levels of process maturity. In a commercial environment, configuration management may make the difference between supporting three computer vendor platforms or four — and that might make the difference between profit and loss.

There is no "typical" software project. Organizations evolve to meet unique product and business requirements. The level of CM required by an organization is driven both by needs and by methodology. No one tool, no single methodology, and certainly no single set of policies will work for everyone. However, there are some basic CM requirements that span nearly all software development environments, because they face many common challenges:

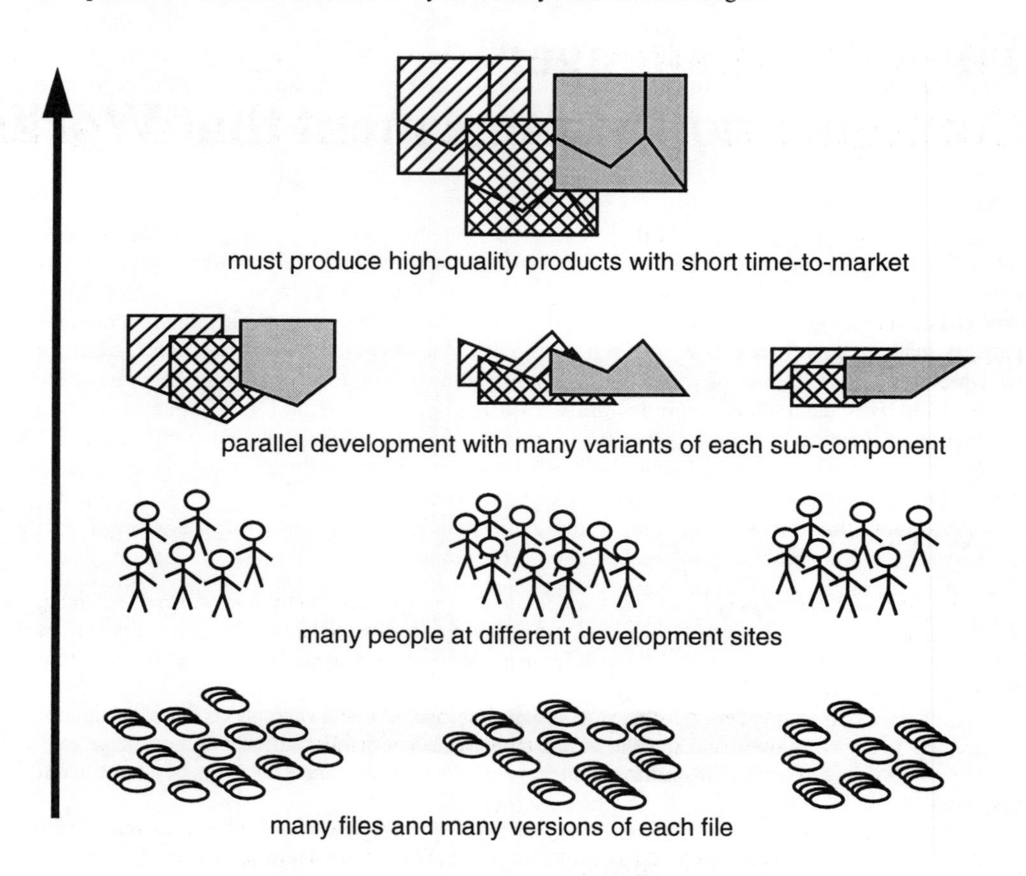

Figure 1.1 The CM challenge

- Constant pressure for aggressive schedules without sacrificing quality.
- Concurrent demands for producing new major software products, adding competitive features to existing products, and providing maintenance releases to thousands of current users [Ols93].
- The requirement to support many target platforms — sometimes more than 100.
- Critical bug fixes must be coded, tested, and released quickly — perhaps in only a day.

- Subcomponents of a product are developed by different groups; these groups may be separated by great distances (perhaps across national boundaries), but still must share common source code.
- Design, documentation, QA, and development must proceed concurrently [Dew93].
- Absolute accountability is required without a slow "approval" process.
- The CM system must improve the productivity of individual engineers, or else they will find ways to subvert it.
- CM must be integrated with the overall development process.

1.2 SCM FUNDAMENTALS

The need for "configuration management" is not unique to the software industry. In a mechanical design and manufacturing environment, a CM system is used to keep track of how components change over time, and how particular versions of specific components are combined to produce the final assembly. The CM system keeps component-level change logs and produces bills-of-materials, complete with version numbers of the components used and complete assembly instructions. The system records the development history in a form that can be used to reproduce the manufactured item.

Just as in hardware and mechanical systems environments, *software configuration management* (SCM) is the art of keeping track of what has changed and how things are combined. The software engineer edits (changes) some files, and then builds (combines) the software in steps that link the changed elements with the remaining unmodified files. An SCM system must include a history of changes made to each file. It also must reliably record in a software "bill-of-materials" the process by which specific versions of these files are combined to produce a complete software system ("release"). This guarantees reproducibility of running software and thus enables the later production of maintenance releases that vary from the base release in a well-defined way. The SCM system is responsible for the collection and reliable retention of the "who, what, when, how, and why" of every source code change and every software system build.

SCM is more than just version control; it is more than just process control; it is more than just bookkeeping. The basic SCM requirements encompass four categories: version control, environment management, build management, and process control. Each of these categories is defined below. Different CM systems address these categories differently; various approaches are compared and contrasted in this paper.

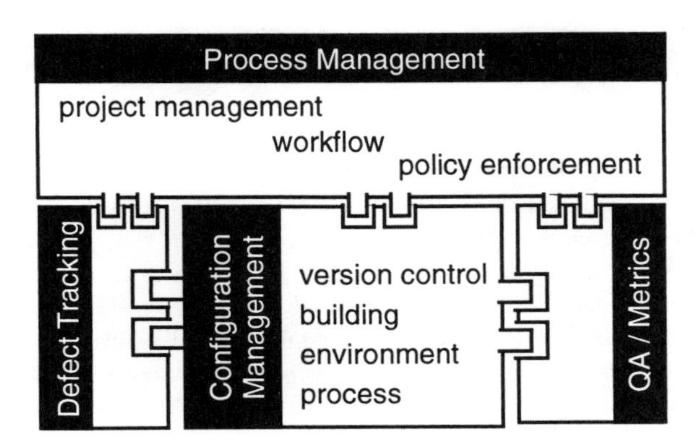

Figure 1.2 CM is part of an overall process

1.2.1 Version Control

A version control system keeps track of all changes to every file and supports parallel development by enabling easy creation of variants (branching) and the later reintegration of the variants (merging). The version control system manages access to objects; "controlled sharing" is essential in a multi-user parallel development environment.

Every type of object that evolves in the software development environment must be version-controlled, including binary objects such as word-processor documents, executable programs, and bitmap graphics objects. Classic version control tools such as SCCS and RCS [Tic85] do not efficiently store this type of data. Other version control features missing from SCCS and RCS are discussed below.

In large-scale engineering efforts the development staff usually consists of several teams or sub-projects. These sub-projects may be using the same source files but may not be located at the same geographic site: some may be in the U.S., while others are in Europe and Asia. The version control system should allow these teams to see each others changes (including change comments, labels, etc.) and also provide controlled access to the sources.

1.2.2 Environment Management ("Sandboxes")

Environment management provides each developer with a consistent, flexible, inexpensive, and reproducible file system environment that selects and presents the appropriate versions of each file. In a large project, developers must stay isolated from changes made by others; but at the same time, they must be able to unit-test their changes with the changes made by certain other users. To be successful, an SCM system must provide fine-grained control over both sharing and isolation.

When performing maintenance on older releases, a programmer must be able to view old source versions, binaries, documents, tests, tools, and other objects. In a way, the SCM environment manager must provide a *time machine,* which makes *everything* in the environment, not just the sources, appear as they did at some point in the past. This is difficult to achieve with classic copy-modify-merge systems because the large number of directories that would require shadow copies makes the task of setting up the "old" environment extremely unwieldy. In fact, a programmer may not even know what the set of relevant objects *were* two years ago. In any case, the time machine mechanism must be able to determine which versions of objects to show, using concise rules that define the desired configuration.

1.2.3 Build Management

Build management controls the building and rebuilding of software to produce *derived objects* which are the final software products. Build management includes *minimal rebuilding* – reusing as many derived objects as possible and only rebuilding those objects that had a dependency change. It also includes the automatic and reliable production of "bills-of-materials" (BOM) that document software system builds, and that can be used to recreate the complete file system environment of any build. The reliability of this process is essential: if the correct objects are not built, or if the bill-of-materials reflects what developers *think* went into a build, rather than what actually *did* go in, the value of the CM system is greatly reduced.

Closely related to build management and version control is *release management:* long-term storage of final software products. The products may be documents, derived objects like programs and libraries, or other objects. These final products require version control just like source code. The bills-of-materials associated with derived objects must be stored along with released derived objects.

1.2.4 Process Control

Process control and project management mechanisms support the enforcement of organization-specific software development policies and procedures. SCM is an important part of the overall software development process because it holds all of the key information resources (sources, documents, and final released products). The SCM system must interact with various processes, such as design methodologies, quality assurance policies, and customer support programs.

Specifically, the version control system must interact with higher-level process management functions such as *change grouping* and *defect tracking*. These processes relate specific versions of source files with a defect report or a generic work activity.

In addition to tracking what is being changed and by whom, the SCM object base must prevent changes by unauthorized personnel, or at inappropriate times. The SCM system should support any and all access-control policies, not just simple access-control lists. For example, the system might permit source files to be checked-in only if they satisfy a specific complexity metric.

There is a wide-spectrum in both the type of process control desired and the demand for process control. Some software engineering teams operate under specific and documented procedural guidelines; others prefer a minimalist approach to policy enforcement. The SCM tool must be flexible, enabling a development organization to customize its environment to support its chosen policies. The SCM tool is not the only tool used in the development process, so it must be easy to integrate with design tools, software quality tools, test coverage tools, and with sophisticated customer call tracking and problem tracking systems. In general, the SCM system must be "open" and easily integrated into existing environments.

1.3 REPOSITORY ACCESS

Version control and configuration management systems are a repository for sources, binaries, and other project objects. The nature of the repository can differ greatly from one system to another. Not only can the feature set of the repositories differ, but so can the basic way objects inside the repository are accessed.

1.3.1 Vaults

RCS, SCCS, PVCS, and most other systems are built on the notion of a *vault*. Work environments are created by extracting source file versions out of a central repository and depositing them in a private work area ("sandbox") that is unique to a particular desired configuration. Changes are made to the sources in a private location which is outside the control of the version control system. The changed sources are eventually put back into the vault.

It is necessary to extract sources because the vast majority of software development tools, including compilers, debuggers, and editors, cannot read the sources directly from the repository. In order to compile software, or run to a metrics tool across all the sources, or simply to search the sources for a string, you must extract *all* of the sources from the vault — even sources which you do not plan to change.

Vaults result in many copies of each source file, because each developer must extract all the sources in order to form the desired configuration. Parallel development results in even more copies. These copies are not under the control of the CM system; thus, there is no global locking agent to coordinate concurrent updates to the sources. Eventually a variety of problems occur, including lost changes. Coordination of all the copies of all the sources imposes a practical limit on the amount of parallel development that is possible.

A wide variety of tools have been implemented on top of classic version control systems, attempting to organize and control the many "sandboxes" created for parallel development. CVS and ODE are examples of such tools built on top of RCS. These tools improve the management of the sandboxes, but don't really solve the fundamental problem inherent in vaults: the software development tools cannot directly access the version controlled objects.

1.3.2 "Standard" Repositories

PCTE [PCTE], Atherton, and some university systems are based on a *standard repository* model. These systems attempt to solve the problem of direct repository access by providing an application programming interface (API) to the repository. The programming interface is declared to be a "standard" and *all* software development tools are expected to use the repository's access interface. All tools in the development environment must be changed in order to achieve direct repository access. If important tools, like the compiler, debugger, and editor are not "converted," then the repository must be treated like a vault.

Some software tools, such as front-end design tools, are closed subsystems — they operate primarily on their own proprietary database of objects. SCM tools are different —business factors demand that they operate on objects produced by commercial software products, such as Microsoft Word documents, source files produced by Emacs, and binaries produced by a compiler. In addition, "direct access" to the repository must include direct access by third-party software tools and system utilities such as "copy", "print", and "grep."

A drawback of attempting to impose a standard interface is that it will quickly become outmoded. Computer vendors are proposing a number of different "object" interfaces that are richer than the current file system interfaces. There are proposed object-oriented database standards, and there are proposals for extended file system interfaces. (No clear trend has emerged yet, and in the meantime, most tools continue to produce files.)

1.3.3 Virtual File Systems

DSEE [Leb84], and later, NSE, TeamNet, and ClearCase solved the problem of direct repository access through the use of a *virtual file system* (VFS). Each of these SCM systems took a different approach, but they all have one thing in common — instead of defining a programming interface for tools, they intercept native operating system I/O calls, such as open(), read(), and write(), and redirect them to the repository. Rather than copying versions into a physical workspace a *virtual workspace* is created. The overall effect is *transparency*: the version-control system becomes invisible, so that the repository appears to be a standard directory tree. These virtual directory trees hook into the regular file system at user-defined points.

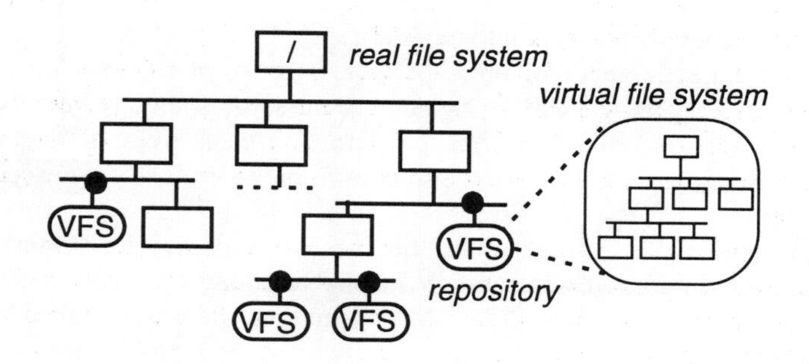

Figure 1.3 Repositories appear as directory trees

Transparency enables the SCM system to work smoothly with standard system software, third-party commercial applications, and a development team's "home-grown" software tools. Users do not have to discard their accustomed ways of working, or their existing tools. For example, such standard programs as *grep*, *more*, *ls*, and *cc* will work the same way on version-controlled objects as they would on ordinary files.

The details of SCM systems based on virtual file systems vary greatly — for example, TeamNet layers its VFS on environment hierarchies while ClearCase defines *views* where the correct versions are accessed dynamically according to user-specified rules called a *configuration specification*. The underlying operating system also affects the VFS: a Unix-based VFS intercepts a completely different set of system calls than a Windows-based VFS. But in all cases, the virtual file system looks like a device driver to the operating system, and the repository looks like a source tree to the user.

Some SCM systems attempt to simulate a virtual file system by providing a run-time library that replaces common operating system calls; the SHAPE AtFS [Lam91] is an example. This approach will work with some applications, but not all, because some system services access files through a layer that cannot be intercepted by this approach. In addition, the performance of user-space file system emulators is not as good as device driver level implementations.

1.4 A CLOSER LOOK AT CLEARCASE TRANSPARENT ACCESS

A ClearCase *versioned object base* (VOB) is a permanent, secure data respository. It contains data that is shared by all developers: this includes current and historical versions of source files, along with derived objects built from the sources by compilers, linkers, and so on. In addition, the repository stores detailed "accounting" data on the development process itself: who created a particular version (and when, and why), what versions of sources went into a particular build, and other relevant information.

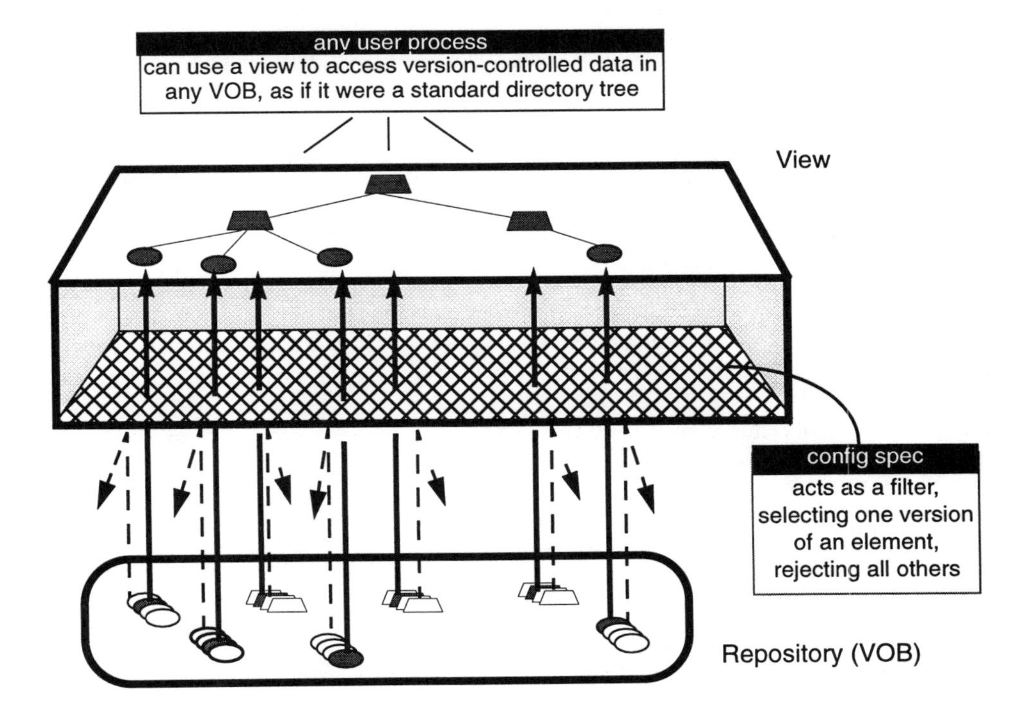

Figure 1.4 ClearCase transparent access

There are many versions of each file in a VOB, and there may be many names and directory structures for the files (reflecting reorganizations of the source tree over time). A ClearCase *view* is a VFS-based virtual workspace, which makes a VOB look like an ordinary file system source tree.

A view enables its users to "see" the repository by selecting a single directory structure and one version of each file; it projects that structure and those versions to the user as an ordinary source tree.

A VOB is a repository intended to be seen by (some or) all developers. By contrast, a view is not itself a repository; rather, it is a tool for *seeing* the repository. Moreover, a view is much more likely to be intended for the private use of one developer than for use by all developers. Associated with each view is a set of user-specified rules, called a *configuration specification* (config spec), which determines which version of each file is seen. For example:

- If I have the file checked-out use the checked-out version.
- Use the version, if any, that went into "bugfix 295".
- Otherwise use the version labelled "Release-2.0".

1.4.1 Deferred Evaluation

ClearCase defers evaluation of the config spec until an element is actually referenced. The view caches the result (i.e. which version of the element was selected) until the element changes or the rules change. Once a version is selected there no static copying or linking operation. The actual contents of the selected version remain in repository storage; the version is merely mapped into the environment's file name space.

When the version's data contents are actually read the view may automatically construct *cleartext* for the version from deltas or some other type of compressed storage. The resulting cleartext for that version is stored in a network-wide on-disk cache so that other people accessing the same version do not have to uncompress the data. Cleartext remains in the cache until a user configurable space or time limit is exceeded. In practice, the cleartext cache has a nearly 100% hit rate (99.5% in a recent sample) so views very, very rarely spend any time extracting deltas (with lots of people compiling or reading sources all of the "popular" versions tend to be cached). The entire cleartext construction and caching mechanism is totally invisible to users; at most, someone might notice a second-or-two delay when first accessing a version that no one has looked at for a long time.

1.4.2 Extended Naming

For ordinary pathnames, like "/vobs/vega/src/zbuf.c", the view automatically selects a version in accordance with the current config spec. However, automatic version selection does not prevent developers from explicitly accessing other versions. A ClearCase *extended pathname* can override the view and specify any version of any element, or the version of an element selected by some other view.

Any version of an element can be specified by appending its version-ID to its standard pathname, forming a *version-extended pathname*. For example:

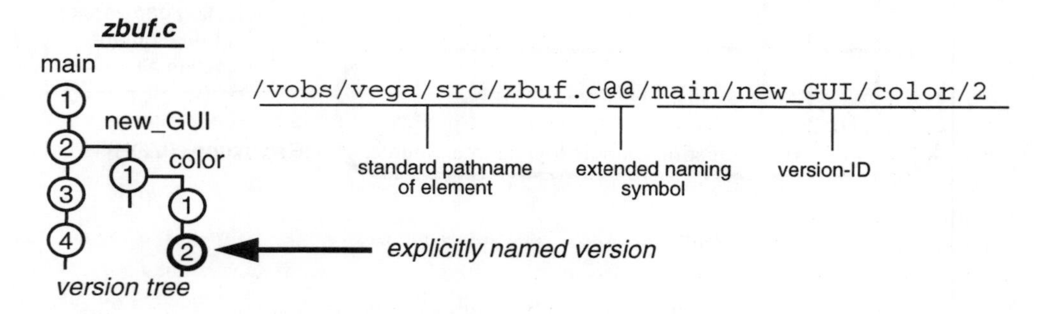

Figure 1.5 Version-extended pathname

Essentially, ClearCase grafts an element's version tree into the file system naming tree. When the ClearCase virtual file system sees the special extended naming symbol (which defaults to "@@") it makes an element act like a directory tree rather than a file. That is, it makes each branch look like a file system directory, which contains a file for each version and a subdirectory for each sub-branch. In the example above, if you set your working directory to src/zbuf.c@@/main you would see four files ("1", "2", "3", "4") and one sub-directory ("new_GUI").

Version labels act like links to the appropriate version, so that a version-extended pathname can also use a version label; this enables developers to reference versions mnemonically:

```
util.c@@/REL2
messages.c@@/REL3_BSLVL2
mgrs.h@@/NEW_STRUCT_TEST
```

Version-extended pathnames can be used in standard commands, either alone or in conjunction with standard pathnames. For example, to compare the version labelled "REL2" of util.c to the version currently being seen by the view:

```
% /bin/diff util.c@@/REL2 util.c
```

Another type of extended naming is *view-extended* naming. A view-extended name overrides the current view by specifying a different view:

```
/view/marys_view/vobs/vega/src/util.c
```
(version seen by Mary's view)

1.5 REPOSITORIES IN A DISTRIBUTED ENVIRONMENT

Nearly all software development today is done in a distributed network environment, often with a heterogeneous mix of development platforms. Simple source control systems, like SCCS, rely on a remote file system to access objects. More sophisticated CM systems typically use a commercial database which must be accessed via some type of client/server protocol. The communication protocol usually handles low-level data representation issues, making heterogeneous access possible.

A large software development effort may have many thousands of source files, binaries, and documents. There are a variety of reasons why it is not always possible, or desirable, to store these objects in a single repository:

- scalability: must avoid network, disk, and other computing resource limitations.
- different sub-components are "owned" by different groups, with separate administrative policies.
- security concerns.
- desire to have independent shared repositories of reusable components.

Large software projects generally divide the sources up into a collection of source trees; each tree roughly corresponding to a major sub-component in the product. Often, a backbone directory tree is created with symbolic links, creating a single logical tree. Sources in one source tree may "include" header files from another; thus, in order to build the software several different source trees must be accessible at the same time.

Conceptually, the ClearCase repository is a globally accessible, central resource. The implementation, however, is modular: each source (sub)tree can be a separate *versioned object base* (VOB). VOBs can be distributed throughout a local area network, accessed independently or linked into a single logical tree. To system administrators, modularity means flexibility; it facilitates load-balancing in the short term, and enables easy expansion of the data repository over the long term. A single system build can simultaneously access as many VOBs as needed to perform the build.

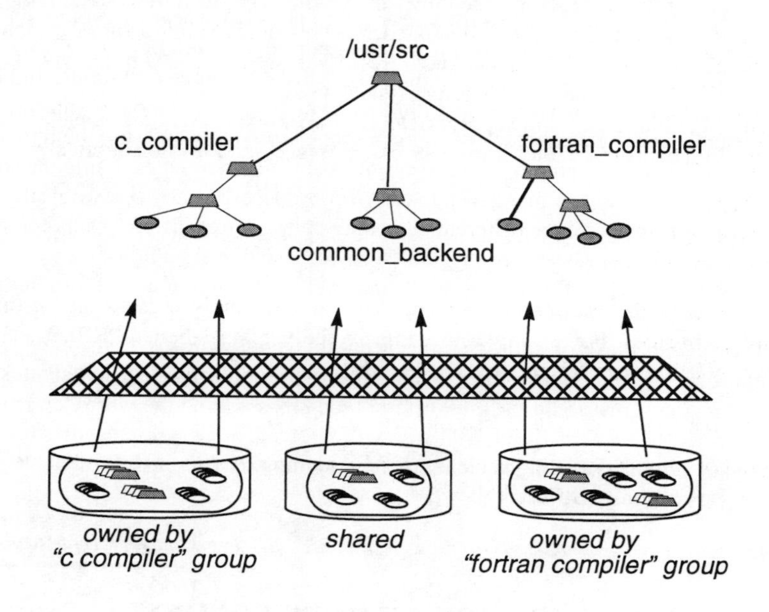

Figure 1.6 A project may have many VOBs; Many projects may share a VOB

ClearCase VOBs act as a *federated database*, that is, they are independent but will cooperate with each other. For example, a computer vendor has a "c" compiler group and a "fortran" compiler group. Each group has its own VOB for the front-end (parser) of their compiler. However, they share a VOB which holds the common back-end (code generator) used by both compilers. When building ("make'ing") the fortran compiler the fortran front-end VOB and the common back-end VOB are accessed. A user may ask to see the history of changes made today in both the fortran front-end VOB *and* common back-end VOB; these changes will be displayed interleaved together (chronologically) making the VOBs appear to be a single entity:

% **lshistory -all -since today /usr/src/fortran_compiler /usr/src/common_backend**

12-Jan-94.10:37 **/usr/src/fortran_compiler/lex.c** version 19 created by Mary Smith
"add support for double precision constants"

12-Jan-94.10:15 **/usr/src/fortran_compiler/parse.c** version 27 created by John Jones
"fix bug 267: core dump on empty input file"

12-Jan-94.09:57 **/usr/src/common_backend/opt.c** version 134 created by Ken Davis
"better branch shadow usage"

12-Jan-94.09:44 **/usr/src/fortran_compiler/lex.c** version 18 created by Mary Smith
"print better error message when label missing"

1.5.1 Geographically distributed development teams

Most large corporations develop software at more than just one physical site; each site develops one or more sub-components of a large system. Sites may be physically near each other and connected by a high-speed network, or they may be on different continents with poor network connectivity. Sites may have private sources but they also may need to share sources, libraries, and header files with other sites (particularly header files and libraries, which act as component interfaces).

Companies usually take a snapshot of the sources at one *master* site and ship them to other *remote* sites. If changes are made at a remote site they must be carefully merged back into the sources at the master site. The process is largely manual and very error prone, especially if several sites are making changes to the same sources. Since different sites may be master of different sub-components it is sometimes difficult to know where the "original" copy of a source actually is.

In many ways, the problem of geographic distribution is analogous to the problem of parallel development at a single site.

The ClearCase MultiSite tool addresses the needs of geographically distributed development teams by supporting parallel development at multiple, geographically-distributed sites. ClearCase can create *VOB replicas,* distribute them to different locations around the world, and automatically synchronize them as changes are made. Multisite will work even if the remote sites have limited or *no* network connectivity (using FTP or magnetic tape as the transport medium).

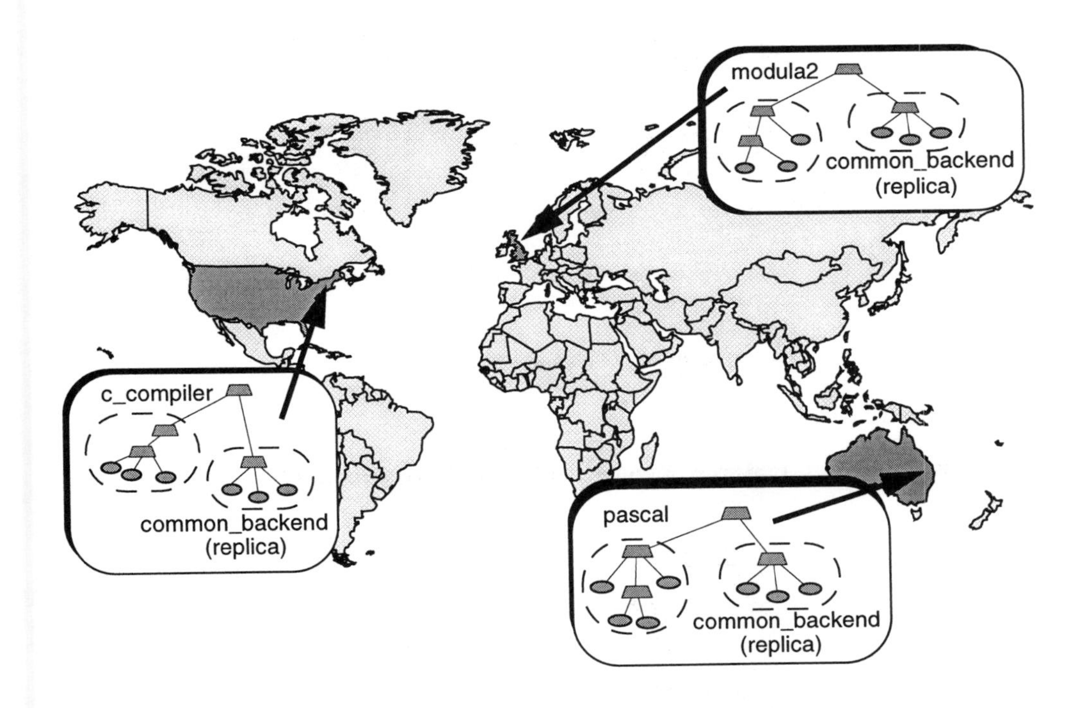

Figure 1.7 Multi-national project sharing sources

The original VOB, its replicas, and their replicas form a *VOB family*. All members of the family are peers, there is no "master" VOB: any one can be modified, any one can spawn a new replica, any one can be deleted when no longer needed, and any one can send updates to any other.

Since all the replicas may be updated (new versions checked-in, files renamed, etc.), the replicas will diverge over time. In the background, a periodic and automatic synchronization mechanism exports changes from one replica and imports them into the others. The update topology may be a star, a multi-hop chain, or any graph that enables updates to eventually flow from one replica to the others. Administrators configure the frequency and topology of updates.

ClearCase's normal parallel development model uses branches to support parallel development (i.e. each effort works on a different branch). Continuing the compiler group example above: when the fortran group makes changes to the shared "common back-end" VOB, it makes those changes on a "fortran_group" branch. The "c" group makes its changes on a "c_group" branch. At integration points, the changes are merged together, typically into the "main" branch.

The only difference between local parallel development and multisite parallel development is that ClearCase MultiSite *enforces* the rule that different sites work on different branches by assigning mastership to individual branches. This ensures *automatic resynchronization*, because only one site can extend a particular branch; thus, all those changes can be trivially grafted onto the corresponding branch at other sites. When a remote effort is complete, or at a convenient integration point, it can be merged into an integration branch; integration of parallel work, testing, and release, can happen at any site. (Local parallel development is discussed below.)

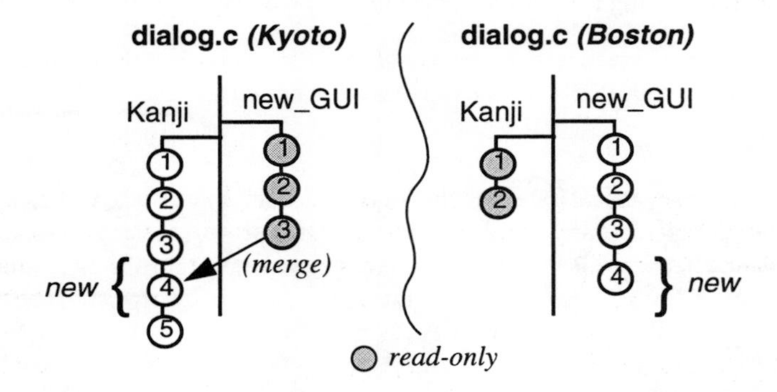

Figure 1.8 Replicas diverge over time ...

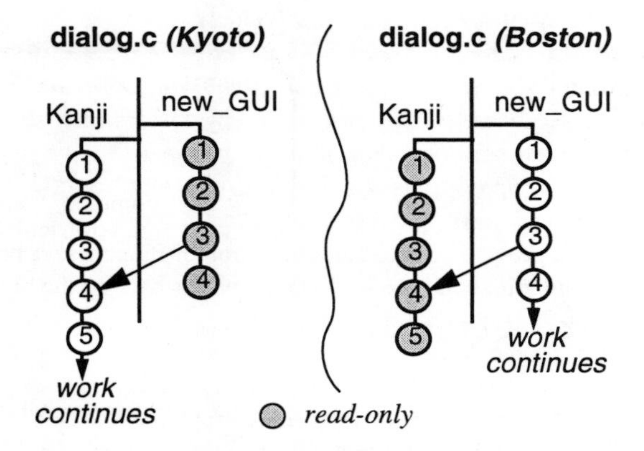

Figure 1.9 ... Until the next periodic update

Mastership for individual branches provides the right level of mastership granularity for parallel development. Courser grained mastership, such as at the element (file) level, precludes parallel development because two people can't work on the same file at the same time. Without any mastership, where any site can change anything, automatic resynchronization is not possible.

Since projects move and are reorganized, ClearCase Multisite must support a mastership exchange mechanism that allows mastership to change at resynchronization points. There are many subtleties involved in the creation and synchronization of replicated object bases, enough so that the details of ClearCase MultiSite must be discussed in a separate paper. In any case, a solution for geographically distributed sites is key to supporting the type of very large, multinational software development efforts found today.

1.6 VERSION CONTROL

As the complexity of software projects has increased over the years, so has the need for more sophisticated version control systems. A number of version control features are discussed below. Many of these features are not found in the "status quo" version control systems, for example, the ability to send change notifications through email or the ability to ask queries that span multiple files. The lack of a true database limits the capabilities of SCCS and RCS and of other systems which are implemented as scripts around these classic tools.

The term *element* is used here to refer to the object that represents all of the versions of a particular file. An SCCS "s." file and an RCS ",v" file are examples of elements.

1.6.1 Parallel Development

Large projects need to have several independent "lines of development" active at the same time. The process of creating and maintaining multiple variants of a software system concurrently is called *parallel development*. Creation of a variant might be a major project (porting an application to a new platform), or a minor detour (fixing a bug; creating a "special release" for an important customer) [Rei89].

Both RCS and SCCS allow for the creation of a *variant branch* off of an existing version. This feature alone makes parallel development possible, but not easy. A significant problem is coordination — when a change spans multiple elements, the variant branch created on one element is not easily associated with the variant branches on other elements created as part of the same activity. For example, a subproject is adding a new product feature, such as a Windows GUI, and wishes to isolate its work for the several months it will take to complete the task. The project creates a variant branch on the source elements it changes. In some elements the branch might be called 1.7.1 while in other elements it might be called 1.18.3. The more parallel development activities in progress, the more confusing the number scheme becomes. Poor support for branching is one of the principal reasons SCCS and RCS are usually surrounded by custom shell scripts.

ClearCase uses symbolic names for branches. In the example above, the sub-project would create a "new_GUI" branch off the appropriate versions. In this way, developers would be able to distinguish "new_GUI" changes from "performance_improvements" changes. ClearCase also has the notion of *branch types* to provide central administration of branches. A branch in an element is really an instance of a particular branch type — that is, it points back to the branch type for common information such as the branch name, access control rights, and comments describing the purpose of the branch. Renaming branch type "new_GUI" to "Windows_GUI" changes all instances. *Locking* branch type "new_GUI" prevents check-ins on that branch for all elements (*freezes* the branch).

SCCS, RCS, and ClearCase all use a similar *branching* graph model. That is, a version has a single distinguished linear successor and may have several variant successors. ClearCase also has *mergers*, which are discussed later.

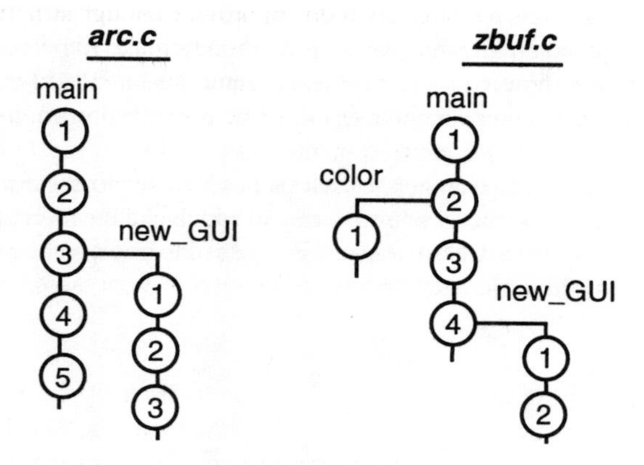

Figure 1.10 Symbolic branch names

Other variant models are possible. For example, CAD systems sometimes use an *arbitrary graph* model with versions linked together by predecessor/successor relationships [Kat88]. Arbitrary graphs tend to lack the structure needed to organize a large scale parallel development effort. Another model creates variants by copying all sources into a new environment, thus branching all elements at the start of the parallel development rather than branching individual elements as needed. This *super-branching* or *sub-environment* model, as found in the NSE or TeamNet, is similar to the manual process implemented by many organizations. Super-branching tends to be too inflexible for projects with a great deal of parallel development; it also makes prodigious demands on disk resources, because there are many complete copies of the source tree, or at least many copies of binaries generated from the source tree. (These issues are discussed more in the section on environment management.)

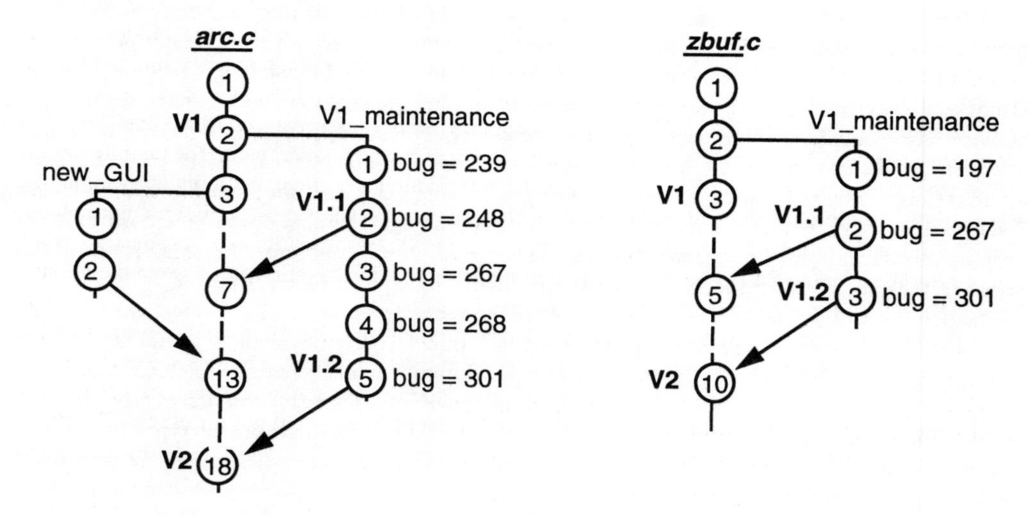

Figure 1.11 Major development lines and change sets

Another popular feature is *change sets:* groups of related changes. For example, fixing a bug may involve creation of new versions of several files; the change set for that bugfix records which versions are involved. Change sets by themselves do not provide enough structure to support parallel development efforts — for example, a 50-person project may make hundreds of changes a week. Some of the changes are bug fixes to a prior releases, other are intended for a future release, still others are for a specific new feature. The changes must be organized in development lines such as "V1_bugfixes", "IBM_port", and "V3_development".

ClearCase supports branches *and* changes sets. Branches are used to organize broad development lines ("V1_maintenance"); change sets are used to record which changes went together for a specific change request ("fix bug #293"). ClearCase change sets are implemented with a user-defined *attributes,* which are discussed more fully below.

1.6.2 Merging

Parallel development efforts are usually merged (integrated) back into a main development line. This enables several parallel efforts to be combined and released together. In the diagram above, maintenance release bug fixes are integrated back into the "main" branch prior to the next major release. Major functional changes, such as the "new GUI," are integrated when completed — if not in time for the next major release, then for a later release. ClearCase records information about mergers in its database.

In a large development project, hundreds of files may have been modified and need to be merged. An *automatic merge* facility can help with the mechanics of merging source code changes. A merge tool that knows the *common ancestor* of the versions being merged can generally merge with little or no human interaction. Experience with DSEE and with ClearCase has shown that over 90% of changed files can be merged without asking the user any questions. The merge tool asks the user to resolve a conflict in the other cases. In about 1% of the cases, the merge tool inappropriately makes an automatic decision, but nearly all of those cases are easily detected because they result in compiler syntax errors. For a large merge, the chances of the ClearCase automatic merge tool making an error are lower than the chances that a human would make an error — and the automated tool is many times faster.

In order to make automatic merge decisions, the tool must know the common ancestor (the *base*) of the versions being merged (the *contributors*). When the contributors differ, the base version is used to tell which contributor to use in the merged result. For example, if the base version has the line "x = 0" and contributor "A" has "x = 1" and contributor "B" has "x = 0" then the merge tool can tell that the result should be "x = 1" because it is contributor "A" that has changed.

In addition to ordinary merges ClearCase supports *ladder mergers, additive mergers,* and *subtractive mergers*. Most branches, like the new_GUI branch above, merge into the mainline at the end of their lifetime. Long-lived branches, like the V1_maintenance branch shown above, may be merged into the mainline at some point but then continue to evolve. It may be merged again later. ClearCase detects repeated mergers and takes into account the results of the earlier mergers when performing the new merger. (The term *ladder merge* describes this situation, because in the version tree graph, the multiple mergers resemble the rungs of a ladder.)

Sometimes a project will make a change in one development line and later want to propagate the change — and just that change — to another development line. For example, a bug is reported in the V1 release of a product. It turns out that the bug has already been fixed as part of general V2 development. You want to extract the changes made for the bug fix — but not for other V2 features — and apply it to the V1_maintenance branch. A ClearCase *additive merger* will do this. It takes a range of versions and merges the changes made inside that range into another branch.

Changes are sometimes made which need to be undone at a later time. For example, a change is made to take advantage of a new OS feature. Later, after several more unrelated changes have been made to the same file, you decide that it is not acceptable to have a dependency on the new OS. A ClearCase *subtractive merger* removes the changes made in a range of versions, resulting in a new version that includes all changes except those that were explicitly excluded.

1.6.3 Labels, Attributes, and Hyperlinks

Over time a project will produce thousands of source modules with hundreds of versions each. *Version labels* are symbolic names for particular versions. For example, *foo.c* version 2.1.3.1 might be given the label RLS2. Most modern version control system support version labels because they are extremely helpful in organizing releases. As with branches, ClearCase has the notion of *version label types* to provide central administration of labels.

Label types, like all ClearCase objects, may be *locked*. Locking label type "RLS2" prevents any "RLS2" label from being moved, deleted, or added. ClearCase locks may have an exceptions list, so a label can be locked so that *only* the project leader can move or apply a specific label. ClearCase maintains a detailed history of *all* changes to the object base, so when a label is applied to a version ClearCase records who applied the label, when and why it was applied. The same is true for attributes and hyperlinks.

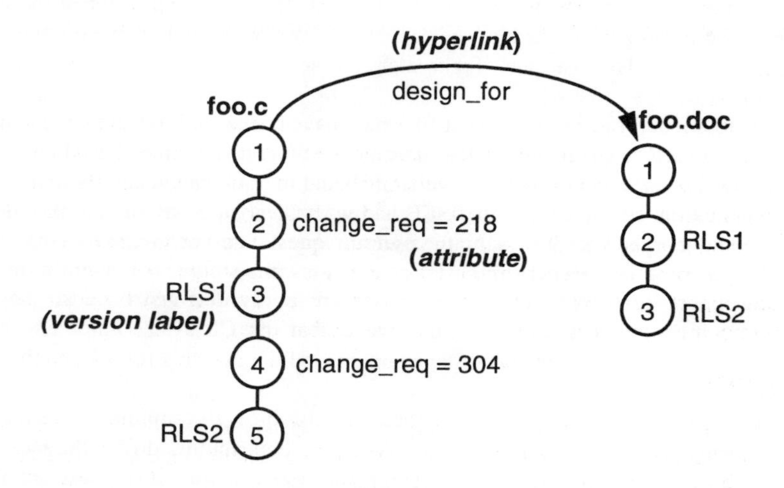

Figure 1.12 Labels, attributes, and hyperlinks

Attributes are name/value pairs which represent state information about a version. ClearCase *attribute types* can define attributes with many value kinds, such as integer, string, enum, and date. The attribute type can optionally define value range constraints. For example, a "change_request_number" attribute type could be defined to be an integer value in the range 1 to 9999, representing the number of the change request for which a version was created. Attributes may be applied to individual versions or entire branches or elements. Attributes are very useful for integrating process control mechanisms with the version control system, and are becoming more popular as the desire for integrated process control increases.

Hyperlinks enable users to define structured or ad hoc relationships between objects. For example, foo.c points to foo.doc via a "design_for" hyperlink. Hyperlinks are useful for requirements tracing and, with a graphic display of the relationship network, navigating between related objects. ClearCase hyperlinks may connect an object in one VOB to an object in another, and remain valid even if objects are renamed or moved. Although hyperlinks relate objects at the file level, they may also include *sub-object locators* for identifying a sub-object inside of a file.

1.6.4 Triggers

In a large development project, it is often important to receive notification when certain objects are changed. For example, the technical writing group may wish to be informed when the functional specification changes. A trigger mechanism causes an arbitrary action to be executed when a particular event occurred. For example, send e-mail to bill_shakespeare when func_spec.doc changes. Most object-oriented database systems have a trigger mechanism.

ClearCase provides a trigger mechanism to help users monitor objects in the version control system. Many different kinds of events can be monitored, and there are many ways to state which set of objects should be watched. An example is *monitor checkin of all files of type "design_document"*. A ClearCase trigger may be defined to run before the operation is executed (pre-event) or after the operation is complete (post-event). A pre-event trigger may return an exit status indicating that the operation should not be allowed. For example, a pre-event trigger on check-in could verify that the source code being checked-in meets certain coding guidelines – if not, the trigger can disallow the check-in. Post-event triggers are generally used to send e-mail notification.

1.6.5 Change Sets

As discussed above, ClearCase implements both branches and change sets. In fact, ClearCase can support two different kinds of change sets: attribute-based and hyperlink-based. In both cases triggers are used to associate an object that is being checked in with the change set. Attribute-based change set triggers use an attribute type, such as "change_request_number", and attach the attribute to the version being checked in. The actual "change request number" is taken from the user's environment or prompted for. Hyperlink-based change sets are similar but they "hyperlink" the version to a bug report (or *task*) object. Hyperlinks, attributes, and triggers are the key building blocks used to implement process-control policies with ClearCase.

1.6.6 Annotation

While change sets, labels, and attributes describe changes at the version level, it is also sometimes necessary to view changes at the line-of-code level. ClearCase can produce an annotated report that describes the origin of each line. The amount of information displayed and the report format are customizable and may include change set attributes, labels, and other data.

```
30-Jul-93 dave      /main/80     |   if (st != TBS_ST_OK) {
02-Mar-93 debby     /main/74     |      if (view_get_view_info (dir_pname
17-Jan-92 bill      /main/32     |         if (!silent)
02-Mar-93 debby     /main/74     |            imsg_print(IMSG_ERR, NO_VI
12-Feb-92 debby     /main/35     |      return st;   /* return status */
17-Jan-92 bill      /main/32     |      }
17-Jan-92 bill      /main/32     |   }
12-Feb-92 debby     /main/35     |   /* If an extended pathname was given
12-Feb-92 debby     /main/35     |    * the @@ on the end of the view tag
28-Sep-93 paul      /main/87     |   if (tag_buf != NULL)
28-Sep-93 paul      /main/87     |      cmd_utl_elem_strip_ext(tag_buf);
26-May-94 gary      /main/115    |
26-May-94 gary      /main/115    |   if (t_stat != TBS_ST_OK)
26-May-94 gary      /main/115    |      return t_stat;
22-Feb-94 gary      /main/108    |   return TBS_ST_OK;
26-May-94 gary      /main/115    | }  /* cmd_utl_resolve_to_vobh */
```

Figure 1.13 Annotated report

Annotated reports may also be used to gather metrics for process management. Unlike complexity metrics and other "code" based metrics, an annotated report contains "change" metrics:

Lines	Week	Week%	Month	Month%	Quartr	Quart%	Year	Year%	File
1201	0	(0%)	0	(0%)	78	(6%)	254	(21%)	cmd_do.c
1993	0	(0%)	15	(0%)	257	(12%)	1286	(64%)	cmd_evnt.
1210	0	(0%)	0	(0%)	7	(0%)	767	(63%)	cmd_find.
2318	0	(0%)	0	(0%)	25	(1%)	2318	(100%)	cmd_mrg.c
...									...
55057	7	(0%)	202	(0%)	3219	(5%)	22517	(40%)	55 files

Figure 1.14 Cummulative "lines changed" over past periods of time

1.6.7 Namespace

Some version control systems are good at tracking the changes to the *contents* of files, but have little or no ability to handle changes to the *names* of files. Name changes are a fact of life in long-lived projects, as are changes like creating new files, deleting obsolete files, moving a file to a different directory, or completely reorganizing a multi-level directory structure.

For example, at release 1.0 an element had the name "proj/gui_src/arc.c" but by release 2.0 the sources had been reorganized and that same element had become "proj/gui/src/arc.c". Assume that a critical bug fix is needed to the 1.0 release. The release 1.0 makefile will no longer work due to name changes and the release 2.0 makefile may be wildly inappropriate for a rebuild of release 1.0. In practice, projects tackle this problem by keeping whole copies of earlier source trees.

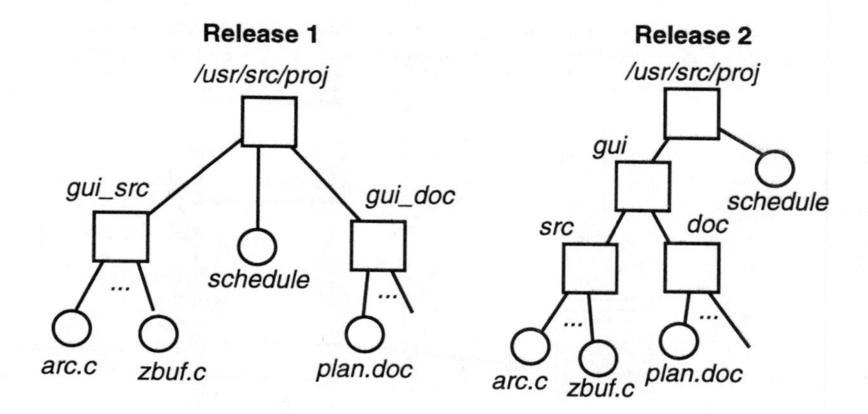

Figure 1.15 Reorganizing a source tree

ClearCase manages whole directory structures, not just individual file elements. The organization of the source tree seen by the user will depend on the rules (configuration specification) used to select versions. This enables users to automatically recreate the names and locations of files for maintenance of a prior release, allowing the old makefiles and source-inclusion (#include) statements to continue to work.

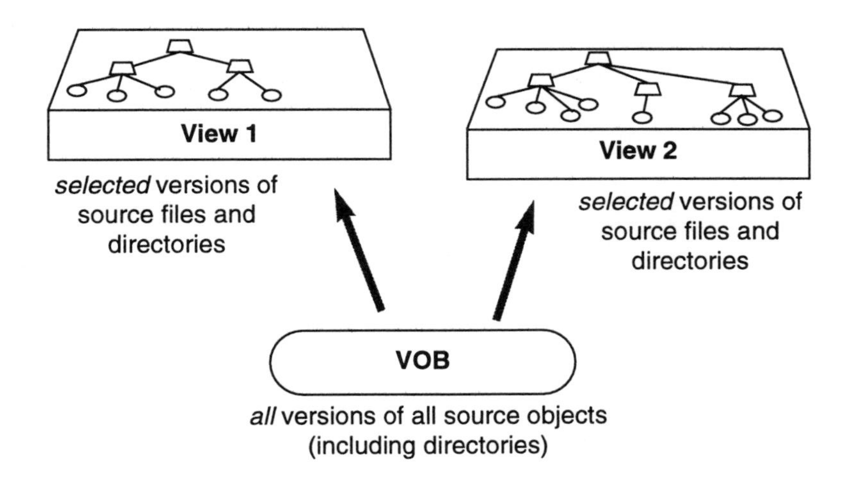

Figure 1.16 Different views of the namespace

ClearCase directories are elements with branches and versions just like the individual source elements. A user may *checkout* a directory, rename or move an element, and then check-in the directory creating a new version of that directory. The old version of the directory shows the element by its old name, the new version shows the element under its new name. The element itself is unmodified and all versions of the element can be accessed under its new name.

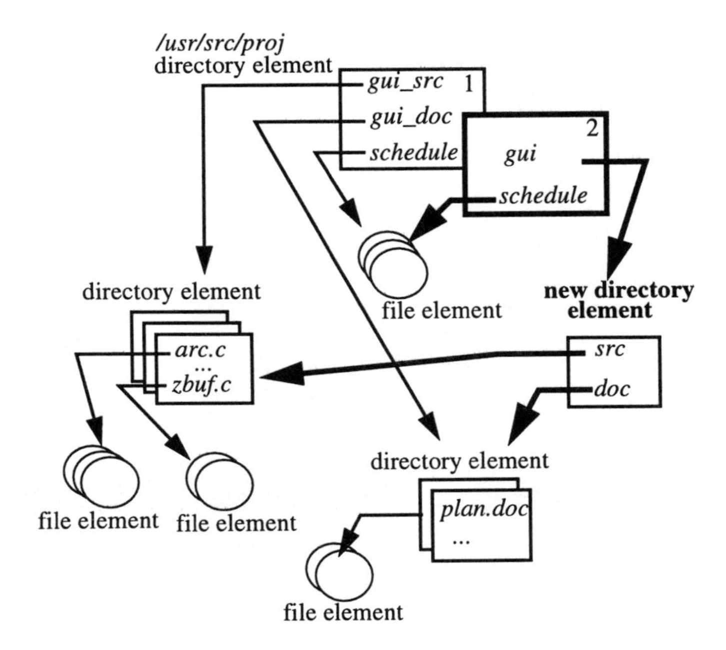

Figure 1.17 Detailed look at the evolution of namespace directories

A ClearCase directory version is very much like a standard operating system directory: it contains a list of names, each of which has a pointer to an element. Each pointer is really an internal identifier that is independent of the "name" of the element (like Unix inodes). Moving and renaming elements do not create a new versions of the element, just the directory. In fact, if an element has become obsolete its name can be removed from a new version of its directory; the element disappears but isn't deleted, it still is accessible through older (or variant) versions of the directory. ClearCase supports graphical comparisons and mergers of directories.

1.6.8 Object Types

As mentioned above, one problem with most version control systems is that they don't efficiently support non-text objects. ClearCase solves this problem by providing plug-in *type managers*. A type manager implements (or inherits) a well-defined set of methods that are required to participate in the version control system. The methods include a "store new version" operation (for check-in), a "construct old version" operation (for check-out), and a few other operations like diff and merge. When a user issues a command, like check-in, the correct method is run, based on the type of the object.

Some operations are optional, for example, "graphical display of differences". Object types form an inheritance hierarchy so a type manager doesn't have to implement all of the operations, just the ones unique to a new object type. ClearCase provides several built-in type managers, including one to store binary data in a highly compressed form; new types usually inherit from these predefined types.

1.7 ENVIRONMENT MANAGEMENT

Long-lived software projects typically involve many developers, each performing software builds that use tens, hundreds, or thousands of source files. The developers work at different rates, and on different tasks: new coding for the next release; fixing bugs in one or more old releases; porting to new platforms; unplanned special releases for important customers.

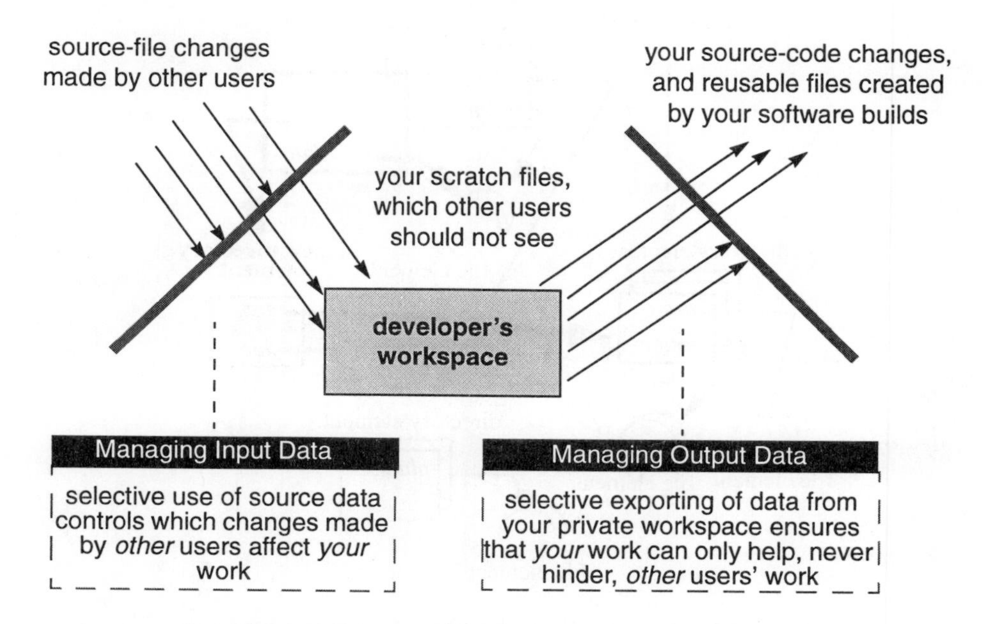

Figure 1.18 Requirements for a development workspace

Each developer needs a certain set of sources with which to work. Different tasks (for example, bugfixing vs. new development) require different versions of the sources — that is, different *configurations* of the source tree(s).

Moreover, the developer's workspace needs to be isolated, for purposes of editing, compiling, testing, and debugging. Ideally, the isolation should be relative, not absolute:

- Others should be able to track the developer's work, and selectively integrate it into their own work.
- Conversely, others should be able to shut out (until a subsequent integration period) those changes that prove destabilizing to their own work.

A key aspect of any CM system is its ability to define a workspace that contains the "right" set of source versions. There are a variety of ways to establish a workspace; four common models are:

- *unconstrained* – there is no well-defined environment, users extract sources from a vault and put them into private areas of their own choosing.
- *hierarchical sub-environments* – the workspace is defined to be a copy of a parent workspace plus all local changes.
- *change sets* - the workspace is constructed from a base version plus a selected set of changes.
- *rule-based environment* – a set of rules define which versions are seen in the workspace. A *static* rule-based system evaluates these rules only at environment creation time (or build time). A *dynamic* rule-based system interprets the rules as objects are accessed. If the rules are powerful enough, a rule-based system can simulate other models; for instance, ClearCase's rule-based environment can simulate hierarchical environments and also change set models.

It is *possible* to develop software using any environment model. In fact, most software is developed in a largely unconstrained environment: SCCS or RCS with a few home-grown shell scripts layered on top. It is very difficult to have a predictable and repeatable process in an unconstrained CM environment. Hierarchical models do not provide the level of flexibility needed in a large development effort; change set models do not work well when there are many changes or when there are many variants; rule-based models are flexible and handle variants well; but only dynamic rule-based models scale-up to very large projects.

	vault	**virtual file system**
unconstrained	RCS/SCCS/PVCS	
hierarchical	Teamware	NSE/TeamNet
change set	Aide-de-Camp	
static rule-based	CaseWare	DSEE
dynamic rule-based		ClearCase

Figure 1.19 Models for environment construction

1.7.1 Unconstrained

Most university and commercial software is developed using the standard "free" tools such as RCS and SCCS. These tools provide only version control so each site must develop and maintain its own scripts for environment management. The scripts usually provide a per user *sandbox* into which the user extracts a copy of the source tree from the vault, makes changes, and puts the changed files back. These scripts generally start out simple, but they are enhanced over time, becoming more and more complex (and less and less maintainable).

1.7.2 Hierarchical

Hierarchical models are sometimes called *copy-modify-merge* models because a user takes a physical or "virtual" copy of a baseline of a source tree, modifies some files, and copies the changed files back to the parent source tree. Changes made by others are incorporated into a child source tree through a *synchronize* operation: new versions are copied or merged from the parent to child. This model essentially perpetuates the sandbox model familiar to SCCS/RCS users.

There are several disadvantages to the hierarchical sub-environment model related to the inflexibility of a hierarchy: in order to integrate changes made in one environment with changes made in another environment, there must be a common parent; that parent must be irreversibly modified in order to integrate changes. Also, a change in one sub-environment cannot be easily propagated to a sibling environment without updating the parent and thus affecting all siblings. This makes pairwise integration and unit testing difficult because you must create an intermediate level environment for integration *before* either sub-environment was created. In a large project, with a dozen sub-projects, you cannot always predict the order in which sub-projects will complete so it is difficult to pre-plan all of the integration environments. For example, consider a manufacturer of cellular communications systems who creates several variants of a release of its software: (a) bug fixes, (b) support for more cells, (c) support for voice mail, and (d) support for FAX. At some future time, this manufacturer finds the need to create a configuration of the software for a new customer which includes features (b) and (c), plus a only the highest-priority bug fixes selected from (a).

A hierarchy is insufficient for creating the new configuration in which features from only selected siblings are combined. The manufacturer needs a mechanism that has the flexibility to combine arbitrary configurations and even parts of a configuration, as in the case of selecting some but not all bug fixes. This is not just a theoretical example; in practice things go wrong and flexibility is required: some features are late and must be dropped from a release at the last minute, some features are integrated into a release but must later be backed-out for business reasons.

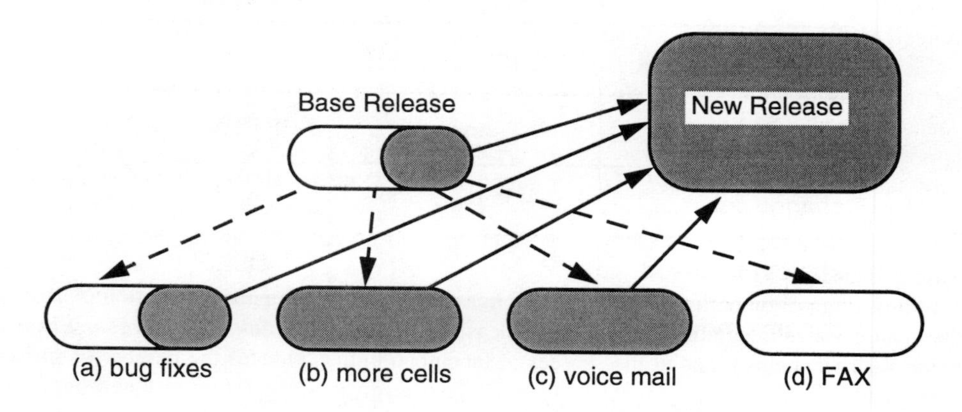

Figure 1.20 When hierarchies are not enough

The cellular communications example illustrates how course grained version selection, such as "copy the entire parent", makes it too hard to mix and match changes. Some other examples of where finer-grained version selection is needed:

- "I want to build my graphical user interface with different versions of the Motif libraries for testing or for different platforms."
- "I want different versions of just system header files and libraries in order to build a product that will be compatible with a specific version of the operating system."
- "I (or my coworker) broke something in one particular change of many, the problem was not detected until just now, I want to back out just that change until it can be fixed."
- "I want my environment to see bug fixes as soon as they are tested, but I don't want to see any functional changes until I'm done with my task."

It is difficult to back-out changes because once a change is put back in the parent environment it replaces the prior version. Even if the old versions are archived it is very difficult to build a mix of old sources and new sources because there is no "correct" parent to copy from; users must manually copy individual source versions into their environments, violating the hierarchy and making synchronization very hard.

In general, sub-environments provide too much isolation of work activities; this makes it hard to integrate work and limits communications among developers. For example, in sub-environment systems you don't learn that two people are changing the same file until the second person tries to put back their work. It is also difficult to get a global view of development activities — for example, who are all the people currently working on various versions of a particular file. Lack of global information makes it hard to get a "big picture" of the state of the development effort; that, in turn, makes it hard to manage and control the project.

1.7.3 Change Sets

As discussed above, change sets are a valuable tool for grouping related changes. But by themselves, they do not provide enough structure to define environments for large scale development efforts. For example, a customer encounters a known bug (say #239) in a particular component, and requests a patch. If the user has received any patches in the past for that component, sending a patch just for problem #239 would cause the customer to lose earlier fixes. The customer needs a cumulative patch, which includes all earlier patches to component X. A change set system would theoretically allow you to build a release that picks and chooses the exact set of changes required by that specific customer; in practice, however, it is not cost-effective to build a custom release for each individual customer, especially if you have thousands of customers. In addition, it would benefit the customer and reduce support calls to the software vendor if the customer were to receive a patch with fixes to other high-priority problems as well (problems found by other customers, which they would likely encounter eventually).

In practice, a commercial software vendor organizes changes so that one bugfix builds on earlier bugfixes. These so-called *patch-bundles* or *jumbo-patches* combines all fixes to date in a particular product component (for example, the spelling checker tool in a desktop publishing product). At some point, the patch-bundles from all product components are combined, and a maintenance release is issued.

Building changes on earlier changes results in an early and incremental integration of changes, rather than massive integration just before a release. This type of *continuous integration* discovers problems earlier, helps pinpoint the sources of incompatibilities, reduces the number of software releases, and increases the amount of testing each bugfix receives (since testing each new bugfix also retests earlier fixes). In addition, since a single incremental fix requires much less testing than a fix based on a customized combination of versions, less time is needed to get a patch built, tested, and shipped to the customer.

Change sets work best when changes are organized into development lines that form an evolving base for changes that will be released together. With ClearCase, branches form a development line for change sets. The ClearCase rule-based environment mechanism can select whole development lines (branches), individual change sets if needed, or some combination of the two.

1.7.4 Rule-Based Version Selection

A rule-based version selection mechanism uses a set of rules to determine which versions should be seen in an environment. Each rule is essentially a query which, when applied to a particular element, returns zero, one, or more versions of that element. Rules are usually evaluated in order: the system attempts to locate a version of the element that satisfies the first rule. If this fails, it proceeds to the next rule and, if necessary, to succeeding rules until it locates a version satisfying the rule's query. If a query is ambiguous (returns more than one version) then either the most recent of those versions is selected, or an error is reported (depending on the CM system).

Rules that select versions by attribute value, such as "bug_num == 291", provide the features of change set type models. Rules like "what I have checked-out else the version labeled RLS2.0" provide the features of sub-environment models. In ClearCase, these types of rules, and other types of rules, can be freely mixed and result in a very powerful environment-control mechanism.

rule 1: bug_num > 267
rule 2: Status == working && Owner == Joe
rule 3: latest on "new_GUI" branch
rule 4: the version labeled RLS2.0

Figure 1.21 Rules

Rule-based systems vary in the power and flexibility of their rules. CaseWare/CM has static attribute/value style rules that are evaluated against a fixed set of items (defined in a system model); the selected versions must be copied into a work area. If conditions change (for example, a label is moved, a new file is created, or the rules change), the environment will be out-of-sync with the rules until the user explicitly asks for copies in the work area to be resynchronized.

ClearCase supports many types of rules, including attribute/value, branch, label, and time-oriented rules. ClearCase rules are dynamic: rules are evaluated as objects are accessed through the virtual file system, so that the sources are always synchronized with the rules. Dynamic rules are essential for partial sharing with other developers, without them a developer must issue an explicit "resynch" request whenever a change of interest is made in *another* developer's workspace.

ClearCase environment management is discussed in more detail in the next section.

1.8 A CLOSER LOOK AT CLEARCASE ENVIRONMENT MANAGEMENT

The ClearCase *view* facility, which implements independent, user-configurable workspaces for software development, play a major role in environment management.

A user can create any number of independent views. Each view is a flexible and inexpensive workspace, which accesses the correct set of source versions for the task at hand (bugfix, port to a new architecture, new development, and so on). Just as each workstation window (process) has an associated working directory, a process that works with ClearCase data has an associated view. That is, any reference to a location within a VOB must be interpreted in the *context* of some view. Typically, a developer enters a command to "set a view", which establishes a view context both for the current process and for any child (subsidiary) processes created subsequently. All those processes will see a particular configuration of the data repository.

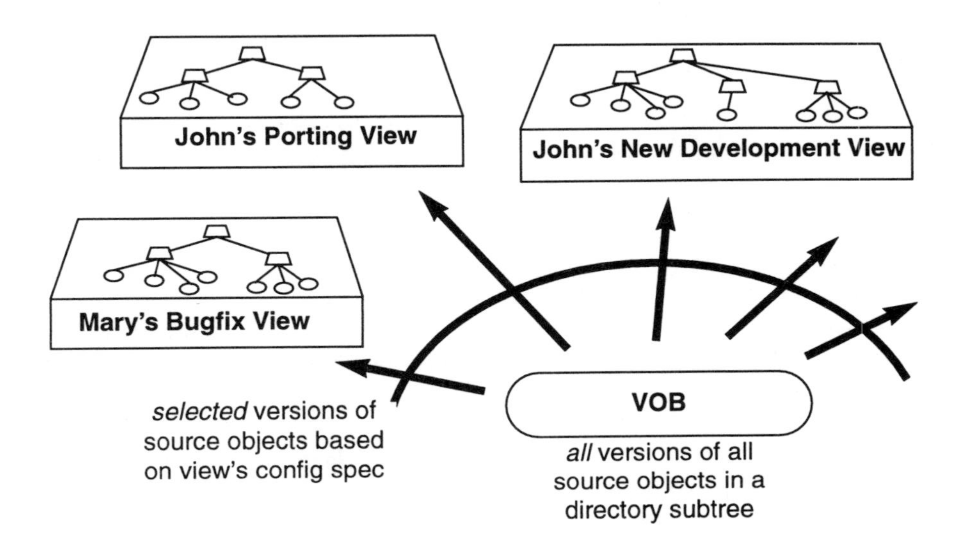

Figure 1.22 Many *views* of the same versioned object base

A developer might set different views in different windows, in order to work with two or more configurations at once. It is even possible to use multiple views in a single command.

A view can be completely private to an individual developer, or shared among developers. A view can be accessed on a single host, or from any host in a local area network. Transparent access makes views compatible with all software development tools, not just ClearCase's own programs. Developers working in views can use system-supplied programs, home-grown scripts, and third-party tools to directly access versions.

1.8.1 Configuration Specifications

ClearCase views are rule-based: an ordered set of rules, called a *configuration specification*, governs which version of each element is seen by the view's users. ClearCase config specs support many different types of rules. Each rule contains a *wildcard* restricting which elements the rule applies to, and a *query* which selects a version of the element. If a query finds exactly one version, that version is used. If no versions are found the view skips that config spec rule and tries the next rule. If the query finds more than one version, and all the versions are on the same branch, the latest of those versions is used (otherwise an error is printed).

A user's "environment" is largely defined by the rules in the config spec, for example:

- A developer working on the "latest and greatest" software versions:

```
element * CHECKEDOUT          (if the file is checked-out use that version)
element * /main/LATEST        (otherwise, use the latest version on the main branch)
```

- A slightly more isolating config spec (for Mary):

```
element * CHECKEDOUT          (if the file is checked-out use that version)
element * {created_by(mary) && created_since(15-Mar)}
```

(use versions checked-in by Mary on or after Mar 15)

```
element * /main/LATEST -time 15-Mar
```

(otherwise, the latest as of 15-March)

Note that the "time rule" above allows you to see sources (and source tree organization) as they were at any time in the past.

- Someone performing maintenance to an old release:

```
element * CHECKEDOUT            (if the file is checked-out use that version)
element * .../v2_fixes/LATEST     (use latest version on maintenance branch)
element * V2 -mkbranch v2_fixes
                                  (otherwise, the official V2 released version)
```

The "-mkbranch" clause causes ClearCase to automatically create a "v2_fixes" branch off the V2 label when the user checks out the element (if the branch doesn't already exist). In essence, this last rule defines and enforces a policy: all bugfixes to V2 go on the "v2_fixes" branch.

- Building a new Fortran compiler front-end but linking it with a stable backend:

```
element /usr/src/backend/... V2  (released version for all in backend sub-tree)
element * CHECKEDOUT
element * /main/LATEST
```

- Building a patch version that includes just a single bug fix:

```
element * {bugnum == 297}          (version with "bugnum" attribute set to 297)
element * V2
```

- Building a new program based on the same versions used in a previously-built release of the program, using a released executable as a guide for picking versions:

```
element * {bugnum == 297}
element * -config /vobs/releases/prog@@12-Dec-93
```

ClearCase queries support numerous other built-in functions and operators (such as *and, or, not*). To facilitate implementation of group-wide policies, an "include" directive allows a config spec incorporate administrator-defined rules.

1.8.2 Flexibility of Rule-Based Version Selection

This rule-based scheme for defining source configurations provides power and flexibility, supporting both "broad-brush" and "fine-tuned" approaches. The entire source environment can be configured with just a few rules, applied to all file and directory elements. When required, fine tuning can be implemented at the individual file or directory level.

For example, a developer might discover that someone has created a new version of a critical header file (say, *base.h@@/main/17*) — a change that causes the developer's compilations to fail. A config spec rule can "roll back" the critical file (in that developer's view) to a known "good" version:

```
element base.h /main/16
   ... or ...
element base.h /main/LATEST -time 11:30
```

(The use of the time rule in the second alternative is very useful when an application compiles correctly before lunch break, but not after.)

It is also easy to achieve "special effects" with config specs. For example, if *no* version of an element matches any of the config spec's rules, the element is suppressed from the view. Neither standard UNIX tools nor ClearCase programs using that view will "see" the element. This feature can be used to configure views that are restricted to accessing a particular subset of sources.

1.8.3 Open-Endedness of a View

The view delays evaluation of the config spec until an element is actually accessed through the virtual file system. For example, assume that a view has a rule requesting "the version with the RLS2.0 version label". A user who accesses file "foo.h" through that view will see the version currently labelled RLS2.0, say version 29. If for some reason the RLS2.0 label were to move to another version, say version 30, the user will see version 30 on the next access of "foo.h".

Since the rules in a config spec typically involve pathname patterns (wildcards) that apply to many files and/or directories, a view is open-ended — new files, new directories, or even entire newly-mounted VOBs on new servers are automatically incorporated into a view. There is no need to "add files to a view" explicitly. Continuing the example above, if the developer with a "RLS2.0" config spec were to suddenly look into a VOB owned by the technical writing group and located on the other end of the network, he would see the RLS2.0 version of the product documentation.

1.8.4 Storage Efficiency of a View

Since access to shared versions is accomplished by mapping, rather than by copying, a view is storage-efficient. For example, several views might select the same version of a source file; the actual uncompressed source text for the version is shared in a network-wide cache so the incremental storage cost to a view for accessing this version is *zero*. In addition, the views can share access to object modules built from shared source files through the *wink-in* feature (discussed later), sharing binary derived objects can save an enormous amount of space.

1.8.5 Checked-out Files

Normally, all files in the VOB appear to be read-only, that is, the permissions on the file (as seen through the virtual file system) state that *no one* has write permission. Attempts to modify the file, no matter what your user identity, results in a "permission denied: read-only file system" error. (This is similar to attempting to modify a CD-ROM file system.)

A developer, working in a view, enters a *checkout* command to make a source file editable. This seems to change a file element in the data repository from read-only to read-write. In reality, ClearCase copies the read-only repository version to a writable file in the view's private storage area. This writable file, the "checked-out version", appears in the view at the same pathname as the file element; the view accesses this editable, checked-out version until the developer enters a *checkin* command, which updates the repository and deletes the view-private file.

An element may have more than one branch checked-out. For example, "Marys_view" may check-out the "mainline" development branch (utils.c@@/main) while "Johns_view" checks-out maintenance branch (utils.c@/main/v2_fixes). By default, when you check-out a branch you have *reserved* the exclusive right to check-in — that is, only you may extend the branch with a new version. ClearCase also supports *unreserved* check-outs, which allow several views to check-out the same branch. The first one to check-in "wins"; all others must merge their changes before checking-in. Reserved check-outs are like the locking check-outs of SCCS, RCS, and DSEE; unreserved check-outs are more like the model used by NSE and TeamWare.

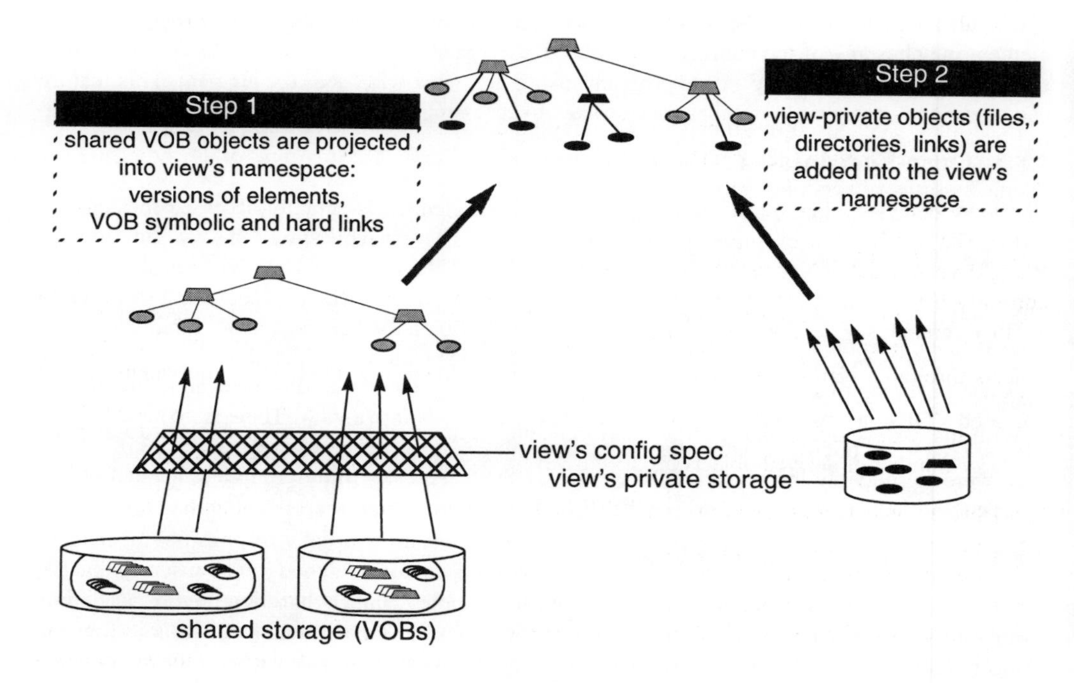

Figure 1.23 The *view* combines VOB objects with private objects

The CHECKEDOUT config spec rule selects the version of an element checked-out to the current view. If a config spec doesn't have a CHECKEDOUT rule, it won't see the view-private checked-out file, rather, it will show the version selected by the other rules. This can be very convenient: suppose you check-out several files and make changes; the resulting program doesn't work because of problems in one of the changed files; you want to temporarily back-out the changes made to file util.c and build and test the other changes without losing your changes to util.c. Your config spec might be:

```
element util.c /main/LATEST      (for just file, don't use checked-out version)
element * CHECKEDOUT             (use checked-out versions of other files)
element * /main/LATEST           (otherwise, latest checked-in version)
```

With the config spec above, the latest checked-in version of util.c will be selected, the view-private checked-out version will be *eclipsed* by the VOB version. Although the editable copy of the checked-out file is stored in the view, the VOB records and controls all check-outs. This means that global information about check-outs is available:

```
% lscheckout

30-Mar.10:15  util.c@@/main by Mary in Mary_new_devel
"Implement faster sorting algorithm"

30-Mar.10:00  message.c@@/main/v2_fixes by John in John_bugfix
"Fix spelling error in message"
```

```
28-Mar.19:30 util.c@@/main/v2_fixes by John in John_bugfix.
"sort core dumps when passed 0 length list"
...
```

In addition to checked-out files the view may hold other private files, such as editor "backup" files, temporary scratch files from command piping (grep "x=0" *.c >mytmp), or any other file not deemed worthy of version control.

1.9 BUILD MANAGEMENT

Ultimately, source code must be built into *derived objects*: binaries, executable images, and other objects that constitute a final product. Derived objects are produced from sources and other derived objects through a series of translation steps, typically defined in a makefile or equivalent system model.

With many developers, many target platforms, and many releases, it can be difficult to manage the large number of derived objects produced. Several key problems must be addressed:

- Derived objects must be built from the "correct" version of the sources using the correct tools and build options. The "environment management" system is usually responsible for making sure that the right sources are used. Most CM systems do not do a good job or ensuring that the right version of the tools (like compilers) as used, or that the right build options are used. For example, standard Make [Fel79] would not rebuild if you switched the compiler flags from "-g" (debug) to "-O" (optimize). Ideally, tool versions, build options, and environment variables would play a role in the rebuild logic.
- Derived objects produced by one person must not "interfere" with the derived objects produced by others; ideally, users should be able to share each others derived objects when appropriate. Sharing derived objects saves both time and space.
- Software rebuilds must rebuild all derived objects that have been invalidated due to changes in the sources or changes in some other factor; ideally, the build management tool will support *minimal rebuilding*.
- After a derived object is produced, it must be possible to determine a reliable "bill-of-materials" (BOM) describing all of the constituent parts of that object; ideally, the BOM should be absolutely correct and detailed enough to easily reconstruct the complete source environment in effect at the time the object was built.

Standard "Make" will rebuild a *target* (usually a derived object) if one of its dependencies has a modification-time that is newer than the target. Make, and other tools that base rebuild decisions on modification-time, do not allow users to share derived objects in a parallel development, because there is a single time scale. For example, suppose John and Mary were each working on a variant of "foo.c" and have both finished changing the source and have checked-in their changes. If John builds "foo.o" and places it in a shared binary area, Mary will find that it post-dates her "foo.c" — so her changes will not get built. Similar problems result if John were to decide to back-out a change and use an earlier version of a source file. Most development teams "solve" this problem by simply not trying to share binaries.

In order to share derived objects, the build system must know exactly which source configuration the developer wants to build with, and have an exact bill-of-materials for all existing derived objects. Reuse of derived objects must be based on matching the developer's desired build configuration against the known configurations (BOMs) of the existing derived objects.

Minimal rebuilding and generation of a bill-of-materials require that the CM build system have knowledge of inter-component dependencies. Traditional system builders require the user to specify the dependencies in some sort of system model, such as a makefile, a DSEE system model, or a CaseWare/CM assembly model.

System models require the proper declaration and maintenance of dependencies. If a dependency is not declared, it will be mistakenly ignored; any extra declared dependencies may cause unnecessary rebuilds. In practice, maintaining dependency information is an unwanted and unwieldy task, which leads to makefiles (or equivalent system models) rapidly becoming out of date. System model generators attempt to partially automate the maintenance of dependencies. Unfortunately, they are usually language-specific, do not properly calculate dependencies in the presence of conditional compilation, and are slow enough to discourage frequent use.

In addition to being hard to maintain, system model dependency graphs are too static to be accurate for a large software build: they would have to be regenerated after every source change, and a different dependency graph would be needed for every possible source configuration. Also, dependency graphs fail to reflect build dependencies that are not source-code based, such as the version of the compiler, the type of target system, or the version of the operating system itself. Moreover, they don't reflect dynamic environmental factors, such as search paths, conditional compilation, and builder options (for instance, MAKEFLAGS and CDEBUGFLAGS=-O).

In order to rebuild correctly and maintain a bill-of-materials accurately, the rebuild logic and bill-of-materials mechanism must not rely solely on user-provided dependency information. Rather, it must operate at a fundamentally lower level in the system build process. ClearCase solves the problem by having its virtual file system, which lives inside the native operating system, gather a bill-of-materials by monitoring the file I/O done by the compiler and other tools during a system build. The ClearCase bill-of-materials mechanism operates in a way that is similar to the way a high security operating system audits all file system access.

1.10 A CLOSER LOOK AT CLEARCASE BUILD MANAGEMENT

ClearCase views provide a software build environment that allows developers to build ClearCase-controlled data using their hosts' native "Make" programs, their organization's home-grown shell scripts, or third-party build utilities. ClearCase includes its own build utility, *clearmake*, which uses "traditional" makefiles but which has many features not supported by other build programs:

- *build auditing*, with automatic detection of source dependencies (including header file dependencies)
- automatic creation of permanent "bill-of-materials" documentation of the build process and its results
- sophisticated build-avoidance algorithms, guaranteeing correct results when building in a parallel development environment
- sharing of binaries among developers' views, saving both time and storage space
- parallel and distributed building, applying the resources of multiple processors and/or multiple hosts to builds of large software systems

Developers use clearmake in the same way they would use Make to perform builds; they can even use existing makefiles. Builds (along with all other ClearCase-related work) take place in a *view*. The view's config spec determines which source versions are used for the build. Typically, developers work in separate, private views; sometimes, a group shares a single view — for example, during a software integration period.

A file produced by a software build is termed a *derived object* (*DO*). Initially, derived objects are stored in the view's private storage area. They are treated like view-private files and projected into the virtual file system. Associated with each derived object is a bill-of-materials called a *configuration record* (*config rec* or *CR*) which *clearmake* can use during subsequent builds to decide whether or not the DO can be reused or shared.

A makefile describes a number of *target* objects, such as "myprog" or "util.o". Usually, each target in the makefile lists dependencies and provides a *build script* for producing the target derived object from the dependencies. A configuration record contains the list of versions that were read or written during the execution of a single target's build script. For example, when building foo.o the source versions foo.c@@/main/17, foo.h@@/main/bugfix/22, and bar.h@@/main/5 were read, and foo.o@@17-Jan.10:52.11 was written. It also includes the text of the build script itself and other environment information, such as username, date, and OS version.

ClearCase may know about several instances of a derived object, each with a different configuration record, each potentially built by a different person. The "lsdo" command (list derived objects) lists all the instances of a DO with a given pathname or in a given directory. For example:

```
% lsdo foo.o
foo.o@@10-Jan.09:01:30 built by Jones at host Neptune
foo.o@@8-Jan.17:15:08 built by Smith at host Pluto
foo.o@@8-Jan.15:31:00 built by Smith at host Pluto
foo.o@@30-Dec.23:40:58 built by Markus at host Saturn
```

The "catcr" command lists the contents of a derived object's configuration record. An abbreviated example:

```
% catcr foo.o@@8-Jan.17:15:08
Derived Object foo.o@@8-Jan.17:15:08 built by Smith (John Smith)
Built at host Pluto (Sparc-10 running Solaris-2.3)
read versions
parse.c@@/main/17
parse.h@@/main/7
lex.h@@/main/93
produced derived objects
parse.o@@8-Jan.17:15:08
parse.lst@@8-Jan.17:15:08
EVs: CDEBUGFLAGS = -g, CPU = sun5
Build script: /bin/cc -g -l -o parse.o parse.c
```

The "diffcr" commands shows the difference between two CRs. With the "-r" option, this command will recursively walk down to sub-derived objects and show their differences, as well. When a newly built program doesn't work, but a previous version does, this command is invaluable for describing "what changed" between the two program builds. An abbreviated example:

```
% diffcr -r myprog@@12-Jan.11:50 myprog@@13-Jan.09:00
target foo.o
< foo.c@@/main/17
> foo.c@@/main/18

target bar.o
< CDEBUGFLAGS = -g
> CDEBUGFLAGS = -O
```

1.10.1 Automatic Dependency Auditing

In order to get an accurate list of the objects accessed, ClearCase *audits* all file I/O done to ClearCase-controlled objects during the execution of the build script. Auditing is a feature provided by the ClearCase virtual file system. Clearmake turns on auditing just before executing the build script, and turns it off when the script completes. Clearmake then creates a new configuration record by combining:

- audit information from the virtual file system
- target build script and options from the makefile
- environment information from the current process
- 'stat' information for non-ClearCase objects in the makefile (e.g. /usr/include/stdio.h).

When the build script completes, clearmake tells the ClearCase object base to associate the new configuration record with the newly produced derived objects. Notice that configuration records are maintained at a per-target granularity, rather than one config rec for the entire build. This enables reuse and sharing of derived objects at the individual target level. If a derived object is built from other derived objects, like a program linked together from binaries, the new configuration record contains references to the configuration records of the sub-derived objects. Even if the sub-derived objects are deleted their configuration records will be preserved as long as they are needed by the higher-level object.

ClearCase also provide a tool called *clearaudit*, which can be used to produce configuration records without using *clearmake*. Clearaudit runs an arbitrary script with auditing enabled, and then records a configuration record. For example, you can use *clearaudit* when writing a source snapshot to a tape (with tar or some other tool). This will create a configuration record listing all the versions written to tape.

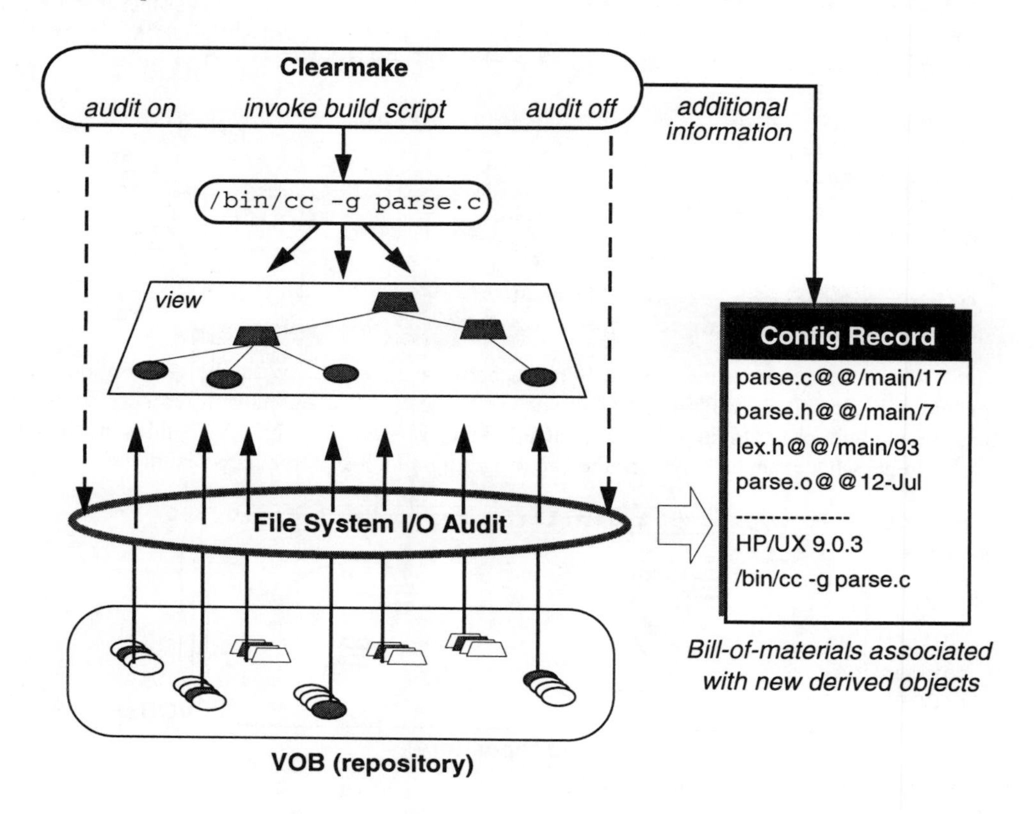

Figure 1.24 Automatic dependency gathering

1.10.2 Reusing and Sharing Builds

As a build environment, each view is "semi-isolated" from other views. Building software in one view can never *disturb* the work in another view — even another build of the same program taking place at the same time. But a developer can examine and *benefit* from work previously performed in another view. When a developer runs clearmake to build a target derived object, say util.o, one of three things can happen:

- clearmake can decide to reuse the util.o currently visible in the current view.
- clearmake can decide to build util.o by executing the build script in the makefile.
- clearmake can locate a past build of util.o in some other view and cause it to *wink-in* (appear) in the current view, replacing any prior instance of util.o. This saves the time and disk space involved in building new objects that duplicate existing ones.

The key to this scheme is the fact that each derived object and its configuration record (bill-of-materials) is registered in the development team's VOB. Even though the physical storage for the derived objects is initially spread among the views that built them, the development team's VOBs constitute a globally-accessible index for all derived objects.

Clearmake decides to reuse, rather than rebuild, a derived object if all of the versions listed in the derived object's configuration record correspond to the versions currently requested by the current view's configuration specification. In addition, the build script, options, and environment variables in the current makefile must match those recorded in the configuration record.

If the derived object in the current view is not acceptable, clearmake will look at other instances of the derived object (potentially built by other developers) registered with the VOB. If a suitable instance can be found, *clearmake* will use it.

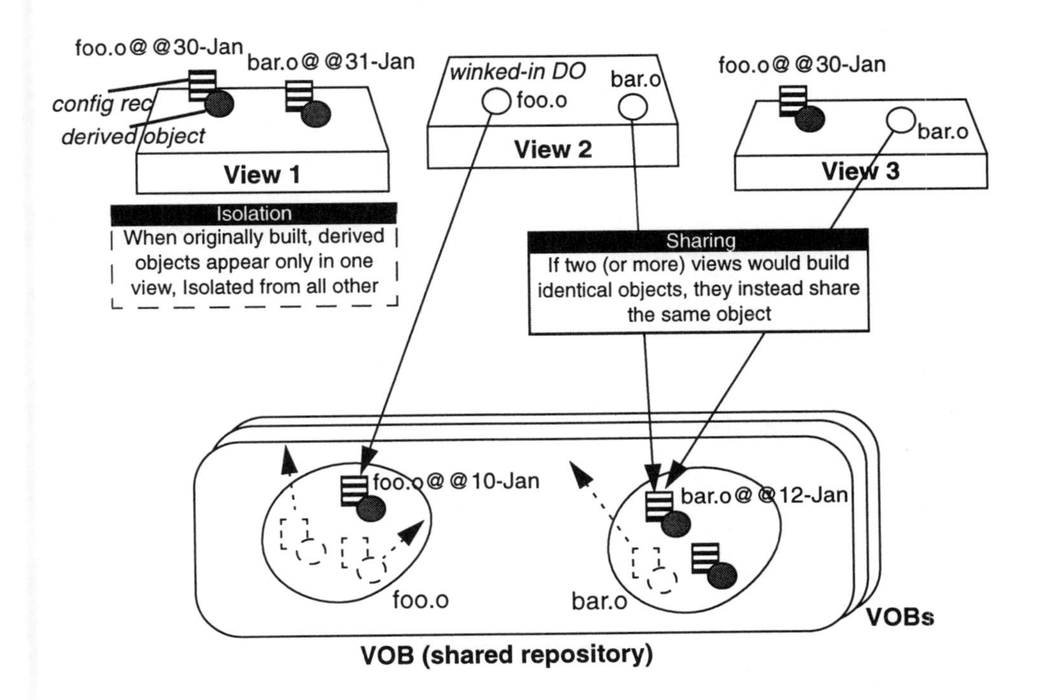

Figure 1.25 VOBs hold information about derived objects

If the desired DO is in another view's private storage area (i.e. it is not yet shared) clearmake will first *promote* the DO to a shared storage pool in the VOB by moving the DO's physical storage from the view to the VOB. This process is invisible to the original view, and is really just an optimization that helps to balance storage and to ensure the availability of shared resources. If the DO is already shared among other views, it does not need to be moved. In any case, clearmake will then *wink-in* the DO by creating what appears to be a hard-link to the DO in the view.

A reference count is maintained for all derived objects; it counts the number of views using a particular DO. A background process, called the *DO scrubber*, periodically deletes derived objects that have a zero reference count. DOs that never became shared are deleted as soon as their view deletes or rebuilds the object.

1.10.3 No header dependencies

There are really two types of dependencies listed in a makefile: *header* dependencies, such as "util.c includes arc.h, util.h, and zbuf.h," and *build-order* dependencies, such as "util.o must be built before myprog can be built." It is the header dependencies that are particularly difficult to maintain. When using clearmake, header file dependencies are unnecessary, because they are automatically recorded during the build audit. In order to change dependencies, such as adding a header file to a ".c" file (or to a ".h" file), that "parent" file would have to be changed — which would result in a rebuild. The audit of the rebuild would detect and record the new dependency. In practice, having correct rebuilds, without having to list header file dependencies, is a major advantage to using clearmake. Given a built program (with a configuration record) the "catcr -makefile" command will generate a makefile with full dependency information so that sources and a makefile can be exported to non-ClearCase sites.

1.10.4 Checking-in Derived Objects

As discussed in the section on version control, ClearCase can version any type of object, including derived objects such as executable images. When you check-in a derived object it becomes a permanent "released" derived object. Its configuration record is kept with it. Checked-in derived objects are first-class versions and can be used in config specs, for example, you could use a previous release of a utilities library rather than building one:

```
element libmotif.a RLS2.0
```

1.10.5 Parallel distributed building

In addition to its configuration management related features clearmake also provides heterogeneous parallel distributed building [Leb87]. That is, clearmake analyzes the build reorder dependencies in the makefile and then submits multiple compilations at once to various machines on the network. Clearmake takes into account how busy each potential build server host is when choosing hosts to build on. Clearmake supports client user preferences ("only use machines more than 75% idle") as well remote server access-control rules ("between 9am and 6pm only group 'r&d' can use this server, and then only if it is greater than 80%").

Parallel distributed build can greatly reduce the time required to build a large system, sometimes by a factor of ten. The combination of parallel distributed building and wink-in (automatic build sharing) can result in even larger performance gains.

1.11 PROCESS CONTROL AND PROJECT MANAGEMENT

In general terms, a "software development process" consists of *everything* involved in the conception, creation, deployment, and maintenance of a software product. Configuration management is usually a large and important part of the process; but problem tracking, activity definition and scheduling, automated testing, metrics monitoring, and other tasks also have their own unique roles. The development process can vary greatly from company to company, and from project to project. The level of formality, the amount of automation, and the tools used must be tailored to each business.

Although software development policies and procedures vary widely from organization to organization, they share a common goal: improving the predictability, quality, and time-to-market of the software under development. In order to achieve these goals, a process needs some level of formality, or *maturity* [Hum89]. Software engineers often fear that "process" means wasteful bureaucracy; it can, but it doesn't have to. There are "bad" processes and "good" processes: a bad process adds overhead without producing sufficient increased organization or quality to pay for itself; a good process can organize a large, complex, and vague task into series of well-defined and manageable tasks.

An important aspect of the SEI maturity model is that an organization must start by writing down the current process so that it can be repeated, measured, and gradually improved. While SEI CMM is an evolutionary approach to process improvement, *business process reengineering* [Ham93] is a revolutionary approach. Corporate reengineering advocates starting by defining the organizational structure and processes you *wish* you had and then transforming the existing corporation into the "ideal" structure as rapidly as possible.

Regardless of how the software development process is developed, once there are well-defined rules it is possible to start automating the process. There are commercial tools that help automate many parts of the software development process, but the tools by themselves do not constitute a process. Rather, the process is the *rules* for how the people, objects, and tools interact.

A class of tool called *workflow managers* attempt to automate business processes with the goal of reducing costs and increasing the overall quality of products and services. The key concept in workflow tools is *action-response*: there are a number of tasks, assigned to various people, which must be accomplished. When an action is taken on one of the tasks, a response is automatically generated: typically an e-mail notification or the creation of a new task. Various state-transition rules govern which actions can be taken.

Enforcing process control rules, with or without an automated workflow system, is a highly desirable goal. Enforcement requires the integration of individual development tools with each other and with the process control mechanism. For example, the process may insist that the configuration management system correlate source changes with defect reports in the problem tracking system. Another example is that the process may require that source code pass a certain metric before it can be checked-in.

1.11.1 ClearCase Process Integration

The ability to enforce process rules places requirements on a CM system. ClearCase does not currently provide a process modelling capability however it does include a flexible, powerful process control toolset, which administrators can use to implement an organization's existing policies. ClearCase process-management tools enable:

- monitoring of the entire development rocess
- fine-tuned management of development activities — controlling who, how, and where changes can be made
- automated communications, targeted as required at individual developers, development groups, and managers
- organization and cross-referencing of all development data: source code, memos, design proposals, technical manuals, and so on
- sample policies for tight integration with several popular commercial defect tracking systems

The process control toolset comprises both with static mechanisms (control structures) and dynamic mechanisms (procedures). Some of the mechanisms are completely automatic; others are created and/or controlled by users and administrators.

When ClearCase client programs make changes to the development environment, they automatically store *event records* in VOB databases. An event includes who made the change, when, why, from where, and the exact nature of the change. ClearCase maintains event records for all kinds of changes, not just the check-in of a new version. For example, ClearCase records who attached an attribute to a version.

Any process-management scheme requires an *access control* component: limiting the use of individual data objects and commands to particular users or groups of users. ClearCase provides a static permissions model (like Unix permissions), a static *lock* mechanism (like access control lists), as well a dynamic policy enforcement mechanism. The dynamic mechanism is based on *triggers*. A *pre-event* trigger is an arbitrary shell script that runs (*fires*) before an operation is performed; the script, based on the user, attribute values/states, the source, or any other factors, can decide to allow or disallow the operation. An administrator can define a trigger for any update operation. A *post-event* trigger fires after the operation completes, typically performing some type of notification.

ClearCase triggers, combined with ClearCase attributes, provide the mechanism necessary to define and enforce many kinds of process models, including state transition models. For example, assume your process model states that only "priority 1" bug fixes are permitted on an integration branch after the branch is declared "frozen". The model is implemented by:

- a "status" attribute on integration branches, with the value "open" or "frozen"
- a lock on the status attribute preventing anyone from changing the value of the status attribute, except for the project administrator
- a "bugnum" attribute on versions, whose value is a key for locating a bug report in a third-party defect tracking system
- a pre-event trigger on the integration branches, monitoring check-ins

When any user attempts to check-in a version on the integration branch, the trigger will fire. The trigger script always allows the check-in if the integration branch is in the "open" state. When it is "frozen", the script:

- fetches the value of the "bugnum" attribute from the version being checked-in
- uses that value to query the defect tracking system for the priority of the bug
- if there is no bugnum attribute, or if the bug is not "priority 1", disallows the check-in

Since trigger scripts are just ordinary shell scripts, and since ClearCase can be queried from a shell, it is very easy to develope sophisticated policy enforcement triggers. In practice, the power and flexibility of the trigger mechanism has made it the most frequently used ClearCase policy enforcement tool.

1.12 CONCLUSIONS

Configuration management is a key part of any mature development process. The CM problems faced by organizations today are very challenging: large projects, geographically separated teams, many platforms, and extreme time pressures. In order to meet these challenges a CM system must: provide comprehensive version control and change management, provide environments for large-scale parallel development which enable sharing as well as isolation, provide a mechanism for tracking software builds and their bill-of-materials, transparently fit into the existing environments, and be closely integrated with the development process and other development tools.

Only if these challenges are met will the CM system avoid being shelf-ware and provide a solution that really works.

ACKNOWLEDGMENTS

Thanks to John Posner for reviewing and editing this material. The author can be contacted at leblang@atria.com; additional information about ClearCase can be obtained from info@atria.com.

REFERENCES

[Cle93] *ClearCase Concepts*, Atria Software Inc., Natick, Mass., 1993.

[Dew93] P. Dewan, J. Riedl, "Toward Computer-Supported Concurrent Software Engineering", *IEEE Software*, Jan. 1993, pp 17-27.

[Fel79] S. Feldman, "Make: A Program for Maintaining Computer Programs", *Software Practice and Experience*, April 1979, pp. 255-265.

[Ham93] M. Hammer, J. Champy, Reengineering the Corporation, HarperBusiness, 1993

[Hum89] W. S. Humphrey, *Managing the Software Process*, Addison-Wesley, 1989

[Kat88] R. Katz, *Towards a Unified Framework for Version Modeling*, Report No. UCB/CSD 88/484, Univ. of California, Berkeley, CA , Dec 1988.

[Lam91] A. Lampen, "Advancing Files to Attributed Software Objects", *Proceedings of Winter '91 Dallas USENIX Technical Conference*, USENIX Association, Jan. 1991.

[Leb84] D. Leblang, R. Chase Jr., "Computer-Aided Software Engineering in a Distributed Workstation Environment", *ACM SIGPlan Notices*, May 1984, pp. 104-112.

[Leb87] D. Leblang, R. Chase Jr., "Parallel Software Configuration Management in a Network Environment", IEEE Software, Nov. 1987.

[Ols93] N. Olsen, "The Software Rush Hour", *IEEE Software*, Sept. 1993, pp 29-37.

[Pau93] M. Paulk, et al., "Capability Maturity Model, Version 1.1", *IEEE Software*, July 1993, pp 16-27.

[PCTE] *PCTE: The Standard for Open Repository*, Prentice-Hall, 1991

[Rei89] C. Reichenberger, "Orthogonal Version Management", 2nd Intl. Workshop on SCM, *ACM SIGSOFT Software Engineering Notes,* Nov. 1989.

[Tic85] W. Tichy, "RCS - A System for Version Control," *Software Practice and Experience*, July 1985, pp. 637-654.

2

A Bi-Level Language for Software Process Modeling

Gail E. Kaiser, Steven S. Popovich and Israel Z. Ben-Shaul
Columbia University, Department of Computer Science, New York, NY 10027

ABSTRACT

Most software process modeling formalisms are well-suited to one of two levels of specification, but not both. Some process languages concentrate on the *topology* of control flow and synchronization. These languages make it easy to define the broad outline of a process, but harder (or even impossible) to refine the process definition by expressing policies concerned with individual tools and data classes. Other process formalisms stress *constraints* on individual activities: it is easy to define the prerequisites and consequences of a process step, but far from straightforward to express the workflow among steps. These languages also tend to be more difficult for humans to understand. We advocate combining topology-oriented and constraint-oriented formalisms, to produce *bi-level* process modeling languages suitable for expressing and enacting both aspects of complex, large scale processes. We present one complete example of this approach, the Activity Structures Language, which employs rules for constraint specification and an extended form of regular expressions for topological specification. ASL has been implemented on top of the MARVEL rule-based process-centered environment.

2.1 INTRODUCTION

A *process* is the set of steps performed during development and/or maintenance of a software system. Different (sub)processes may be suitable for different personnel roles, lifecycle phases, projects, organizations, application domains, etc. A *process model* defines a process in some formal notation, called a process modeling language (PML). The concept of process modeling and research on process modeling languages has increasingly attracted attention in the software engineering community, as evidenced by the series of International Software Process Workshops and International Conferences on the Software Process. A dominant theme

Configuration Management, Edited by Tichy

is the notion of a process-centered environment which operates as an "enaction" engine for a specific PML. Environment instances are maintained by trained process engineers who define and evolve project-specific process models. Enaction usually enforces and/or automates (portions of) the desired process on behalf of a team of environment users (see, e.g., [Sch93, ICS93]).

Many PMLs are based to some extent on notational paradigms originally devised for other purposes. For example, APPL/A [Sut90] extends Ada, Funsoft nets [Gru91] are based on Petri nets, AP5 [Coh86] uses OPS5-like production system rules, Darwin [Min91] employs Prolog-like logic programming rules, Adele [BEM91] follows database triggers, HFSP [Kat89] is similar to attribute grammars, *etc.* Many PMLs have successfully been used to model part or all of the ISPW6 [KFF+91] or ISPW7 [HK91] "example problem", but it is generally agreed that some language paradigms are better than others at expressing different aspects of software processes [KR90].

One of the most significant distinctions among different styles of PMLs is their affinities towards control flow and synchronization, or the topology of the workflow, *vs.* constraints on isolated process steps. *Topology* specifies the required and/or prohibited (partial) orderings among process steps, generally but not always at a relatively global level of abstraction, i.e., perhaps covering the entire process, but at least a coherent process fragment consisting of multiple steps. In contrast, *constraints* restrict the applications of individual tools, and their access to and manipulation of process state and product data. Nearly all proposed PMLs are reasonably well-suited to one or the other aspect, and most are sufficient for both in the same sense that a Turing machine can express any computation, but few handle both kinds of modeling issues equally well. We believe that PMLs would best be constructed by selecting a *pair* of complementary formalisms, one oriented towards topology and the other towards constraints, and then combining these formalisms in a *bi-level* fashion that facilitates enaction of both kinds of process model requirements.

The two styles of process formalisms addressed here are both distinguished from the *action languages* that appear in many process-centered environments, either to directly implement new tools or to "wrap" existing tools. For example, AP5 specifies the process in a rule-based form whose actions are implemented in Common Lisp. Adele triggers have two distinctly different syntaxes for their condition and action parts. Darwin's object scripts can be implemented in any programming language, whereas its rules use a Prolog-like notation. The action language thus constitutes a third linguistic formalism necessary for process enaction, but separate from process modeling, *per se*. Further discussion of action languages is outside the scope of this paper.

We present a working multi-user implementation of a bi-level PML. We selected our own MARVEL Strategy Language (MSL) [HKBBS92] to express constraints, and a variant of constrained expressions [ADWR86][1] due to Riddle [Rid91] for the topology component. MSL provides planning system-style rules for specifying the prerequisites and consequences of the tool invocations of each individual process step, usually applied to the tool's data parameters and related objects. Constrained expressions support regular expression operators and concurrent shuffle of process fragments, as well as send/receive primitives for synchronization among concurrent subexpressions — thus directing the overall workflow. Constrained expressions were originally developed as an alternative to path expressions [CH74] for specifying

[1] This use of the term "constrained" should not be confused with the "constraints" discussed in this paper.

event patterns in concurrent systems, and similar formalisms have been widely used in both sequential [BH83] and concurrent [Bat88, PHK91] debuggers.

Our resulting PML is called the Activity Structures Language (ASL). MSL is a proper subset of ASL. The rest of ASL consists of Riddle's activity structures extended with parameter variables, whose classes (types) are defined by object-oriented data modeling facilities already provided by MSL. (MARVEL's action language was used "as is" for interfacing to commercial off-the-shelf tools through what is often called tool envelopes [GK91].) ASL was implemented by *translation* of the extended constrained expressions into MSL, followed by normal enaction of MSL using the multi-user MARVEL kernel [BSKH93]. The only modification to MARVEL itself was the addition of a 750-line module in the process engine. The idea of implementing constrained expressions in terms of MARVEL was first suggested by Williams [Wil88], although he did not express the idea as a multi-level process language, and did not undertake any implementation effort.

We motivate our approach by presenting a small process fragment — taken from the ISPW7 example problem — that requires modeling of both topology and constraints. We then sketch the two process modeling formalisms adopted, explain our designs for the ASL notation and its enaction model, and describe the implementation. We show a portion of our solution to the example problem using ASL, and briefly compare to related work on topology-oriented, constraint-oriented, and bi-level process modeling formalisms. The paper ends with a brief summary of the main contributions of this research.

2.2 MOTIVATION

The ISPW7 example problem, which involves specifying a process for making several common types of modifications to a large software system, is probably the closest the software process modeling community comes to a widely recognized "benchmark". We consider one representative subprocess, that of making the design and code changes necessitated by a requirements change. This subprocess begins after the proposed requirements change has been approved and completed. It includes four distinct user *roles*:

1. The designers, who are responsible for maintaining the design specification documents.
2. The reviewers, who must approve the modified design before updated source code can be deposited into the baseline.
3. The programmers, who make all changes to the actual code.
4. The quality assurance engineers, who perform unit tests on the changed system components and ensure that they meet the current design specification.

As illustrated in Figure 2.1, design and code changes may begin in parallel with the reservation of the appropriate design documents and source code modules, respectively. Boxes represent high-level process steps; solid arrows represent control flow of the process within each role, and dashed arrows the synchronization between roles. Once the design has been modified, the review team must approve before it can be deposited into the public repository. This completes the modification of the design, but the code modifications are still pending. In the meantime, the programmers have been performing an edit-compile loop to change the code. They may have already completed their modifications, but are not allowed to deposit their code until the design modification has been accepted. Note that the the "Design Modified" synchronization may occur at any point during the programmers' subprocess before the

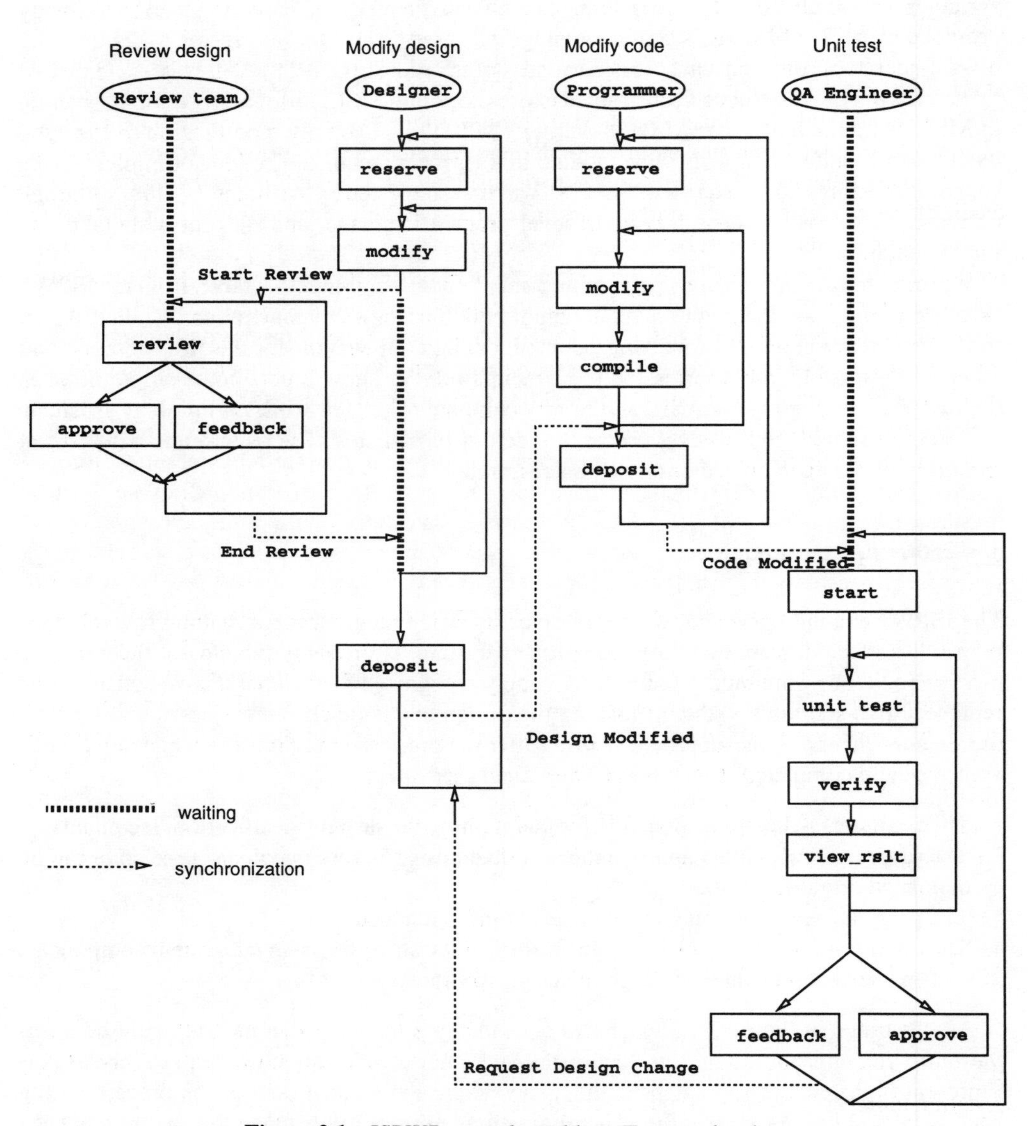

Figure 2.1 ISPW7 example problem: Teamwork subset

deposit, but we only illustrate the latest possible time in the figure. Once the programmers have deposited their changes, the QA engineers can begin their work. These testers may either approve the code, in which case the entire subprocess is complete, or may give feedback to the design team as to which tests failed. The designers in turn may modify the design and/or require the programmers to fix the bugs found by the unit testers. This repeats until the code passes its unit tests.

Figure 2.1 shows an abstract *topology* that hides the *constraints* that determine selection of alternative paths, e.g., whether or not to iterate. For example, the topology's synchronization aspect indicates only that the designers must wait until the review team has completed either an approval or a feedback step before completing their modification process fragment. Thus it would appear to be valid for the designers to deposit their changes immediately after receiving feedback from the reviewers stating that more changes are needed! Instead, the designers' choice of which branch to take should consider the actual decisions of the review team. In particular, they should not have the option of exiting the loop and depositing the design unless the reviewers have approved it. Another example is the programmers' edit-compile loop, where the criteria for whether or not to iterate may depend on the outcome of a tool invocation, i.e., whether or not the compiler detects syntax errors. Further, the programmers should not be permitted to deposit code that has not compiled successfully.

Some but not all topology-oriented PMLs omit constructs for succinctly expressing such decision criteria while all constraint-oriented PMLs (by definition) provide facilities for indicating the conditions under which an individual process step should (or should not) be enacted. In contrast, topological PMLs (by definition) always state control flow paths and synchronization (if there can be multiple participants in the process) directly, but the constraints of the other style of PMLs usually imply only *potential* precedence relationships among process steps, not all of which are appropriate. Both kinds of requirements are stated statically in the process model, using either style of PML, but are fulfilled dynamically during process enaction.

Besides enforcement of both topology and constraints, this subprocess presents several opportunities for automation. Each of the synchronizations shown could be enacted by automatically notifying the recipient role, e.g., automatically generating electronic mail from the review team to the designers when either feedback or approval is complete. Once the code modifications have been made, the compilation process could be triggered automatically. Similarly, the relatively mechanical procedure of running unit tests and verifying the result of each test can sometimes be automated. Many process-centered environments automate portions of the process as well as prevent violations.

2.3 BACKGROUND

Our Activity Structures Language combines two pre-existing notations, Activity Structures due to Riddle and our original MARVEL Strategy Language (MSL). We employed the MSL notation more-or-less "as is",[2] but extended the original activity structures notation in several ways as explained in the following section. Here we briefly introduce the two original notations, reducing the relatively large MSL to focus on those portions relevant to the main points of this paper.

---

[2] We made one change in the semantics of MSL, to allow multiple rules with the same signature but different bodies. This has proved to be useful in general, but first came up during the ASL implementation.

2.3.1 MARVEL Strategy Language

MSL assumes that the process state and product data are stored in MARVEL's object-oriented database; we omit details here, see Section 2.4.1.

Each process step is encapsulated in a *rule* with a name and typed parameter variables. The body of each rule is composed of a *condition*, an optional *activity*, and a set of *effects*. The condition has two subparts: queries, to gather local variables (e.g., included ".h" files when compiling a ".c" file), and properties, which must evaluate to true prior to invocation of the activity. Both queries and properties may include a complex nesting of conjunctions and disjunctions of navigational and associative predicates (which have no side-effects).

The activity names a tool envelope and specifies its inputs and outputs. *Envelopes* are stylized shell scripts, which permit conventional file-oriented tools to be integrated into a process without source modifications or recompilation. Each envelope implicitly returns a code that uniquely selects the specific effect from among those given in the rule, to assert the actual result of the tool on the objectbase (returning 0 selects the first effect, returning 1 the second, *etc*). For example, a successful compilation would probably map to a different effect than one that detected syntax errors.

Separate effects are necessary since an external off-the-shelf tool can directly modify files referred to in the objectbase, through the shared file system (the values of file attributes are pathnames), but cannot directly manipulate the internals of the objectbase. If there is no activity, then there is only one effect. Each effect is a conjunction (treated as an ordered series) of assignments, which perform the specified update operation. The condition and effects together define the constraints on the process step.

When a user enters a command, the MSL process engine selects the matching rule(s) considering multiple inheritance on the classes of the supplied arguments (rule names can be overloaded, for instance, `edit` a source code module *vs.* `edit` a technical report). There may be more than one match, e.g., the same signature but a different condition; the matching rules are considered in an implementation-specific order,[3] but only the first one whose condition can be *satisfied* is actually enacted.

The condition of a rule is satisfied if its properties evaluate to true for every possible value of each local variable (in the case of `forall` queries) or for at least one value of each local variable (`exists` queries), considering also the values of the parameter variables (i.e., the actual parameters supplied to the rule). If the condition of a selected rule is not satisfied, backward chaining is attempted. If the condition is already satisfied or becomes satisfied after a backward chain, the activity is initiated; otherwise the user is informed that the process step cannot be carried out at this time. After the activity, the appropriate effect is asserted. This triggers forward chaining to any rules whose conditions become satisfied by the effect, all of which are enacted in an implementation-specific order obeying the annotations below. The asserted effects of these rules may in turn satisfy the conditions of other rules, and so on. Eventually no further conditions become satisfied and forward chaining terminates.

Forward and backward chaining through condition predicates and effect assignments is controlled by chaining annotations. Each predicate/assignment is annotated as either *atomicity*, enclosed in square brackets "[...]", or *automation*, enclosed in parentheses "(...)". All forward chaining through an atomicity assignment in an asserted effect to rules with satisfied conditions must be completed as part of an all-or-nothing transaction. In contrast, forward chaining from an automation assignment is optional, and can be "turned off" wholesale or explicitly restricted

[3] Always the same order, there is no non-determinism.

through `no_forward` or `no_chain` annotations on individual (automation) predicates in the condition (preventing forward chaining into that rule) or assignments in an effect (preventing forward chaining out). Backward chaining into either atomicity or automation assignments is considered a form of automation chaining, and thus optional. Backward chaining can be restricted by `no_backward` or `no_chain` annotations on individual predicates in the condition or assignments in an effect (preventing backward chaining out of the rule or into it, respectively). The allowed backward chaining and forward chaining over the rule base implicitly define the topology of the process; since it is rather difficult to discern this topology from inspection of the rule base, MARVEL provides a tool for browsing the rule network constructed by matching predicates in rule conditions with assignments in effects.

MSL does not provide any explicit synchronization primitives. Instead, individual rules and/or atomic rule chains enacted on behalf of different users that attempt to access the same data at the same time in incompatible modes (e.g., one reads while another writes or both write) are resolved through a semantics-based concurrency control protocol [Bar92]. There are also coordination modeling facilities for defining project-specific collaboration policies, which also apply reactively to concurrency control conflicts that happen to come up; see [Hei93b].

Figure 2.2 shows a representative rule from the C/Marvel process we used in MARVEL's own development; the full process consists of 40 classes, 184 rules and 46 tool envelopes.[4] This `arch` rule's queries gather up all the C, yacc, lex and ar files included in the module value of its parameter variable ("?m"), as well as in any nested modules.[5] The properties check whether the module has already been archived, and if not, permits backward chaining to attempt to compile everything in the module (that have not already been compiled) and to archive all its components (that have not already been archived). However, separately executing the appropriate archive rule on one of these components does not automatically forward chain to trigger this `arch` rule on the enclosing module, because that is denied by the `no_forward` annotation. Whenever `arch`'s second effect is asserted, then all other rules whose conditions are satisfied by setting the status of a related ar file to archived are executed as part of a transaction; if for some reason it is not possible to complete all these rules, then the whole chain (including the original `arch` rule) is rolled back and any side-effects undone.

2.3.2 Activity Structures

Activity Structures are oriented towards expressing topology of process fragments. Riddle's activity structures notation consists of regular expressions extended with two concurrency operators, *shuffle* and *concurrent repetition*. The usual sequencing, alternation and iteration apply to named activities, or subexpressions composed of the various operators and activities. Each activity corresponds to a process step. Shuffle allows its operands to be interleaved in any arbitrary order, except as restricted by embedded send and receive primitives (which may substitute anywhere for an activity operand). To permit process steps to execute truly concurrently, the activities mentioned in the shuffle operands could represent "begin-step" and "end-step" rather than whole steps. Concurrent repetition allows zero or more instances of its operand to be interleaved in any arbitrary order.

---

[4] These statistics are for the C/Marvel process released with MARVEL 3.1; there have been several earlier processes with the same name.

[5] The complicated-looking `config` and `MACHINE` references are there because C/Marvel supports multiple configurations, i.e., with and without ASL, and multiple machine architectures, particularly SparcStation, DecStation and IBM RS6000.

```
arch [?m:MODULE]:
    (and (forall CFILE ?c suchthat
           (and no_chain (member [?m.cfiles ?c])
                (or (?c.config = ?m.config)
                    (?c.possible_config = ""))))
         (forall YFILE ?y suchthat
           (and no_chain (member [?m.yfiles ?y])
                (or (?y.config = ?m.config)
                    (?y.possible_config = ""))))
         (forall LFILE ?x suchthat
           (and no_chain (member [?m.lfiles ?x])
                (or (?x.config = ?m.config)
                    (?x.possible_config = ""))))
         (forall MODULE ?child suchthat
           no_chain (member [?m.modules ?child]))
         (exists AFILE ?a suchthat
           (and no_chain (linkto [?m.afiles ?a])
                (?a.config = ?m.config)))
         (forall MACHINE ?mc suchthat
           no_chain (member [?a.machines ?mc])))
    :
    (and no_chain (?m.archive_status = NotArchived)
         no_forward (?m.compile_status = Compiled)
         no_forward (?c.archive_status = Archived)
         no_forward (?y.archive_status = Archived)
         no_forward (?x.archive_status = Archived)
         no_forward (?child.archive_status = Archived))

    { ARCHIVER mass_update ?m ?mc.afile ?a.history }

    (and (?m.archive_status = Archived)
         no_chain (?mc.time_stamp = CurrentTime)
         [?a.archive_status = Archived]);
    no_chain (?m.archive_status = NotArchived);
```

Figure 2.2 A rule from C/MARVEL

```
(
    (
        ( Edit ( send 1   receive 3   ( Edit | λ ) )* )
      Δ
        ( Edit ( send 2   receive 4   ( Edit | λ ) )* )
      )
     Assemble   Distribute
  Δ
    ( ( receive 1   Proof   send 3 )
      |
      ( receive 2   Proof   send 4 )
    )*
)
```

Figure 2.3 An activity structure

There are multiple plausible semantics that can be associated with the notation. We outline several possibilities in Section 2.5. Neither data nor any association of process steps with actual tool invocations is mentioned in the notation, which is purely concerned with the topology of the process.

Figure 2.3 shows a simple example taken from Riddle's paper. Activities are identified by name, with λ representing the null activity (usually as an alternative for an optional activity). The `send` and `receive` primitives are always associated with a number, for matching up each `send` enaction with its corresponding `receive` to synchronize parallel subprocesses. Juxtaposition of subexpressions is the (implicit) sequencing operator; vertical bar (|) the alternation operator; and star (`*`) the repetition operator. Δ is the shuffle operator; concurrent repetition is not used in this example.

2.4 ASL SYNTAX AND SEMANTICS

Our Activity Structures Language (ASL) combines activity structure definitions (henceforth *AS-defs*) with MSL in a single but bi-level PML. ASL's notation for activity structures differs from Riddle's notation both cosmetically, in the concrete syntax of operators, and in the abstract syntax and semantics of the shuffle operator. We use semi-colon (";") to denote sequencing, prefix each activity structure definition with a name for that process fragment — followed by a colon (":"), and use ampersand (`&`) to denote shuffle. We also use the keyword `epsilon` to represent the empty activity, as opposed to Riddle's lambda (λ). Unlike Riddle's infix shuffle (Δ) of two operands, `&` is a prefix operator with a parenthesized, comma-separated list of an arbitrary number of operand subexpressions; this more clearly expresses multi-participant processes and better fits our representation of concurrent roles, as explained in Section 2.5. More significantly, the default is for shuffle operands to execute truly concurrently, i.e., causally independent (except for obeying any embedded send/receive primitives). There is no restriction to "atomic" activities.

2.4.1 Data Constraints

MARVEL stores process state and product data in a repository defined by object-oriented classes specified in the data modeling subset of MSL. Classes declare attributes of *primitive* (e.g., integer, string) or *enumerated* types; *file* attributes, either text or binary; *composite* attributes, an instance or set of instances of a given class (or its subclasses); and *link* attributes, also an instance or set of instances of a given class. Initial values may be specified for primitive and enumerated attributes, and filename extensions for file attributes (the values of file attributes are pathnames in the regular file system). Composite attributes allow construction of hierarchical object structures, i.e., when a parent object is deleted all of its descendents are also deleted, while link attributes support an arbitrary graph of relationships among objects. Multiple inheritance is supported, with naming conflicts among inherited attributes treated as errors. All of these facilities come "as is" from the original MARVEL system.

While MSL rules have parameter variables and local variables, Riddle's activity structures do not explicitly specify the data manipulated by activities, since he intended to admit a wide range of interpretations. In the process fragment shown in Figure 2.3, for example, each instance of the `Proof` activity might apply to the document file just `Edited`, and `Assemble` and `Distribute` to the manuscript consisting of all document files previously `Edited` and `Proofed`. But an alternative interpretation that allowed `Edit` of anything to be followed by `Proof` of anything probably would not be ideal for real-world software processes.

In order to bridge between MSL's data-centered (i.e., constraint-oriented) rules and activity-centered (i.e., topology-oriented) constrained expressions, and to devise a practical implementation, it was necessary to choose a specific (and compatible) model. Activity signatures similar to those used in programming languages and MSL rules, to specify only the number, order and types of parameters, would be insufficient. It must also be possible to specify *semantic* constraints such as a requirement, considering Figure 2.3, that after each `receive` on "1", the proofreader `Proofs` the same document file that the first editor had just `Edited`. Thus we introduced in ASL a notion of parameter variable *bindings*. This is accomplished by treating each parameter variable as bound to a specific object (or to a set of objects), where the scope of each variable is the enclosing AS-def (rather than just the individual activity), and thus every occurrence of the same variable within a single AS-def refers to the same object (or to some member of the set). A parameter variable must be designated as *multiple* to be bound to multiple objects at the same time.

The desired binding option is represented in ASL by declaring each parameter variable with a keyword indicating how that variable should become bound and can be rebound. The keywords are `set`, `use`, `reset`, `multiset`, `multiuse` and `multireset`; `set` is the default and may be omitted. We explain the meaning of each keyword through short examples:

```
( edit[set ?c:CFILE] ; compile[use ?c:CFILE] )*
```

indicates that the argument provided to both `edit` and `compile` must be an instance of `CFILE` (or one of its subclasses), as usual. But, in addition, the object provided by the user on the first invocation of `edit` becomes bound to the "?c" variable (according to the `set` directive), and the current object already bound to "?c" is required as the argument to `compile` (by the `use` directive). Any other object supplied by the user would be rejected. This process fragment is even more restrictive, in that the second and any subsequent iteration must `edit` and `compile` the same `CFILE` as the original, because "?c" is bound to `edit`'s argument only if it is not already bound to some other object; otherwise, the `set` directive is effectively the same as `use`.

However, the `reset` directive in

```
( edit[reset? c:CFILE] ; compile[use ?c:CFILE] )*
```

allows "?c" to be rebound by every enaction of the `edit` command, using the object selected by the user, while the `compile` is still limited to the last object that was `edit`ed. In contrast,

```
( edit[multiset ?c:CFILE] ; compile[multiuse ?c:CFILE] )*
```

constructs a group of objects, all bound to "?c", consisting of every actual parameter selected (over time) by the user when he or she invokes the `edit` command. This form further permits the user to select any object in this group as the actual parameter to `compile`. The `multireset` option replaces the entire group of objects bound to a parameter variable with only the newly selected object, to start over on collecting the bindings.

Finally, the process fragment

```
( edit[multiset ?h:HFILE] ; compile[multiuse ?c:CFILE]* )*
```

allows the user to edit any header file and then compile zero or more source files previously selected by the user (e.g., in some prior `edit` activity with the same parameter variable, "?c", in some enclosing expression). Note that this approach cannot enforce that only source files actually *including* the modified header file are recompiled.

In addition to this *implicit* data binding mechanism as a side-effect of users' activity invocations,[6] the ASL implementation also supports two *explicit* binding commands, `Bind` and `Unbind`. These allow a user to establish single or multiple bindings to particular parameter variables *a priori*, before a (sub)process begins, and/or to change and remove bindings established by the implicit mechanism. It is possible to effectively disable implicit binding and require explicit binding, by declaring all parameter variables as `use` or `multiuse`. Likewise, explicit bindings can effectively be disallowed for a process step by declaring its parameter variables as `reset` or `multireset`.

2.4.2 Tool Constraints

Riddle's activity structures cannot specify constraints on tool invocations, only the topology of control flow and synchronization. For example, a process might require that a module be `reserved` before `editing` and that it be `edited` only by the same user who currently held that module in `reserve`. A process might further require that a module's source timestamp be more recent than its executable timestamp in order to be `compiled`, but that the timestamp not be updated if there were no changes made during an `edit`.

There are various ways to enforce these restrictions. For example, MARVEL's access control mechanism (similar to the one used by the UNIX file system) could support the owner restriction. The relative ordering of `reserve` and `edit` could be specified in the process model topology, with the same-user requirement indicated by enclosing these activities within the same shuffle operand. Separate `edit` and `view` activities could distinguish between update and read-only operations, although then the decision whether or not to modify would have to be made in advance. But these and similar requirements may often be more easily specified using *rule skeletons*. An example is shown in Figure 2.4.

The rule skeleton's signature must match the activity name, parameter order and types as

[6] The data bindings apply to all participants in the same process fragment.

```
edit[?z:CFILE]:
    :
    (and no_chain(?z.locker = CurrentUser)
         no_chain(?z.reserve_status = CheckedOut))
    { EDITOR edit ?z.contents }
    no_chain(?z.time_stamp = CurrentTime);
    no_assertion;
```

Figure 2.4 ISPW7 example problem: Simple rule skeleton

they appear in the AS-def (parameter names are not significant for matching purposes between a rule skeleton and an activity, only between activities). The apparently extra colon (":") in the second line is there because the queries part of the condition is empty in this example. "?z.<attribute_name>" specifies an attribute that must be defined in the `CFILE` class or one of its superclasses. `CurrentUser` and `CurrentTime` are built-in functions that return the current userid and timestamp, respectively, while `CheckedOut` is one of the enumerated values for the `reserved_status` attribute. When the tool returns a status code of 1, the corresponding `no_assertion` effect indicates "no change" in the process state.

The `no_chain` annotation on every predicate in the condition and the first (status code 0) effect's assignment are needed to "turn off" MARVEL's default behavior of automatically backward and forward chaining whenever possible. If either of the two `no_chain` annotations in the condition were not present in Figure 2.4, the process engine would automatically invoke `edit` on a file as soon as the file was `reserved` and automatically invoke `reserve` on a file whenever a user attempted to `edit` it; the former case would probably be more disruptive than the latter, since backward chaining occurs only if the rule's condition is not already satisfied.

A more complex constraint might restrict the set of `HFILE`s that can possibly be included in a `CFILE`, e.g., those that are components of the same `MODULE`. This could be enforced by automatically gathering these `HFILE`s as *local variables* of the `compile` activity, retrieved through a query in the rule's condition. This example is shown in Figure 2.5. The `exists` clause finds the `MODULE` containing the supplied `CFILE` and assigns it to local variable "?m". Then the `forall` clause collects the set of `HFILE`s contained in its `includes` attribute, assigning all of them to "?h". Since "?h" is associated with a `forall` clause, the predicate referencing "?h.<attribute_name>" is applied (separately) to every member of "?h". Note that the same purpose could be attained in ASL by employing the `Bind` command and the `multiuse` designation for an explicit "?h" parameter (since a rule skeleton can have any number of parameters), but our alternative lessens the burden on users, who would otherwise have to select actual parameters for each activity invocation — even when the parameter variables have already been bound.

For ASL we use the term "rule skeleton", rather than simply "rule", since the ASL translator treats each rule as a *template*. In particular, it inserts additional condition predicates and effects assignments to enforce the topology specified by activity structures. When the same activity occurs multiple times in an AS-def, its rule skeleton is cloned so different such predicates and assignments can be added separately for each occurrence. Williams proposed an alternative approach, where conditions and effects as well as control flow are specified separately for each occurrence of an activity.

```
compile [?c:CFILE]:
    (and (exists MODULE ?m suchthat (member [?m.files ?c]))
         (forall HFILE ?h suchthat (member [?m.includes ?h])))
    :
    (or no_chain(?c.time_stamp > ?c.object_timestamp)
        no_chain(?h.time_stamp > ?c.object_timestamp))

    { COMPILER compile ?c.contents ?c.object_code
                       ?h.contents "-g" }

    (and no_chain(?c.status = Compiled)
         no_chain(?c.object_time_stamp = CurrentTime));
    no_chain(?c.status = ErrorCompile);
```

Figure 2.5 ISPW7 example problem: Rule skeleton with local variables

2.5 ASL ENACTION MODEL

Depending on the capabilities of the supporting environment infrastructure, several alternative enaction models are possible. We have identified four distinct points on the spectrum from prescriptive (system-driven) to proscriptive (user-driven) [Hei90]:

1. The straightforward prescriptive interpretation of an AS-def "generates" an actual process instance as a sequence of activities, so we call it the *Generation* approach. If one thinks of an AS-def as defining a language, the process engine then amounts to a generator of strings in the language (i.e., traces of activities). Choices among alternatives including whether or not to repeat a cycle could be requested from the user in a "live" environment, or selected randomly in a simulation. The generation approach has been explored by Gaede on top of the single-user MARVEL 2.6 [GNR91].
2. In what we call the *Passive Recognition* approach, the environment's enforcement capabilities would be used to "recognize" a process, given an actual sequence of commands (activities) entered by the users. Thus the process engine would function as a parser of strings in the language defined by AS-def. This could support either an *a posteriori* analysis of a completed process instance, or dynamic acceptance/rejection of each command as a process unfolds.
3. An *Active Recognition* extension of the above option is possible only if the system underlying the ASL implementation provides a backward automation capability. The process engine would treat each user command as a goal to be achieved, and automatically enact other commands first, as necessary, to match the AS-def. The difference between the two options is that some prefixes disallowed by Passive Recognition could be allowed by Active Recognition, when the process engine is able to insert the missing commands into the trace just before the point where the recognizer would have entered an "error state". This makes sense only in the context of dynamic parsing of prefixes.
4. In a *Hybrid* approach, Generation and Active Recognition would be combined, using both forward and backward automation capabilities of the environment. The process engine would wait for a user to enter a command before doing anything, and then perform backward

automation as in Active Recognition to attempt to enable the command. After completion of this command, the process engine would treat the command as an event, triggering forward automation to attempt to carry out the direct implications of that command — up until the next choice (branch) point in the AS-def. It would then stop and wait for the next user command.

The distinctions among these options may be clarified by considering some plausible enactions of the activity structures operators, particularly the decisions implied by alternation, repetition and concurrent repetition. For example, say the process model specifies a process fragment as "A | B"; then it is necessary during enaction to determine whether to do A or instead do B. For "A*", it is necessary to decide how many times to actually do A — possibly but not necessarily in on-the-fly rather than in advance, e.g., after one execution of A ends it might then be decided whether or not to do it again. Concurrent repetition ("@A") is even more complex, because the number of users must be determined, and more users than originally anticipated might join in.

Considering alternation "A | B" in the Generation approach, the process engine might ask the user whether to do A or B, and then initiate the chosen activity. In both Recognition approaches, the user simply does A or does B, that is, enters a command corresponding to selecting activity A or a command corresponding to B, and the environment allows either case. There is no real difference between these and the Hybrid approach for this simple example.

For repetition, e.g., "(A; B)*", a Generation environment might ask the user how many times to repeat, and then do A automatically followed by B, followed by A, and so on. A Passive Recognition environment would allow the user to repeat "A; B" an arbitrary number of times by hand, but would not permit B unless already preceded by A. An Active Recognition environment would behave the same way, except whenever the user attempted to do B without having already done A (since the last B), the process engine would attempt to automatically do A first. A Hybrid system would add to Active Recognition the functionality of automatically doing B whenever the user did A.

The Generation approach might handle the concurrent repetition in "@(A | B); C" by first asking a distinguished user for the desired number of concurrent repetitions and which specific end-users should make decisions within each of the repetitions; then each of these users would be asked to choose between A and B. The environment would realize when all the A's and B's had been completed, and then do C. Or, in a simulation mode, the environment could choose a number of concurrent repetitions according to some specified probability distribution and similarly randomly select between A and B for each of them. An alternative interpretation of concurrent repetition would require each of the instances to follow the <u>same</u> choice, which could be useful for executing a "groupware" tool [DR93].

Passive Recognition might handle "@(A | B); C" by allowing any number of end-users to do either A or B, but not both, until some user happens to do C. C is enabled only when all existing instances of the concurrent repetition have finished, and is disabled by the creation of any new instances. A more difficult alternative (to implement), but one which would have allowed more concurrency, would have been to allow C to be started at any time, but not to be deemed finished until all instances of A and B are finished. Once C had been started, it would prevent any user from initiating either A or B.

Active Recognition could be achieved for "@(A | B); C" by following an approach similar to that suggested above for Generation: Say a user requested to do C. Then the process engine would automatically spawn the concurrent repetitions, although here it would be necessary to ask the user who requested C how many users and which user in particular should take over control of each instance. There seem to be several possible Hybrid models, one directly combining the Generation and Active Recognition behaviors as described here. But another perhaps better approach might support a mixed mode, where a user could select either A or B, initiating forward automation, or C, triggering backward automation.

We have implemented a variant of the Passive Recognition model, where its "parsing" approach applies only to the topological aspect of the process model, i.e., the activity structures definitions. For the constraints aspect, that is, the MSL subset of ASL, we instead apply the Hybrid approach, since that was the original semantics of MSL. MARVEL's process engine is capable of enacting any mix of the four forms outlined above, determined by the actual chaining annotations employed (i.e., `no_forward` and so on). Since the Generation approach had already been tried for activity structures alone, as mentioned above, we chose the opposite extreme in part for comparison purposes (the detailed comparison is outside the scope of this paper).

Thus the bi-level ASL environment does nothing until a user enters a command. If the command corresponds to an activity (as opposed to one of the built-in commands such as `help`), the system accepts the command only if it is valid according to the current AS-def and the past history of activities to this point. It does <u>not</u> attempt to automatically enact predecessor or successor activities in the AS-def, but may automatically fire rules through backward and forward chaining to satisfy constraints.

For example, if the user enters the `compile` command without first executing the preceding `edit` command in

```
( edit[reset ?c:CFILE] ; compile[use ?c:CFILE] )*
```

the `compile` activity would be disallowed. But if the user selected the `edit` command at a valid point, at the beginning of the process fragment or after a previous `compile`, that command would be accepted (with any type-valid argument due to the `reset` data binding directive) and executed <u>if</u> the condition specified in the `edit` rule skeleton (see Figure 2.4) were satisfied. The `compile` command is not automatically initiated afterwards even though it is now valid according to the control flow (and presumably invokes a batch processing tool that does not require user interaction). Instead, the process engine waits for the user to enter the corresponding command, at which time the condition of the `compile` rule skeleton (Figure 2.5) is evaluated.

2.5.1 Process State Representation

Activity structure definitions are presented to the users of an ASL environment instance concretely as *activity structure objects*, or *AS-objects*. Each AS-object is an instance of a class that defines the type of a (sub)process. The attributes of an AS-object maintain the current process state during the enaction of the corresponding AS-def. We represented AS-objects as first-class objects in the same objectbase as the product data so that the process state could be manipulated by MSL rules (i.e., those generated by the translator).

There is always at least one AS-object for each instantiated AS-def (instantiation is explained below), and potentially a composite AS-object hierarchy if the AS-def contains any shuffles or concurrent repetitions. The *root AS-object* will have children representing each of the operands of shuffle or concurrent repetition operators enacted at the top level of the AS-def; its children may in turn contain other AS-object descendents representing shuffle or concurrent repetition operand subexpressions of nested structures, to an arbitrary depth. The hierarchy is displayed to the users, supporting browsing and querying the same as any other part of the objectbase. We chose this granularity of representation to materialize the work breakdown, with each user's role in the process reflected by an AS-object. However, smaller granularities would have been feasible; for instance, Gaede's activity structure implementation represents each individual activity as a first-class object.

The screen dump in Figure 2.6 displays the AS-objects — `task5.1` and its shuffle children — for our example process fragment (from Figure 2.1). A composition relationship between any pair of parent and child objects is represented by a straight line; a link relationship is drawn as a curved arc (such as exists between `task5.1` and each of its parameter objects). The illustrated objectbase is quite sparse, since it was constructed only for testing our ISPW7 process model. For example, the `proj` project contains only one program, `pgm`, which in turn has its entire source represented by a single object, `src`. This is not intended to be realistic: the objectbase containing MARVEL 3.1's own source code consists of over five hundred objects (so the top-level display of the objectbase looks like a black blob, until one uses browsing commands to zoom in).

Most of the pulldown menus list commands available in every MARVEL environment instance. But the menu selected by the "Rules" button includes all the commands corresponding to activities available specifically in the current instance, because they were defined by rule skeletons in the ASL process model; it also includes a (large) number of special commands for statically binding/unbinding data parameters. The menu for our ISPW7 example problem solution (Section 2.7) is shown in Figure 2.7. A separate text window prints various messages and prompts during process enaction, and another window animates the sequencing from one activity to the next with an icon depicting the status of each activity's enaction (all of the activities shown in Figure 2.8 have been completed).

2.5.2 Process Management

To begin a process, a user (usually someone fulfilling a management role) `Instantiates` the top-level AS-object and `Activates` it. This user would then `Assign` each of the roles within each top-level shuffle or concurrent repetition to a particular user (perhaps himself or herself), each of whom can then `Activate` their subsidiary AS-objects to perform their roles. We continue to use the term *role* to mean the part played by a user in a process instance while acting in a particular capacity; for example, each reviewer, designer, programmer and QA engineer in Figure 2.1 fulfills a distinct role. Each role must by executed by a separate user connection to the MARVEL environment instance; that is, a single user may not perform multiple roles simultaneously (but see the discussion of `Attach` and `Detach` below). However, the same human user may be connected to MARVEL multiple times in parallel — in which case he or she is treated as a distinct "user" for each connection. The roles may in turn contain nested shuffle or concurrent repetition operators. When such a subsidiary shuffle or concurrent repetition is reached during process enaction, it is handled in the same way, with all of its child AS-objects first being `Assigned` to particular users, who can then `Activate` them.

A user can suspend his or her current role at any point using the `Detach` command, and resume this or another role later with the `Attach` command (the implementation of the `Attach` command prevents two users from controlling the same role instance at the same time). While a user is attached to an activated AS-object, all commands are implicitly supplied with this object as their last parameter. The topology embodied in the corresponding activity

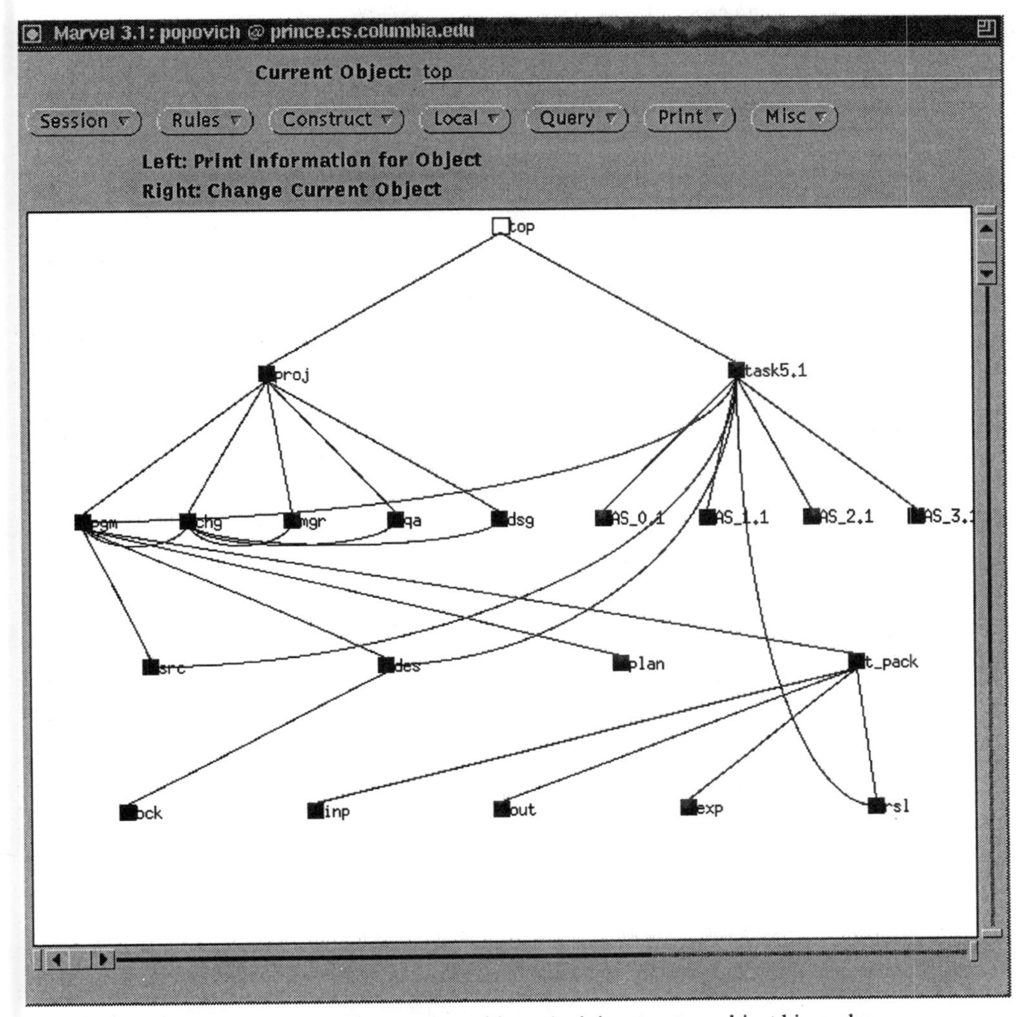

Figure 2.6 ISPW7 example problem: Activity structure object hierarchy

structure definition is enforced on such commands, and successful commands automatically update the state of that AS-object (i.e., the values of its attributes) to reflect progress through the process. When the process fragment for a role is finished, the user reports the successful completion by selecting the `Terminate` command. A role may also be exited unsuccessfully at any point using the `Deactivate` command, but later on it must again be `Activated` (starting over) and eventually `Terminated`. All shuffle or concurrent repetition operands must terminate before the enclosing activity structure (sub)expression will be permitted to continue past that point (in the case of concurrent repetition, one or more operands' terminations may be unsuccessful, i.e., a `Deactivate` command).

Whether `Attached` to an activated AS-object or not, a user can always invoke commands corresponding to normal MSL rules that have been imported into the ASL process model. Such rules enable the same backward and forward chaining (what we call the Hybrid enaction

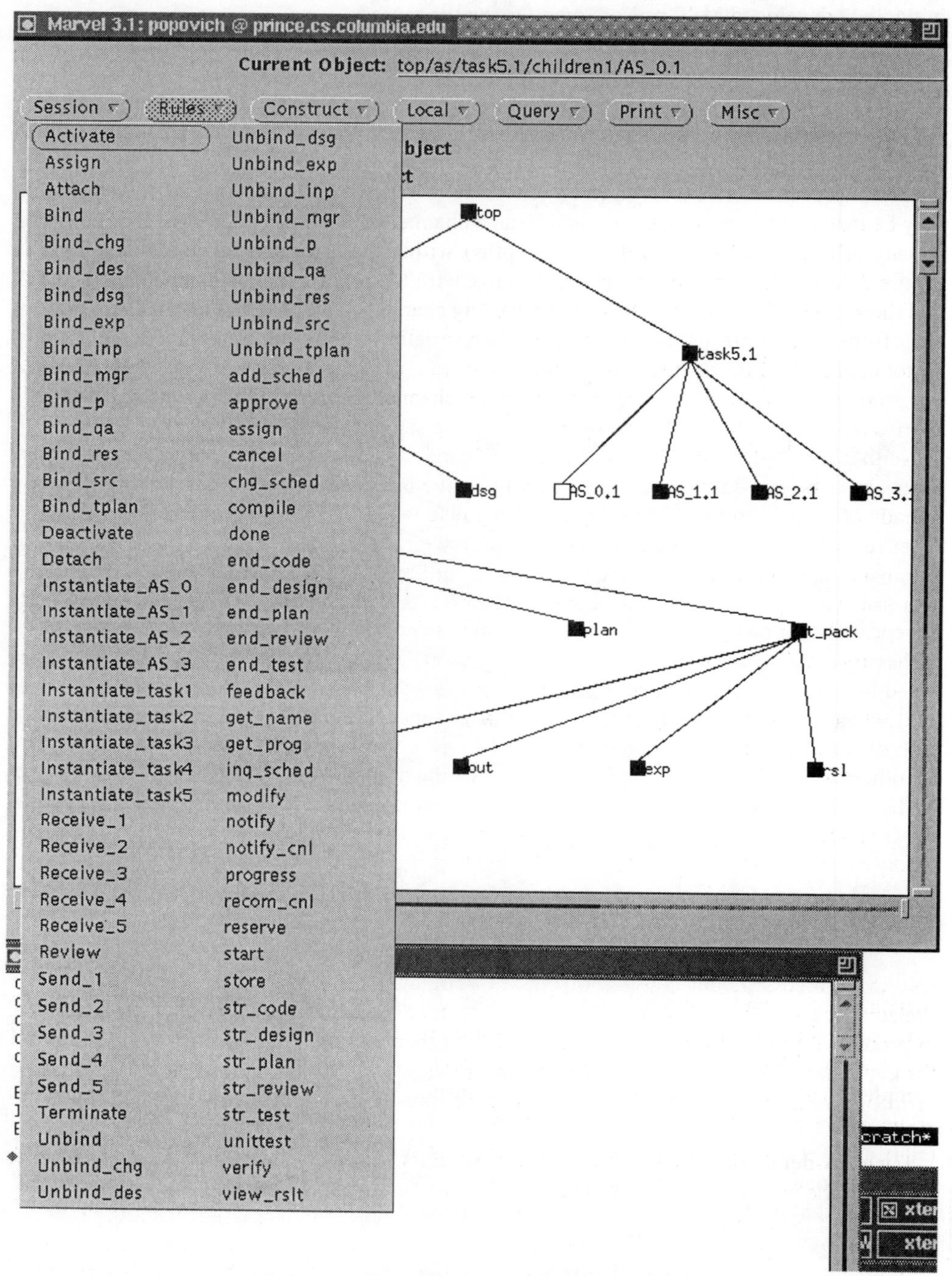

Figure 2.7 ISPW7 example problem: Rule menu

model) normally performed by MARVEL. ASL and MSL are completely interoperable, so previously developed MSL process modules can be reused.

2.5.3 Role Synchronization

As in Riddle's activity structures, ASL's send and receive primitives each take a *channel* number as their (only) argument. These operations are implemented as named `Send_x` and `Receive_x` commands, for each channel number `x`. When a `Send` is executed on a channel, it may be matched by any `Receive` on the same channel number, provided both are embedded (at any arbitrary and perhaps different depths) within the same top-level AS-def. Thus in Figure 2.3, only the first editor can synchronize with the proofreader using channels 1 and 3, and the second editor can synchronize only using channels 2 and 4. Pairs of channels prevent roles from intercepting their own messages. In a variation with a single pair of channels, either editor could `Send` on channel 1 and either editor (not necessarily the same one that requested the proofreading) could `Receive` the reply on channel 2. In any case, however, a `Send` is always matched with exactly one `Receive` on the same channel and *vice versa*.

Neither the `Send` nor the `Receive` command ever blocks, waiting for a rendezvous, because we believed this would be annoying to the user (and in any case, switching among threads of control to be able to do something else when one of them blocks — or for any other reason — is supported by MARVEL's XView graphical user interface but not by its tty command line interface). There is no notion of a "full" channel (the buffer is treated as infinite), so a `Send` always succeeds immediately. A `Receive` on an "empty" channel fails, and must be repeated later on by the user —or the user may select an alternative activity, if provided for in the process. However, to avoid busy-waiting on an "empty" channel, the user requesting the failed `Receive` is automatically added to a list of users who are to be notified by electronic mail when the next `Send` is executed on that channel. When the email notification arrives, each of the affected users can retry the `Receive`, at which point one will be successful and the others will fail again. A simple alternative would have been to notify only the first user on the list, to effect a queuing policy, with automatic removal from the queue if a user goes on to select an alternative activity (e.g., a `Receive` on another channel).

2.6 IMPLEMENTATION DETAILS

An ASL process model consists of classes defining the product data representation, rule skeletons, and one or more named activity structure definitions. The AS-defs are translated to produce a pure MSL process model, which is then loaded by the normal means into the MARVEL kernel for enaction. (An ASL process model can also *import* an arbitrary collection of MSL modules, which are not involved in the translation but are loaded into MARVEL "as is".)

Each AS-def is translated to at least one MSL class whose attributes include state variables that track the progress of process enaction. One such class, whose name is taken from the AS-def, is the class of the *root AS-object* in the composite object hierarchy. Each shuffle operator in an AS-def is translated to a set of MSL classes, one for each operand subexpression, whose instances are also AS-objects. Similarly, a concurrent repetition operand is translated to an MSL class. The top-level AS-def is effectively transformed to a single regular expression, where each shuffle or concurrent repetition operator together with its operand(s) is effectively replaced by a single symbol. Then each operand subexpression is transformed, with each of its own nested shuffle operators replaced, and so on, recursively. A designated string attribute of each AS-object class is initialized to the text of the corresponding regular expression, for display during objectbase browsing.

These regular expressions are translated into a set of rules implementing a deterministic finite state automaton (DFSA). Each transition in this DFSA is implemented by a single rule representing an activity occurrence. Each of these rules is derived from the supplied MSL rule skeleton for the corresponding activity, and contains its signature, queries, properties, tool invocation, and effects. The translator adds predicates on process state attributes to the properties, to restrict each rule to apply only when the DFSA is in the appropriate state, and effect assignments to update the state attributes following a transition in the automaton. An additional parameter is added at the end of each rule skeleton signature, whose type is the AS-object class for the corresponding top-level AS-def operand, or shuffle or concurrent repetition operand, and the formal parameter names are modified to textually include the corresponding binding directives.

Rules are also generated to implement:

- Each `Send` and `Receive` transition, with automaton states handled as above and an auxiliary root AS-object attribute acting as the buffer for each channel;
- The generic `Attach` and `Detach` commands, e.g., the `Attach` condition requires that only the currently `Assigned` user can successfully `Attach` to the given AS-object;
- `Bind` and `Unbind` commands for each parameter variable, which can be repeated arbitrarily for variables designated as *multiple*;
- `Instantiate`, `Assign`, `Deactivate` and `Terminate` commands for each AS-object class, and `Activate` commands for each child AS-object class (top-level AS objects are handled by a general Activate rule defined on the ACTIVITY_STRUCTURE class). For example, figure 2.8 illustrates the automatic rule chaining in response to an `Instantiate` command, to create a root AS-object and its children AS-objects; the screen dump shows MARVEL's normal process animation window.

We added the Activity Structures Manager (ASM) module to the MARVEL kernel to support (1) an extended context mechanism that associates a current AS-object with each user connection and passes that AS-object automatically to all rules generated from AS-defs, (2) the implicit parameter variable binding facility, and (3) an option for guaranteeing truly "atomic" activities as in Riddle's original semantics (this mechanism is not discussed in this paper). When a user command is resolved to the list of possible rules according to the actual parameter types, ASM automatically supplies the current AS-object as the final parameter. ASM is also called when a rule's condition is evaluated, to enforce the variable binding requirements and establish any new bindings.

The translator consists of about 8050 lines of C code (including 350 lines of headers), 3350 lines of Yacc and 800 lines of Lex. Eight files were reused essentially unchanged from MARVEL's loader, which parses MSL into the kernel's internal form. The six added files include approximately 3900 lines of C, 950 lines of Yacc and 80 lines of Lex. ASM is a single file of about 750 lines of C. In comparison, MARVEL 3.1 has about 154,000 lines total, so implementing ASL on top of MARVEL was quite efficient in terms of code reuse.

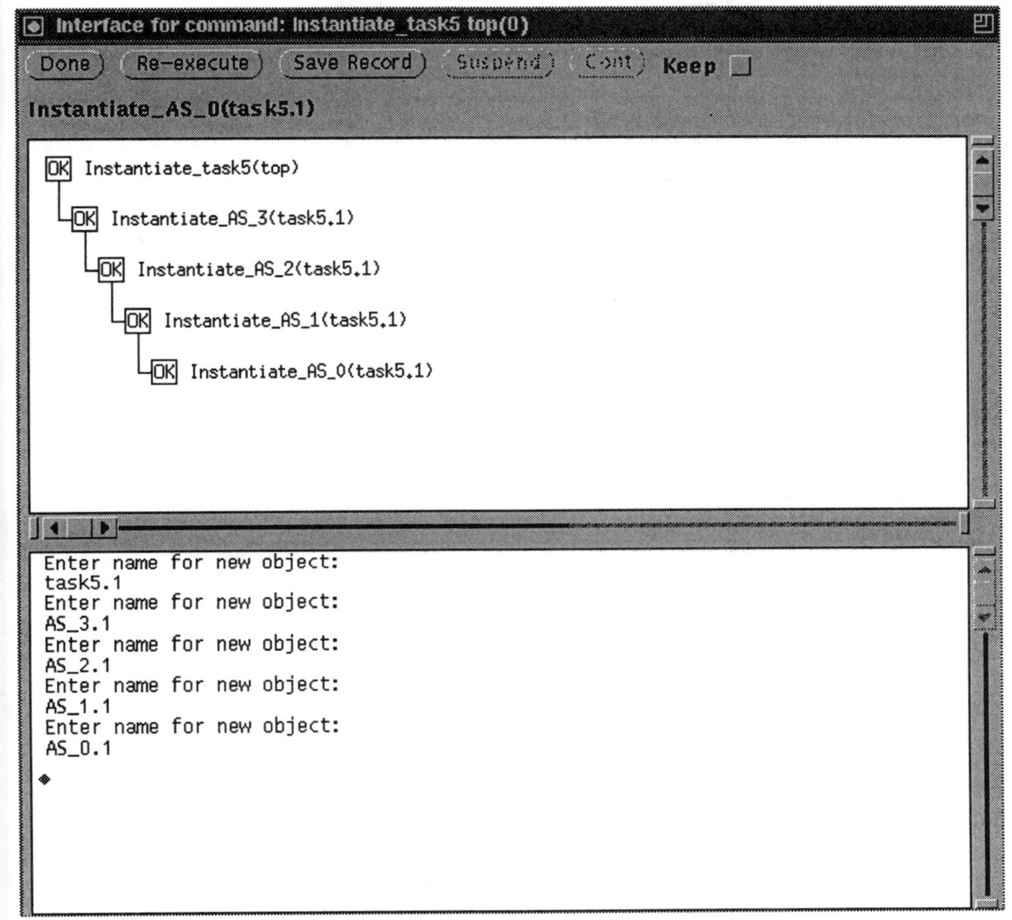

Figure 2.8 ISPW7 example problem: Rule chaining for AS-object instantiations

2.7 ASL EXAMPLE

The process modeling problem of Section 2.2 requires expression of both the topology among process steps and the constraints on individual steps, whereas the purpose of ASL is to add a topological specification (activity structures) to a rule-based exemplar of the constraint-oriented type of PML (MSL). Thus, one would expect ASL to be a good match for this problem, in the sense that the ASL process model should be concise and easily understandable.

Figure 2.9 shows the AS-def specifying the topology. As written, it allows only a single instance of each of the four roles. But concurrent repetition could be nested around the subexpression for a role, to permit any number of instances to be instantiated during process enaction. The three rule skeletons shown in Figure 2.10 define the `modify` activity with respect to a design document and the `modify` and `compile` activities with respect to a source code module.

Figure 2.11 shows the three MSL rules generated for the first two of these three rule skeletons, according to their occurrence of their activities in the activity structure definition. Each generated rule has one parameter added at the end of the formal parameter list, for the

```
task5:
&(
    #
    # review design
    #

  (receive 1; review[?des:DESIGN];
   (approve[?des:DESIGN] | feedback[?des:DESIGN]); send 2)*
 ,

    #
    # modify design
    #

  (reserve[reset ?des:DESIGN]; modify[?des:DESIGN];
   (send 1; receive 2; (modify[?des:DESIGN] | epsilon))*;
   deposit[?des:DESIGN];
   send 3; receive 4)*
 ,
    #
    # modify code
    #

  reserve[reset ?src:SRC];
  (modify[?src:SRC]; compile[?src:SRC])*;
  receive 3; deposit[?src:SRC]; send 5
 ,
    #
    # unit test
    #

  receive 5; start[?p:PROGRAM];
  (unittest[?p:PROGRAM]; verify[?p:PROGRAM];
   view_rslt[?res:TEST_RESULT])*;
  (approve[?p:PROGRAM] | (feedback[?des:DESIGN]; send 4))

 )
```

Figure 2.9 ISPW7 example problem: Teamwork in ASL

```
#
# modify design document. this is fired by forward chaining
# from reserve[?des:DESIGN] rule
#
modify[?des:DESIGN]:
  (and (exists PROGRAM ?p suchthat
         no_chain (ancestor[?p ?des]))
       (exists CHANGE ?chg suchthat
         no_chain (linkto[?p.change ?chg]))
       (exists DESIGNER ?dsg suchthat
         no_chain (linkto[?chg.designer ?dsg])))
  :
  (and (?des.reserve_status = CheckedOut)
   (or no_chain(?des.modify_status = Created)
       no_chain(?des.modify_status = Modified)
       no_chain(?des.modify_status = Feedback)
       no_chain(?des.modify_status = Approved)))
  {MODIFY modify ?des.contents }
  (and no_chain(?des.modify_status = Modified)
              (?des.time_stamp = CurrentTime));

#
# modification of source
# reset compile status
#
modify[?src:SRC]:
  :
  (?src.reserve_status = CheckedOut)
  { MODIFY modify ?src.contents }
  (and no_forward(?src.modify_status = Modified)
       no_chain(?src.compile_status = NotCompiled)
       (?src.last_modified = CurrentTime));

#
# compile source
#
compile[?src:SRC]:
  (exists PROGRAM ?p suchthat (member[?p.sources ?src]))
  :
  { COMPILE compile ?src.contents ?p.exec }
  (and no_chain(?p.build_status = Built)
       no_chain(?src.compile_status = Compiled));
  (?src.compile_status = NotCompiled);
```

Figure 2.10 ISPW7 example problem: Sample rule skeletons in ASL

user's current AS-object, and the binding directives have been concatenated with the formal parameter names. The translator added one state predicate to each skeleton's condition and two state assignments (leaving one state and entering the next) to each skeleton's single effect.

Throughout our example so far, we have made extensive use of links and the MSL navigational query primitives, which resulted in reducing the number of parameters for each AS-def activity and each rule skeleton to one. Neither activities nor rule skeletons are limited to only one parameter, however. For example, instead of maintaining a single test package consisting of the sample inputs and outputs for each program being unit-tested, and requiring a link association in the objectbase between the program and its test package, we could ask the user to specify the desired inputs and outputs (presumably from among multiple possibilities) when the appropriate process steps are enacted. The testing role of the `task5` AS-def might then be written as in Figure 2.12. The rule skeletons for the modified `unittest` and `verify` steps would then be, as shown in Figure 2.13, hardly more than their activities — since most of their queries would no longer be needed. This alternative AS-def fragment would replace the last portion of the `task5` AS-def in Figure 2.9.

The complete ASL process model for the ISPW7 example (without this alternative) contains 36 rule skeletons collectively consisting of 509 lines, including comments, and five activity structure definitions consisting of 113 lines, exclusive of the data model classes. The other four AS-defs deal with the initial approval of the change request, the manager's scheduling of the work to be done, the creation of the testing plan, and the building of the test package to be used by the unit testers. The ASL translator generates 134 rules, exclusive of the numerous `Bind` and `UnBind` rules, totaling 1255 lines with no comments. 35 of the rules handle process management (instantiating, assigning, *etc.*), 41 synchronization (send and receive), 20 internal state bookkeeping, and the remaining 38 rules invoke tools. The generated state machines, five for the AS-defs and four for shuffle operands, contain a total of 40 states.

2.8 RELATED WORK

We present here a summary of related work on three kinds of PMLs, those specifically oriented towards topology and constraints, respectively, and those directly covering both aspects of process modeling.

2.8.1 Topology-Oriented PMLs

Topology-oriented PMLs are naturally strong in modeling the relatively global control flow aspects of both single and multiple user processes (or process fragments). They vary in the degree to which decision criteria, including data- and tool-specific constraints (or policies), can be specified. Those PMLs based on task graphs usually present a hierarchical decomposition of tasks into subtasks down to individual process steps, with explicit predecessor/successor relationships among (sub)tasks and/or process steps. These relationships typically reflect data flow of tool parameters among the nodes in the graph. There are usually no predicates attached to initiation of a task, but a finite state automaton regulates the passage among process states. PMLs based on Petri nets may be hierarchical, with some transitions expanding to a subnet. The marking of input/output places (with tokens) represents both control state and data parameters. A transition is typically associated with a predicate that must be satisfied to fire that transition,

```
modify [?set_des:DESIGN, ?SO:AS_1]:
  (and (exists PROGRAM ?p suchthat
         no_chain(ancestor [?p ?set_des]))
       (exists CHANGE ?chg suchthat
         no_chain(linkto [?p.change ?chg]))
       (exists DESIGNER ?dsg suchthat
         no_chain(linkto [?chg.designer ?dsg]))):
  (and (?set_des.reserve_status = CheckedOut)
       (or no_chain(?set_des.modify_status = Created)
           no_chain(?set_des.modify_status = Modified)
           no_chain(?set_des.modify_status = Feedback))
       no_forward(?SO.state6 = Ready))
  { MODIFY modify ?set_des.contents }
  (and no_chain(?set_des.modify_status = Modified)
       (?set_des.time_stamp = CurrentTime)
       (?SO.state6 = Inactive) (?SO.state2 = Ready));

modify [?set_des:DESIGN, ?SO:AS_1]:
  (and (exists PROGRAM ?p suchthat
         no_chain(ancestor [?p ?set_des]))
       (exists CHANGE ?chg suchthat
         no_chain(linkto [?p.change ?chg]))
       (exists DESIGNER ?dsg suchthat
         no_chain(linkto [?chg.designer ?dsg]))):
  (and (?set_des.reserve_status = CheckedOut)
       (or no_chain(?set_des.modify_status = Created)
           no_chain(?set_des.modify_status = Modified)
           no_chain(?set_des.modify_status = Feedback))
       no_forward(?SO.state1 = Ready))
  { MODIFY modify ?set_des.contents }
  (and no_chain(?set_des.modify_status = Modified)
       (?set_des.time_stamp = CurrentTime)
       (?SO.state1 = Inactive) (?SO.state2 = Ready));

modify [?set_src:SRC, ?SO:AS_2]:
  :
  (and (?set_src.reserve_status = CheckedOut)
       no_forward(?SO.state1 = Ready))
  { MODIFY modify ?set_src.contents }
  (and no_forward(?set_src.modify_status = Modified)
       no_chain(?set_src.compile_status = NotCompiled)
       (?set_src.last_modified = CurrentTime)
       (?SO.state1 = Inactive) (?SO.state5 = Ready));
```

Figure 2.11 ISPW7 example problem: Sample generated MSL rules

```
receive 5; start[?p:PROGRAM];
(unittest[?p:PROGRAM, ?in:TEST_INPUT, ?out:TEST_OUT];
 verify[?out:TEST_OUT, ?exp:TEST_EXPECT, ?res:TEST_RESULT];
 view_rslt[?res:TEST_RESULT])*;
(approve[?p:PROGRAM] | (feedback[?des:DESIGN]; send 4))
```

Figure 2.12 ISPW7 example problem: AS-def for testing with multiple packages

```
#
# execute a program
#
unittest[?p:PROGRAM, ?inp:TEST_INPUT, ?out:TEST_OUT]:
  :
  (?p.test_status = TestIn)
  {TEST unittest ?p.exec ?inp.contents ?out.contents }
  ;

#
# compare output file and expected output file and write
# the result on result file.
#
verify[?out:TEST_OUT, ?exp:TEST_EXPECT, ?res:TEST_RESULT]:
  :
  {TEST verify ?out.contents ?exp.contents ?res.contents }
  ;
```

Figure 2.13 ISPW7 example problem: Rule skeletons for testing with multiple packages

but the predicate is attached to the transition rather than the tool or its data — and thus must be duplicated everywhere the tool or data is used to express tool- or data-specific constraints.

Articulator [MS92] models a process as a hierarchical structure of *task graphs*, in the style outlined above, directly presenting the topology of the process. At the lowest level in the hierarchy, *action* nodes represent individual process steps, and their status is derived from the enactment of that step. At higher levels, the nodes are called *tasks*, and their status is derived from the status of their subtask nodes. In either case, each node passes through a sequence of states, beginning with `None` and normally proceeding through `Allocated`, `Ready` and `Active` before finishing in the `Done` state. Other states may be reached under exceptional conditions, in which case external repair is required in order to continue the process [MS91]. Once a node enters the `Done` state, its successor nodes become enabled (enactable), which appears to be the only kind of constraint enforced. A user has the freedom to choose among enabled nodes, including switching back and forth among in-progress subgraphs. Multiple users are synchronized through the precedence relations among the nodes in their (concurrent) subprocesses.

Melmac [DG90] is typical of the many process-centered environments whose PML is based on Petri nets. In Melmac's *Funsoft nets* [Gru91], multiple transitions can fire simultaneously to reflect multiple participants in the process, so synchronization is treated the same way as other control flow, through the topology and marking of the net. Transitions may be hierarchical, and even replaced with a new subnet on-the-fly during process enaction. *Modification points* control the timing and scope of this replacement. Funsoft nets attach *predicates* and *jobs*, or tools, to transitions; predicates conditionally restrict when the transitions may be applied, while jobs are simply executed as part of the transition. If multiple transitions invoke the same tool, the predicate must be repeated for each case; of course, different predicates may be warranted. Predicates thus provide a limited form of constraints [GJ92].

The Hierarchical and Functional Software Process (HFSP) PML [Kat89] is based on attribute grammars. The topology of the process model is defined through context-free productions, representing sequencing, alternation, iteration and hierarchical structuring (including recursion). The attributes' semantic functions specify computations on input parameters from the parent subprocess and on output parameters from the children. Process fragments represented by symbols can be executed concurrently if there are no data dependencies among their parameters, an implicit form of synchronization. Terminal symbols represent individual process steps, whose tools are invoked through interfaces defined in a *process enaction script*. HFSP's *decomposition conditions* are placed on productions to restrict their application, similar to the predicates of Petri nets.

The PDL project defines processes using context-free grammars [IOIT91], with similar topological properties to HFSP. *Restriction conditions* are placed on data parameters of process steps; it is not clear from the paper whether these restrictions are defined once for each step, matching our notion of constraints, or separately for each occurrence in some production, like the predicates of Petri nets. The enaction model provides a menu-based navigation through the topological framework, although the authors postulate another enaction model analogous to the Passive Recognition of our ASL environment. A process model is translated into a second formalism, the functional Process Description Language (PDL) [IPKT89], which is independent rather than constituting a level of a combined formalism as in ASL. The PDL process program, called a *script*, is then refined manually from an abstract to a concrete form that can be directly enacted by the PDL interpreter. The interpreter supports a general escape mechanism, whereby undefined functions in the process model can be defined interactively during enaction.

ASL is relatively limited compared to the above topology-oriented formalisms, since every activity is necessarily primitive, corresponding to an individual tool invocation. It would be an interesting extension of our work to add hierarchical activities, where each non-terminal activity would correspond to a separately defined AS-def, with the potential recursion of context-free grammars.

2.8.2 Constraint-Oriented PMLs

Constraint-oriented PMLs tend to be good at modeling the local prerequisites (and, possibly, consequences) of individual process steps, independent of where they appear in the topology of the overall process; that is, a step may occur in multiple places with the same constraints. Constraint-oriented PMLs invariably attach some kind of pre-condition to each action, usually representing a tool invocation, that should be satisfied prior to the action and/or whose satisfaction automatically initiates the action. A pre-condition normally inspects the data parameters to the action, but might also consider the overall process state. In a "backward chaining" process engine, the system might automatically invoke other process steps to attempt to satisfy and/or derive the truth value of the pre-condition of a step, treated as a goal. In a "forward chaining" system, the actions and/or post-conditions of steps may result in automatic invocation of additional process steps whose own pre-conditions have become satisfied. Topology with respect to single or multiple users can thus be specified (implicitly) by the constraints of individual process steps, but at a relatively low and non-intuitive level. The Brownston *et al.* OPS5 book [BFKM85] dedicates many pages to "hacking" control flow in rule systems, by introducing state variables to force chaining among rules in the desired order.

The Common Lisp Framework (CLF) [Pro88] incorporates a process model written in AP5, which supports data-driven forward chaining over two separate rule bases [Coh86]. *Consistency rules* have a similar purpose to MARVEL's atomicity annotations and *automation rules* are related to MARVEL's automation annotations, but with nothing akin chaining restrictions; both forms of rules include a pre-condition and an action. A consistency rule's condition may be specified in either of two ways; as a constraint that must *always* be satisfied, or as a trigger that must *never* be satisfied. In either case, process steps whose enaction would violate consistency constraints are either repaired or aborted (by execution of the appropriate consistency rule's action). Automation constraints, which usually specify small bookkeeping chores, are fulfilled only after the corresponding process step has been completed (if the automation rule's condition becomes satisfied, the action is executed). In principle, AP5 rules (like MSL rules) could specify the topology of a process, albeit at a very low level, but they are not used that way in CLF. A process model supports only one participant at a time, so there is no synchronization, *per se* — although data can be imported from another user [NG91].

Adele's *triggers* seem typical of those employed in many modern database management systems, but as far as we know, only Adele has been directly applied to process modeling and enaction [BEM91]. When a trigger's pre-condition is satisfied, its action is executed. PRE and POST triggers are evaluated at the beginning and end of a process step, respectively, within an all-or-nothing transaction. ERROR triggers are considered when such a transaction fails for some reason and AFTER triggers are applied after a transaction succeeds. Triggers effectively implement constraints, but could also express topology at a very low level; however, the examples in the papers show them employed only for local chores associated with a single process step rather than to determine the partial ordering among process steps. Synchronization among roles is specified in a second formalism, called TEMPO [BEM93], with rules built on top of Adele's triggers; this is different from our bi-level breakdown, since TEMPO is concerned with collaboration among what are defined as effectively separate processes rather than topology of a process.

Darwin's *laws* [Min91] define both the process model and the permitted evolution of the process model over time (see, e.g., [MP93]). Laws are syntactically and semantically similar to Prolog rules. Process steps are modeled by *messages* between objects; the objects represent tools and users as well as data. Constraints are enforced *via* Prolog-style unification and backtracking, with messages evaluated as goals with respect to the law. They either succeed, by deriving a delivery to the object, or fail, in which case the message is blocked. The (optional) actions in the law can replace the contents and/or intended recipient of a message. We think it may be even more difficult to specify topology using this approach than the forward-chaining systems. Again, there is no explicit synchronization, although the system has been shown applicable to multi-user configuration management [MR90].

The Process Support System (PSS) [BPJ91] uses a process modeling language called simply PML. PML also represents concurrent roles as instances of classes, which communicate with one another by asynchronous message passing. The bodies of roles are made up of process steps defined as *properties*, each with a name and *guard* conditions that must be satisfied before the step can be performed. Constraints are enforced by an engine that schedules properties corresponding to received messages; when there are no further properties to be scheduled, it constructs an *agenda* containing all the user commands of that role whose guard conditions are satisfied. The user then chooses among those possible actions, at which point the scheduling is resumed. PSS seems to have no structure imposed above that of the individual roles and their interconnections, which implicitly determines the topology.

2.8.3 Bi-Level PMLs

Heimbigner's ProcessWall [Hei92] is not a complete process-centered environment, but an environment component —a process state server with a predefined representation for *tasks*, hierarchical breakdown of tasks into (sub)tasks and individual process steps, and data flow among nodes in the graph. This process state representation is not intended to replace a PML, which is why we do not consider ProcessWall an example of a task graph PML as discussed above. Instead, Heimbigner describes an intriguing notion of *process constructors*, clients (of the process state server) that construct the topological aspects of the task graph using ProcessWall primitives, and *process constrainers*, other clients that enforce constraints on transitions in the graph. The goal of this work is to support interoperability among multiple distinct PMLs, rather than to integrate the two different styles into a single notation.

In ASL, a process constructor would be the instantiation of an activity structure as a (complex) AS object, which defines the inter-activity control flow and synchronization. A process constrainer would be a collection of rule skeletons, which add constraints to the partial order established by the activity structure specification. ASL has an advantage over the ProcessWall mechanisms, in that both levels can (in principle, but not necessarily) be specified in a single unit, which may aid understandability. ProcessWall, however, seems to have an advantage over ASL in flexibility.

Oikos [Cia93] is arguably bi-level, although this nature may not be obvious since the two levels are relatively well-integrated. The topological layer, based on Linda-like tuple spaces [CG89], consists of a hierarchical structure of *blackboards* that represent the work breakdown as mutually recursive *process* and *environment* blackboards. Process blackboards generally represent predefined processes (or process fragments) while environments offer the user freedom to choose among available processes. The constraint layer is an individual blackboard, containing facts and rules expressed in Prolog. These are organized into *theories* that represent process roles, and specify synchronization through insertion and removal of facts on shared blackboards. Theories, data and tools are accessed through predefined *services*.

ASL's structurally similar scheme represents subprocesses as a hierarchical structure of AS objects. Like blackboards, our AS objects contain state information and have separate rule sets (for performing state transitions) for each element in the hierarchy. Oikos, however, shares the topology-oriented languages' general limitation of requiring repetition of constraints at each applicable node in the hierarchy. ASL avoids this problem by merging the constraints specified in an activity's rule skeleton into each instance of the rule (occurrence in an activity structure) automatically.

The Accueil de Logiciel Futur (ALF) environment employs a sophisticated multi-paradigm process modeling formalism, called the Model for Assisted Software Processes (MASP) [OZG91]. In addition to an object model based on PCTE class definitions [Tho89], the MASP notation has five components:

1. A set of *operator types* that define individual process steps in terms of their pre-conditions and post-conditions, expressed in first-order logic.

2. A set of *expressions*. This is an abstraction mechanism for allowing logical sub-expressions to be defined once and then used many times in a process model.
3. A set of *orderings*. These are restrictions on the execution order of operators, and are expressed in a notation based on path expressions. This seems to be the most clearly topology-oriented part of the MASP formalism.
4. A set of *rules*. These define the permissible automation in the environment. In most rule-based PMLs, including the MSL, the rules are the process steps and encapsulate an action that corresponds to what MASP calls an operator, so chaining among rules enacts a sequence of process steps. In contrast, MASP rules are separate from the operators, and although chaining starts from an operator the remainder takes place only between rules and cannot involve another operator.
5. A set of *characteristics*. These are consistency constraints, expressed in first-order logic, that must always be maintained by the environment. This is the most clearly constraint-oriented aspect of the PML, although the operator pre- and post-conditions and rules also seem to be more concerned with constraints than topology.

Boveroux *et al.* provide an extended example of an ALF process model [BCD+91].

APPL/A is a "process programming" language [Ost87] based on Ada. Process roles are represented as Ada tasks and synchronize *via* rendezvous. Subroutines support hierarchical decomposition and conventional structured-programming constructs specify the control flow among process steps. This imperative aspect provides the topology-oriented level of the PML.

APPL/A extends the Ada syntax with relations to store process data, and two constraint-oriented constructs —*triggers* and *predicates* —resulting in a bi-level formalism. Triggers react to operations on relations. There are four such operations (`insert`, `update`, `delete` and `find`) that may be defined on each relation type. Triggers may fire on either `acceptance` events, before the operation is performed, or `completion` events, after the operation has finished. A trigger may contain both a *synchronous* part, which runs while the triggering thread of control is still suspended by the event that fired the trigger, and an *asynchronous* part, which runs after the synchronous part has completed and the thread has been allowed to continue.

Predicates are constraints on the data stored in the relations, expressed in a form of first-order logic. A predicate may be used in two ways in a process definition. It can be called as a function, to return a truth value, or it can be *enforced*. When a predicate is enforced, then no operation may leave the predicate violated, except as specifically allowed within one of APPL/A's "transaction-like" statements [SHO90]. The enforcement of a predicate may be turned on and off dynamically within the process by assigning to its `enforced` attribute, as well as temporarily suspended by the "transaction-like" statements.

2.9 CONTRIBUTIONS

We explained why complex, large scale software processes often require two levels of specification, and that some process modeling languages are more suitable for describing the topology of the process, *via* control flow and synchronization primitives, while others are better suited for expressing constraints on the data and tools employed in individual process steps. We demonstrated through the Activity Structures Language and its Passive Recognition enaction model that process-centered environments could profitably incorporate both styles of process formalisms in a single but bi-level PML. We described a relatively straightforward implementation of this PML on top of the existing MARVEL environment. This system has been used to implement a multi-participant solution to the ISPW7 example problem.

We do not intend to claim that ASL is the "best" bi-level PML that could be developed, far from it: various limitations are mentioned throughout the paper. Our implementation of a bi-level PML by translation of one level into the other has the immediate advantage of implementation efficiency,[7] but experimentation with other approaches is certainly warranted. The whole notion of a bi-level PML may also be suspect, since this approach requires the process engineer to learn two different process modeling paradigms, and to internalize a methodology concerned with which one to choose for each process modeling situation. Experience with using bi-level PMLs in industrial settings, as well as further development of single-paradigm PMLs that cover both topology and constraints, will be needed before the tradeoffs are fully understood and any definite conclusions can be drawn.

ACKNOWLEDGMENTS

ASL was developed in consultation with Bill Riddle and Steve Gaede of Software Design & Analysis and Brian Nejmeh of Innovative Software Engineering Practices. Most of our ISPW7 solution is due to Hideyuki Miki, when a resident visitor at Columbia from Software Research Associates. MARVEL 3.x has been licensed to about 35 institutions to date. Since ASL was originally implemented on top of MARVEL 3.0, some implementation details changed substantially when it was upgraded to become part of the standard 3.1 release. Send email to marvelus@cs.columbia.edu for information about licensing. An abridged version of this paper, based primarily on the initial 3.0 realization, appeared in *Fifteenth International Conference on Software Engineering*, IEEE Computer Society Press, May 1993, pp. 132-143.

During the period when this research was accomplished, the Programming Systems Laboratory was supported by National Science Foundation grants CCR-9106368 and CCR-8858029, by grants and fellowships from AT&T, BNR, Bull, DEC, IBM, Paramax and SRA, by the New York State Center for Advanced Technology in Computers and Information Systems and by the NSF Engineering Research Center for Telecommunications Research. In addition, the authors were supported in part during Summer 1991 by a consulting contract with Software Design & Analysis.

REFERENCES

[ADWR86] George S. Avrunin, Laura K. Dillon, Jack C. Wileden, and William E. Riddle. Constrained expressions: Adding analysis capabilities to design methods for concurrent software systems. *IEEE Transactions on Software Engineering*, SE-12(2):278–292, February 1986.

[Bar92] Naser S. Barghouti. Supporting cooperation in the MARVEL process-centered SDE. In Herbert Weber, editor, *5th ACM SIGSOFT Symposium on Software Development Environments*, pages 21–31, Tyson's Corner VA, December 1992. Special issue of *Software Engineering Notes*, 17(5), December 1992.

[Bat88] Peter Bates. Distributed debugging tools for heterogeneous distributed systems. In *8th International Conference on Distributed Computing Systems*, pages 308–315, San Jose CA, June 1988. IEEE Computer Society.

[7] Another member of our group has implemented the completely independent StateMate process modeling formalism [HK89] by translation into MSLfor enaction; see [Hei93a].

[BCD+91] Ph. Boveroux, G. Canals, J. C. Derniame, C. Godart, Ph. Jamart, and J. Lonchamp. Software process modelling in the ALF system: an example. In A. Fugetta, R. Conradi, and V. Ambriola, editors, *1st European Workshop on Software Process Modeling*, pages 167–179, Milan, Italy, May 1991. AICA.

[BEM91] Noureddine Belkhatir, Jacky Estublier, and Walcelio L. Melo. Adele 2: A support to large software development process. In Mark Dowson, editor, *1st International Conference on the Software Process: Manufacturing Complex Systems*, pages 159–170, Redondo Beach CA, October 1991. IEEE Computer Society Press.

[BEM93] Noureddine Belkhatir, Jacky Estublier, and Walcelio L. Melo. Software process model and work space control in the Adele system. In *2nd International Conference on the Software Process: Continuous Software Process Improvement*, pages 2–11, Berlin Germany, February 1993. IEEE Computer Society Press.

[BFKM85] Lee Brownston, Robert Farrell, Elaine Kant, and Nancy Martin. *Programming Expert Systems in OPS5*. Addison-Wesley, Reading MA, 1985.

[BH83] Bernd Bruegge and Peter Hibbard. Generalized path expressions: A high-level debugging mechanism. *The Journal of Systems and Software*, 3(4):265–276, December 1983.

[BPJ91] R.F. Bruynooghe, J.M. Parker, and J.S.Rowles. PSS: A system for process enactment. In Mark Dowson, editor, *1st International Conference on the Software Process: Manufacturing Complex Systems*, pages 128–141, Redondo Beach CA, October 1991. IEEE Computer Society Press.

[BSKH93] Israel Z. Ben-Shaul, Gail E. Kaiser, and George T. Heineman. An architecture for multiuser software development environments. *Computing Systems, The Journal of the USENIX Association*, 6(2):65–103, Spring 1993.

[CG89] Nicholas Carriero and David Gelernter. Linda in context. *Communications of the ACM*, 32(4):444–458, April 1989.

[CH74] R.H. Campbell and A.N. Habermann. The specification of process synchronization by path expressions. In *Operating Systems*, volume 16 of *Lecture Notes in Computer Science*, pages 89–102. Springer-Verlag, Berlin, 1974.

[Cia93] Paolo Ciancarini. Coordinating rule-based software processes with ESP. *ACM Transactions on Software Engineering and Methodology*, 2(3):203–227, July 1993.

[Coh86] Donald Cohen. Automatic compilation of logical specifications into efficient programs. In *5th National Conference on Artificial Intelligence*, volume Science, pages 20–25, Philadelphia, PA, August 1986. AAAI.

[DG90] Wolfgang Deiters and Volker Gruhn. Managing software processes in the environment MELMAC. In Richard N. Taylor, editor, *4th ACM SIGSOFT Symposium on Software Development Environments*, pages 193–205, Irvine CA, December 1990. Special issue of *Software Engineering Notes*, 15(6), December 1990.

[DR93] Prasun Dewan and John Riedl. Toward computer-supported concurrent software engineering. *Computer*, 26(1):17–27, January 1993.

[GJ92] Volker Gruhn and Rudiger Jegelka. An evaluation of FUNSOFT nets. In J.C. Derniame, editor, *Software Process Technology Second European Workshop*, number 635 in Lecture Notes in Computer Science, pages 196–214. Springer-Verlag, Trondheim, Norway, September 1992.

[GK91] Mark A. Gisi and Gail E. Kaiser. Extending a tool integration language. In Mark Dowson, editor, *1st International Conference on the Software Process: Manufacturing Complex Systems*, pages 218–227, Redondo Beach CA, October 1991. IEEE Computer Society Press.

[GNR91] Steven L. Gaede, Brian Nejmeh, and William E. Riddle. Interim report process management: Infrastructure exploration project. Technical Report 7-48-5, Software Design & Analysis, March 1991.

[Gru91] Volker Gruhn. *Validation and Verification of Software Process Models*. PhD thesis, Forschungsberichte des Fachbereichs Informatik der Universität Dortmund, 1991. Bericht Nr. 394/91.

[Hei90] Dennis Heimbigner. Proscription versus Prescription in process-centered environments. In Takuya Katayama, editor, *6th International Software Process Workshop: Support for the Software Process*, pages 99–102, Hakodate, Japan, October 1990. IEEE Computer

Society Press.

[Hei92] Dennis Heimbigner. The ProcessWall: A process state server approach to process programming. In Herbert Weber, editor, *5th ACM SIGSOFT Symposium on Software Development Environments*, pages 159–168, Tyson's Corner VA, December 1992. Special issue of *Software Engineering Notes*, 17(5), December 1992.

[Hei93a] George T. Heineman. Automatic translation of process modeling formalisms. Technical Report CUCS-036-93, Columbia University Department of Computer Science, November 1993.

[Hei93b] George T. Heineman. A transaction manager component for cooperative transaction models. Technical Report CUCS-017-93, Columbia University Department of Computer Science, July 1993. PhD Thesis Proposal.

[HK89] Watts Humphrey and Marc I. Kellner. Software process modeling: Principles of entity process models. In *11th Internation Conference on Software Engineering*, pages 331–342, Pittsburgh PA, May 1989. IEEE Computer Society Press.

[HK91] Dennis Heimbigner and Marc Kellner. Software process example for ISPW-7, August 1991. /pub/cs/techreports/ISPW7/ispw7.ex.ps.Z available by anonymous ftp from ftp.cs.colorado.edu.

[HKBBS92] George T. Heineman, Gail E. Kaiser, Naser S. Barghouti, and Israel Z. Ben-Shaul. Rule chaining in MARVEL: Dynamic binding of parameters. *IEEE Expert*, 7(6):26–32, December 1992.

[ICS93] *2nd International Conference on the Software Process: Continuous Software Process Improvement*, Berlin, Germany, February 1993. IEEE Computer Society Press.

[IOIT91] Hajimu Iida, Takeshi Ogihara, Katsuro Inoue, and Koji Torii. Generating a menu-oriented navigation system from formal description of software development activity sequence. In Mark Dowson, editor, *1st International Conference on the Software Process: Manufacturing Complex Systems*, pages 45–57, Redondo Beach CA, October 1991. IEEE Computer Society Press.

[IPKT89] Katsuro Inoue, Takeshi Pgihara, Tohru Kikuno, and Koji Torii. A formal adaptation method for process descriptions. In *11th International Conference on Software Engineering*, pages 145–153, Pittsburgh PA, May 1989. IEEE Computer Society Press.

[Kat89] Takuya Katayama. A hierarchical and functional software process description and its enaction. In *11th International Conference on Software Engineering*, pages 343–352, Pittsburgh PA, May 1989. IEEE Computer Society Press.

[KFF+91] Marc I. Kellner, Peter H. Feiler, Anthony Finkelstein, Takuya Katayama, Leon J. Osterweil, Maria H. Penedo, and H. Dieter Rombach. Software process modeling example problem. In Mark Dowson, editor, *1st International Conference on the Software Process: Manufacturing Complex Systems*, pages 176–186, Redondo Beach CA, October 1991. IEEE Computer Society Press.

[KR90] Marc I. Kellner and H. Dieter Rombach. Session summary: Comparisons of software process descriptions. In Takuya Katayama, editor, *6th International Software Process Workshop: Support for the Software Process*, pages 7–18, Hakodate, Japan, October 1990. IEEE Computer Society Press.

[Min91] Naftaly H. Minsky. Law-governed systems. *Software Engineering Journal*, 6(5):285–302, September 1991.

[MP93] Nazim H. Madhavji and Maria H. Penedo, editors. *Special Section on the Evolution of Software Processes*, volume 19:12 of *IEEE Transactions on Software Engineering*. December, 1993.

[MR90] Naftaly H. Minsky and David Rozenshtein. Configuration management by consensus: An application of law-governed systems. In Richard N. Taylor, editor, *4th ACM SIGSOFT Symposium on Software Development Environments*, pages 44–55, Irvine CA, December 1990. Special issue of *Software Engineering Notes*, 15(6), December 1990.

[MS91] Peiwei Mi and Walt Scacchi. Modeling articulation work in software engineering processes. In Mark Dowson, editor, *1st International Conference on the Software Process: Manufacturing Complex Systems*, pages 188–201, Redondo Beach CA, October 1991. IEEE Computer Society Press.

[MS92] Peiwei Mi and Walt Scacchi. Process integration in CASE environments. *IEEE Software*,

9(2):45–53, March 1992.

[NG91] K. Narayanaswamy and Neil M. Goldman. Team coordination: Information sharing + policies. In Ian Thomas, editor, *7th International Software Process Workshop: Communication and Coordination in the Software Process*, pages 99–101, Yountville CA, October 1991. IEEE Computer Society Press.

[Ost87] Leon Osterweil. Software processes are software too. In *9th International Conference on Software Engineering*, pages 1–13, Monterey CA, March 1987. IEEE Computer Society Press.

[OZG91] Flävio Oquendo, Jean-Daniel Zucker, and Philip Griffiths. The MASP approach to software process description, instantiation and enaction. In A. Fugetta, R. Conradi, and V. Ambriola, editors, *1st European Workshop on Software Process Modeling*, pages 147–155, Milan, Italy, May 1991. AICA.

[PHK91] M. Krish Ponamgi, Wenwey Hseush, and Gail E. Kaiser. Debugging multi-threaded programs with MpD. *IEEE Software*, 8(3):37–43, May 1991.

[Pro88] CLF Project. *CLF Manual.* USC Information Sciences Institute, January 1988.

[Rid91] William E. Riddle. Activity structure definitions. Technical Report 7-52-3, Software Design & Analysis, March 1991.

[Sch93] Wilhelm Schäfer, editor. *8th International Software Process Workshop: State of the Practice in Process Technology*, Wadern, Germany, March 1993. IEEE Computer Society Press.

[SHO90] Stanley M. Sutton, Jr., Dennis Heimbigner, and Leon J. Osterweil. Language constructs for managing change in process-centered environments. In Richard N. Taylor, editor, *4th ACM SIGSOFT Symposium on Software Development Environments*, pages 206–217, Irvine CA, December 1990. Special issue of *Software Engineering Notes*, 15(6), December 1990.

[Sut90] Stanley M. Sutton, Jr. *APPL/A: A Prototype Language for Software-Process Programming*. PhD thesis, University of Colorado, 1990.

[Tho89] Ian Thomas. PCTE interfaces: Supporting tools in software-engineering environments. *IEEE Software*, pages 15–23, November 1989.

[Wil88] Lloyd G. Williams. Software process modeling: A behavioral approach. In *10th International Conference on Software Engineering*, pages 174–186, Raffles City, Singapore, April 1988.

3

Variants: Keeping Things Together and Telling Them Apart

Axel Mahler
Lampen & Mahler Software-Engineering

ABSTRACT

Variant management is one of the more obscure issues in software configuration management. Despite its practical relevance, variant control has not yet gained an adequate level of attention in the software engineering community. It is often misconstrued as simply another version control problem. This chapter discusses the background of variant management, and argues that the issue should be clearly separated from classical version control. A number of techniques for maintaining multi variant software products are analyzed along with different tools that implement them. Most software configuration management systems either provide a set of basic mechanisms that, all by themselves, do not represent a compact solution. Or they impose comprehensive source management models that limit the software engineer's flexibility. The shape utility, described in this paper, introduces a meta-mechanism that associates an abstract notion of variant with sets of appropriate basic mechanisms to represent variants technically. Shape's variant definitions provide the missing link between the power of basic software variation mechanisms, and a high-level management concept that is easily custom tailored to the needs of individual projects.

3.1 INTRODUCTION

Versatile management of software variants can help small and medium software development shops stay competitive[1].

While the mass market for standard software is dominated by a few very large companies, small and medium software businesses are often dependent on the development of custom

[1] Good software management will also increase the competitiveness of large companies. It is simply argued that techniques such as variant management are of particular importance to smaller enterprises.

Configuration Management, Edited By Tichy

applications, targeted at a specialized clientele. Today, it is almost impossible to realize the prices that would be necessary to cover the development cost for a complex software system, if the product could be sold to only a few customers. In order to distribute the development cost over more sold copies, the market is expanded by adapting the base product to the specific requirements of numerous users who have somewhat similar applications. The emerging need to maintain a complex system with an ever increasing number of variants can easily turn into a nightmare if no proper variant management is in place. Because the problems involved do not look quite as subtle when a project is just about to be launched, they are easily underestimated. Do not let yourself get fooled, though! Variant management is one of the most cumbersome tasks in software configuration management. It is neither as well understood as *revision control*, nor is it as well supported by tools.

A good way to start a discussion of variant management would be a definition of the notion *variant*. Unfortunately, there is no definition available that is both, general and widely agreed upon. The term variant is frequently used within the conceptual domain of version control. A popular interpretation is that variants are sub-trees of the version tree of a version controlled object. Most software developers who ever participated in a larger software project have an idea about what variants are (at least for them): *parallel versions*. Many version control systems seem to support this view. Tools, such as SCCS [Roc75] or RCS [Tic85] facilitate the archival of successive revisions of a software component—the *mainstream* of development—as well as the representation of deviations from the mainstream, usually called *branches*. While the revisions in a single stream supersede their respective predecessors, the leaves on the various branches represent valid development stages that coexist concurrently. Doesn't this provide a viable basis for managing variants in the software development process ? Unfortunately, this intuitive concept of variants is too simplistic.

3.1.1 Understanding the Nature of Software Variants

There has been a number of more serious attempts to find a useful definition for the fuzzy notion of variant. Tichy proposes a definition that views a variant as a source object linked to another one via the relation *variant-of*, where variant-of is a relation linking two source objects that are indistinguishable under a given abstraction[2]. Another, more technical interpretation stems from the domain of programming support environments for modular languages, such as Gandalf [Hab86] or Adele [Est85]: variants are seen as alternative implementations of the same specification. So far none of the proposed definitions has found general favor. One of the reasons for the lack of a more widely agreed common understanding might be that most definitions are either too technical, too strongly tied to the issue of version control, or so general that they are not really helpful.

In 1988, the first *International Workshop on Software Version and Configuration Control* dedicated a panel discussion to the topic [Tic88b]. Although many aspects of variant configuration management were contemplated, the expert discussion revealed the difficulty of finding a common, and general definition. Viewing the invariant part of an object as an interface that has different—variant— implementations, was considered too restrictive. Instead, it was suggested to consider a number of classes of variants: dependent on the particular development scenario, variants *could be* different implementations of the same interface; variants could also

[2] Tichy contrasts *variant* with the term *revision* which he defines as a source object linked to another one via the relationship *revision-of* where revision-of is a relation linking two source objects if one was produced by changing the other [Tic88a].

be objects with interfaces that differ in irrelevant details, or share a subset of attributes; variants could as well be represented by conditional compilation, or be generated from the same object(s) by varying the tool parameters. The question was raised, how it could be ensured that arbitrary, unanticipated combinations of variants are configured in a consistent manner. It was also held that a distinction should be made between the logical definition of (in-)variants, and the *mechanisms* for representing commonalities and differences between variants.

3.1.2 The Multiple Maintenance Trap

The usual procedure for introducing a new variant into the product library is to establish a baseline copy of the system and to modify it in order to accommodate it to the new target environment. Certain components might be removed, others added, some are modified, but typically many (if not most) components of the original program are reused without modification. The unfortunate need for multiple maintenance arises later, when modifications have to be applied to those parts of a system that ought to be *common* to several variants, but are—for technical reasons—maintained as separate copies for each variant. The resulting situation is confusing: a growing number of product variations must be supported while modification requests for operational releases require immediate reaction, all at the same time the next release of the product is under development. Applying the same modification all over again to all the variants is an extremely tedious job. If this job has to be performed manually, it is very likely that the development state of the variants will go out of sync rather sooner than later, and leave the overall product inconsistent.

In order to evade the described effect, it is advisable to avoid redundancy between system components whenever possible. For the structural organization of a multi-variant software product, avoiding redundancy implies *sharing* of those parts that are identical for more than one variant.

3.1.3 Instantiation of Variants

Sharing of data and source code between variants introduces a new problem: how are the variants kept logically and technically separate from each other ? How exactly is a special product variant composed (what is its configuration ?), and how shall it be built, for example if it is to be shipped ?

In a perfect world, the source library for a software product would be arranged such that inserting a change is as simple as if there were only a single tree of source components from which all variants are built: no need to beat one's brain about where to place the change (which variant shall be the "master" ?), how to make sure that it is propagated appropriately (which "slaves" are affected ?), or how to test if it causes regression in any of the affected configurations. In a perfect world, identifying and building any perceivable variant configuration would be as easy as typing "`make`" at the root of a source tree that leaves no choices unresolved: no need to meditate over obscure compilation flags, compiler versions, optional components, their dependencies, and the corresponding version of the accompanying documentation.

Although there are lots of tools and methods available, the world of software-engineering is everything but perfect. In order to keep the product development process under control, practical software management must address (among other things) the following particular concerns:

Repository organization: finding a representation for the bits and pieces of a variant product that supports sharing of common parts while those parts that reflect the varying constraints be clearly identified and kept separate. This can be considered the *variant control invariant* of the repository (see next point).

Variant change management: developing and defining a software change process that ensures the integrity of the repository, i.e. makes sure that the invariant of the repository (common parts are shared, separate parts are correctly identified) is preserved across changes.

Identification and build of variant configurations: keeping different variants of a product logically separate. This requires a configuration identification process that finds all the constituent parts of a requested configuration in the repository, and a build process that takes the appropriate steps to derive a consistent product.

3.2 REPRESENTATION OF SOFTWARE VARIANTS

Talking about variants of a software object implicitly makes an abstraction: if the subject is "variant foo" versus "variant bar" of an artifact, only the artifact's suitability for a given purpose under certain constraints is considered. In the following discussion, *requesting a variant* is a conceptual operation that instructs the software development environment (SDE) to make a specific instantiation of a software object accessible. When the artifact is requested (e.g. retrieved from the repository, or derived by a build) it is abstracted away from the mechanisms that are employed to maintain whatever makes the "foo" variant of the artifact fit for use under those constraints, and thus different from the "bar" variant. In this section, these mechanisms and their particular characteristics shall be discussed in more detail. A proper understanding of the techniques used to represent and control variants is needed for the definition of variant management procedures that support such an abstract view of variants.

Following the distinction between the two levels of programming that are called programming-in-the-large and programming-in-the-small [DeR76], Winkler distinguishes in his contribution to the first workshop on Software Version and Configuration Control, *program variation in the small* (PVITS), and *program variation in the large* (PVITL). While program-variations-in-the-large typically deal with the building of program systems out of program building blocks (components, modules etc.), program-variation-in-the-small is concerned with intra-component variation [Win88]. From the configuration manager's point of view, this distinction, although appropriate for technical reasons, is undesirable. The following consideration of variant representation techniques shall provide the basis for finding a more general concept of product variation that abstracts from the peculiarities of PVITL and PVITS.

3.2.1 Variant Representation Basics—The Component Level

In most SDEs, there are two basic choices for the representation of variant components:

1. maintaining a separate copy of the component for each variant (this approach shall be called *variant segregation*), and
2. maintaining a single source object for all variants that are extracted as needed (*single source variants*).

Although technically inferior, variant segregation is the mechanism of choice suggested by most source control systems. The subsequent comparison will highlight the specific properties, advantages, and drawbacks of both techniques. In particular, it is argued that the use of *version branches* in source control systems is in most cases unsuitable for the maintenance of variants.

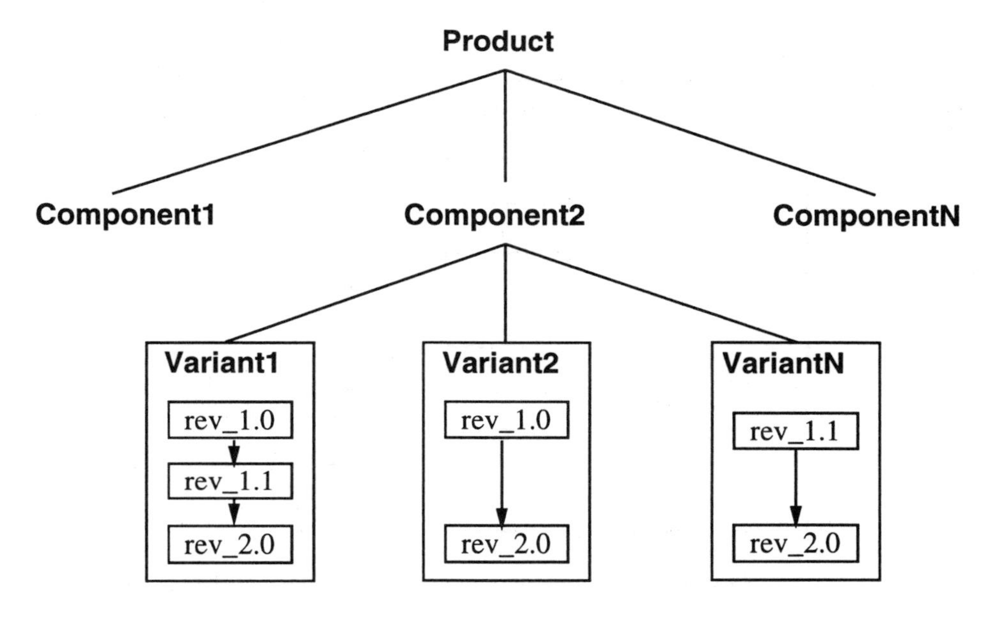

Figure 3.1 Segregated variants in a component directory

3.2.1.1 VARIANT SEGREGATION

There are several different ways to segregate variants of a source component. For project repositories that are based on hierarchical file systems, Figure 3.1 shows the classical source organization scheme. The variant component is made up of a directory that contains the component's variant instantiations (the variant *siblings*). The file names of these instances represent the *variant branches* in the component's development genealogy. Besides its intriguing simplicity, this approach has the advantage that it blends easily with revision control if the variant instances are represented by archives of a version control system rather than plain files. A specific drawback of the described technique is the additional level in the product's component name space that causes a loss of transparency in variant management.

A different technique is suggested by many version control systems. Here, the variant component is represented by a tree of versions that are stored within a single version archive (instead of a directory). Variants are represented as branches that spawn from the tree of revisions (Figure 3.2).

Although most version control systems (with SCCS being a notable exception) provide the possibility to tag branches with symbolic names, caution should be exercised when version control archives must be used for permanent storage of variants. As will be discussed in the section on *Advanced Issues in Variant Management*, below, the main problem with this approach is the unclear separation between real, and temporal variants. Reichenberger discusses the problems of intermixed organization of revisions and variants in greater detail [Rei89].

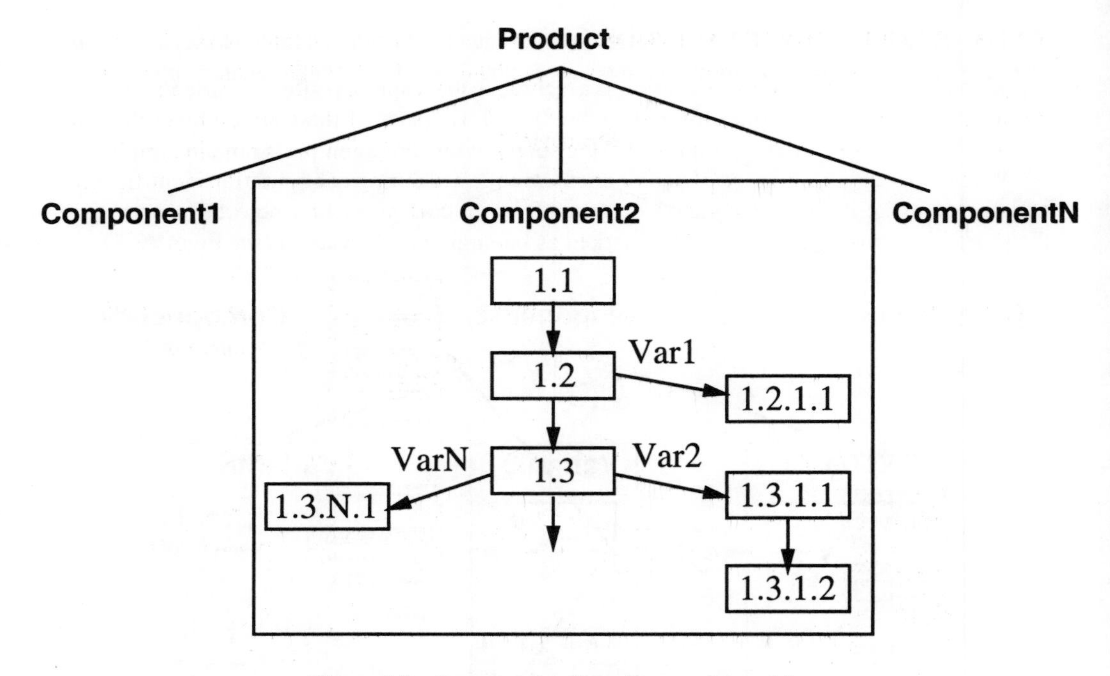

Figure 3.2 Segregated variants in a version archive

These drawbacks are strongly impairing the specific advantages of this approach which are efficient usage of storage capacity (usually, only the differences between successive versions are stored), and the compact representation of all of a component's instances.

Variant segregation is likely to introduce redundancy into the product's source library, because a variant is typically a modified copy of some other source object. As these modifications are often small compared to the amount of data that the variant siblings have in common, this technique is vulnerable to the multiple maintenance problem. Modifications that apply to common parts must be propagated to the other siblings. This is easier said than done, because it is often not obvious, whether a change affects variant specific or common parts, or perhaps *introduces* variant specific characteristics into hitherto common parts.

Another problem is that the same component may be subject to variance in several dimensions. The same source component may, for example, be variant for different operating systems and different functional characteristics such as user interfaces. These dimensions are completely independent of each other, and there is no reason why one of them shall have the privilege of "owning" the branch name. For a further discussion of this problem, see the section on *Multiple Variance*, below.

Due to the above mentioned problems, variant segregation is best suited for the maintenance of components that *localize* variants, i.e. where the different instantiations have no or few source text in common with their siblings (e.g. completely different implementations of functions with the same interface), and that vary only within a single dimension. Localization of variant specific code requires planning for variance and good modular design.

3.2.1.2 SINGLE SOURCE VARIATION

Winkler describes single source variation as a technique that captures different variants forming a family, in one common piece of code [Win88]. Those parts of the source object that are specific for a certain variant are marked accordingly, while common parts remain simply "as is". When a variant instantiation of a component is requested during configuration identification and/or system build, it is automatically extracted from the common source object by assembling the shared sections, and those that are marked as belonging to the variant (see Figure 3.3).

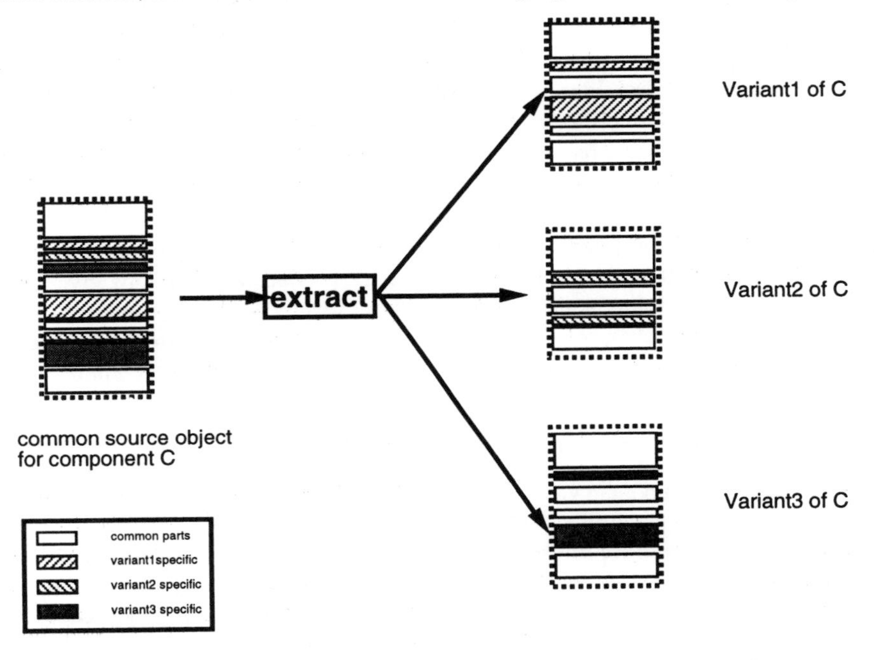

Figure 3.3 Single source variants

Single source variants are a popular component variation scheme in a number of programming languages, such as C, where it is applied as *conditional compilation.*

In comparison with the variant segregation approach, single source variation has two major advantages:

1. redundancy between different variants of a given component can be almost completely avoided.
2. disk space is used very efficiently.

Single source variants have disadvantages, however. Probably the most serious is the obfuscation of the source code by *meta constructs* that control the instantiation process for the different variants. Thus, program source code with scattered meta instructions is sometimes called *meta program.* If a component is affected by variance in several categories, the meta program may rapidly become incomprehensible, and thus unmaintainable. A serious problem is caused by the fact that many single source variation techniques rely on text processing, rather than programming language concepts, such as generic packages in Ada. It is very easy to instantiate inconsistent component versions, for example by passing a wrong flag to the variant extraction tool. Variant management should take extra pains to make sure that variants are extracted such that the object instances are likely to be consistent.

An additional drawback of single source variation is a certain loss of traceability in a variant's change process: because the unit of change is the component that represents all variants, each modification "physically" affects the complete set of variants, even if only one variant is affected logically. As a consequence, the component's change log may document changes that apply only to one variant.

Both, variant segregation, and single source variation have their specific advantages and problems. As a rule of thumb, variant segregation is most appropriate in situations where the amount of data that is common to several variants is small—and vice versa. However, in practice it will often be infeasible to maintain a clear separation. Rather, both techniques will be used concurrently, and intermixed. As will be discussed below, it is not uncommon that a component is variant in more than one respect: Variant property "foo" might be represented by variant segregation, while property "bar" is extracted from each of the segregated instances as needed.

A problem that both representation schemes have in common is caused by their nature as component level techniques. In any non-trivial project, product variation in a given category will likely involve many components. Component level variant control has no means to ensure consistent naming of branches, or consistent use of preprocessor instructions. These are some of the issues that have to be addressed by advanced variant management techniques.

3.2.2 Advanced Issues in Variant Management

Both of the described component variation techniques depend on a *variant management policy* that must either be adhered to by user discretion, or be enforced by the support environment. In order to keep the overall repository structure well ordered, it is necessary to use naming conventions for variants. For segregated variants, it should be ensured that the objects that realize a specific variant are consistently named throughout the product. This applies to file names (as shown in Figure 3.1) as well as branch names in version control systems (Figure 3.2).

Variant objects that are represented as single source variants also depend on naming conventions. Here, the symbols and/or instructions that control the variant extraction tool (e.g. the C preprocessor) need to be standardized.

3.2.2.1 TEMPORAL AND PERMANENT VARIANTS

Another important policy issue is the proper distinction between temporal and permanent variants. Whitgift calls variants that are doomed to being merged with other variants of an object, *temporary variants* [Whi91]. This kind of "variant" is frequently found in software maintenance situations, when multiple developers need to modify the same source component in parallel.

In contrast to temporal variants, *permanent variants* are not intended to be merged with any other variant. Permanent variants represent branches in the product development path that have their own life cycle.

Software development environments that do not clearly distinguish between temporal and permanent variants are vulnerable to confusion in the development process. Shall the branching feature of a version control tool, such as RCS, be used for the support of parallel development, or for representation of permanent variants ? If both uses are intended, how can temporal and permanent branches be distinguished ? Due to the close relationship of temporal variants to a particular concept of the change control process, these should not be regarded as variants at all.

3.2.2.2 AGGREGATE VARIATION

Software variation not only encompasses variance of individual system components, but also variations of the *part list* of composite objects, such as programs or libraries. As the part list of a system varies, it is obvious that the structural relationships between the parts will be different as well. The figure below illustrates this situation. Note that not only the composition of the three variants varies but also their internal dependency structure.

Variant1 = A, B, C, D; A C, B D
Variant2 = A, B, C; B C
Variant3 = A, B, C, D1, E; A C, A D1, B E

Most advanced configuration management systems are based on either or both of the two concepts, *system model*, and *view*. The system model approach employs a database of component versions, and a set of plans for various configurations. Product configurations are identified and built by intelligent tools that select the components from the database according to the plan. The view concept tries to abstract away from versions and variants by presenting a flat view of the system (i.e. all version selection options are resolved) to the user. With views, a user worries about configuration management only when a view is defined. When a product variant is approached through a view, there is almost no need to mind different configurations.

Structural variation of a product can be achieved through variant system models. Because system models are (first class) source objects, they can be varied with the same component variation techniques described in the previous section. The ShapeTools configuration management system, described in the next chapter, for example, uses a special kind of *single source variation* for system models to represent varying aggregate structure.

3.2.2.3 DERIVATION VARIANTS

Derivation variants occur when the same set of source objects is processed in different ways in order to produce a set of variant derived objects. Derivation variants refer to variants of derived objects (so far, only source objects were considered), and variant processes to produce these objects.

Derivation variants often occur *implicitly* if a system is built within a heterogeneous computer network (this is a common problem with different brands of workstations in a shared NFS file system). *Explicit* derivation variants occur typically in cross compilation scenarios. The problem is more general, though. Variance of the build process occurs, for example, when different tool versions are used, or the tool behavior is modified by supplying different sets of options and switches to the tool process (e.g. if the same piece of documentation is formatted for output on A4 or US legal format media).

3.2.2.4 MULTIPLE VARIANCE

It has been mentioned earlier that it is rather the rule than the exception that variant software objects vary in more than one dimension. An interesting problem for configuration identification and build tools is the combination of independent variants. Although the real number of sensible variant configurations may be smaller than the cartesian product of all variant dimensions (because some of the combinations may not make sense) this is a tricky issue. Configuration management systems that suggest one particular representation concept for variants are vulnerable to increased management and maintenance overhead. Variant segregation, for example, implicitly assumes that an instance of a variant object has exactly one distinctive property which is reflected by the branch name.

Source management systems that favor variant segregation as the representation technique of choice will either have to distinguish between major (variant segregation) and minor variants (single source variation), or need a combinatorial number of variants that combine the compatible properties. The first solution is unsatisfying because the distinction between major and minor variants is arbitrary. The second solution would introduce an intolerable amount of redundancy into the source repository. Also, the specification of build requests may be obscure, because building a certain product variant can involve interaction with all of the variant management techniques described above.

3.2.2.5 CONSISTENCY ISSUES IN VARIANT COMBINATION

The possibility to request various combinations of variants for a software object raises the question, which variant parameters can be safely combined. It would be clearly desirable to have a means to prevent variant combinations that would, for example, configure a system to run on an MVS mainframe, and under Unix at the same time. On the other hand, there might be dependencies between different variants that imply requesting of a secondary variant *V2*, each time some primary variant *V1* is requested. For example, the "debug" variant of a program might require a particular compiler that might only be available for the "Unix" variant. So, if the "debug" variant is requested, the "Unix" variant should be requested implicitly.

The issue of configuration consistency has been addressed in depth in the area of programming language oriented configuration management (e.g. [Hab81b, Per87, Est85, Mor88]). While some of this work will be briefly discussed in the next section, a thorough discussion of language oriented SCM is beyond the scope of this article.

3.3 THE STATE OF THE ART AND PRACTICE IN VARIANT MANAGEMENT

Twenty years of research in the field have generated a considerable amount of concepts, techniques, and tools for software configuration management. Much of the corresponding work is described in the proceedings of the *International Conferences on Software Engineering* (ICSE 1–16), and the ACM SIGSOFT/SIGPLAN Symposiums on Practical Software Development Environments (appearing as special issues of ACM SIGPLAN Notices, and ACM Software Engineering Notes). A comprehensive introductory text on practical software configuration management is Whitgift's book [Whi91]. The spectrum of functionality in current software configuration management systems is reviewed and discussed in [Dar90], and [Fei91]. Probably the most interesting material on the subject is contained in the proceedings of the workshop series on software configuration management (see References).

It is surprising that despite a rather extensive body of work in the area of configuration management, variant control issues receive only inadequate attention. There is, for example, no explicit mention of variant management capabilities in Dart's overview [Dar90]. When variants are addressed explicitly within the scope of a tool or environment discussion, they are mostly conceived as a special case in version control (namely when it comes to *branching*). Thus, the discussion of variants remains confined to the component level, and to variant segregation in particular. There are notable exceptions, though. The following discussion is structured along the following lines:

- Component variation
- Variant compositions and configuration consistency
- Variant builds and derived object management, and
- Variant authoring.

3.3.1 Component Variation

One of the problems in component management is the enforcement of consistent naming of variant branches across various components of a system. Classical version control systems, such as RCS [Tic85], provide no support for consistent branch naming but rather rely on user discretion. Miller proposes an inverted approach to configuration management that places variant control at the lowest level of the functional hierarchy of source control [Mil89]. A software system is treated as a hierarchically structured collection of source code components that are consistently tagged with variant attributes. When the system is revised, each revision applies to the entire system rather than individual components. Thus, consistent identification of variant components is preserved. Reichenberger criticizes the intermixed organization of revisions and variants in conventional source control systems, and proposes *orthogonal version management* [Rei89]. Orthogonal version management is similar to the inverted approach proposed by Miller in that the entire project is emphasized over its individual components. In the *Voodoo* system, component variants are created as variant nodes that bear the name of a globally defined project variant [Rei93].

Both approaches support an explicit concept of variant, and imply segregation as exclusive means to keep the variants of a component apart. In contrast, Atria's *ClearCase* system does not provide any explicit notion of variant, but rather provides mechanism. Consistent naming of component variants can be achieved trough *branch types* [Atr92]. In ClearCase, a component's history is represented as a tree of named branches. When a new branch is created it must be associated with a branch type. Branch types are simply names that are defined in advance by the environment administrator.

The ShapeTools SCM system suggests *inverted branching* for maintaining consistency in variant labeling [Lam93]. A structure node is created for each variant. Rather than having the component first, with variant specific branches in the component's version history, inverted branching spawns the variant branch first, and keeps the components and their revisions in the second row. Thus, the branch name implicitly applies to the respective variant instances of all components.

Database, Selectors and Cels (DaSC) is a source control approach that is not based on entire modules[3] as storage granulate but uses meaningful abstractions within a document type's application domain (e.g. procedures and abstract data types for programming languages) as atomic units [Gen89]. In DaSC, modules are represented by selector files that identify in the database the particular granules of code that make up that version of the module. Each possible variant configuration of a system is represented by an inclusion directory that is the root of a respective hierarchy of selector files. The source code granules are arranged in a hierarchy of abstractions where, for example, variants are represented by directories (similar to inverted branching) containing the applicable pieces of code. An advantage of DaSC is that sharing of common code is promoted while variant specific parts are clearly identified. DaSC completely avoids conditional processing of source code, and thereby circumvents a major drawback of the single source approach to variant representation.

A vaguely similar approach was chosen for the design of the EPOS software engineering database [Lie89], and in SMDS' Aide-de-Camp software management system [SMD92]. Both systems are centered around dedicated databases that are tuned for efficient storage and retrieval of document fragments, for example lines of source code. Based on this technology, versions of a module are represented by a base object, and a set of applicable changes. Accordingly, multiple variants of a source object can be represented as a non-variant base object, and a set of variant specific modifications (*change sets*) that are dynamically applied when a particular variant is requested. Change sets are maintained for entire products rather than individual components. In Aide-de-Camp, particular configurations of software systems are described in terms of a simple list algebra. For example, a base configuration could be defined as

$$BASE1.0 = M1 + M2 + M3$$

while an update to the base version could be defined as the base configuration plus a number of change sets:

$$BASE1.1 = BASE1.0 + CS1 + CS2$$

Similarly, a variant of the product could be defined as

$$BASE1.1\,Win = BASE1.1 + WindowsMods$$

Here, the term *WindowsMods* is assumed to be defined in the same manner, as a list of variant specific change sets.

The mentioned systems are based on sophisticated single source variation techniques that avoid the use of conditional constructs in the source pool. A drawback of these approaches is their dependency on either highly specialized, proprietary databases, or source organization schemes that might be considered fragile. In contrast to these approaches, the NORA environment, developed at the Technical University of Braunschweig, makes heavy use of the C preprocessor to control document variants. The problems of using conditional constructs within a complex, multi-variant source object are tackled with inference based re-engineering tools [Kro93]. Mathematical concept analysis is employed to infer variant structures from complex conditional structures in existing source code. Visual aids are used to present the inferred logical structure to the user. An outgrowth of this work is Zeller's concept of configuration management with feature logics [Zel94]. In this model, components are tagged with *feature terms*. When a system is to be composed, a set of valid variant combinations is inferred

[3] the term module shall refer to a relatively large collection of source code that is maintained as a single component or file

and presented as an interactive control panel. The control panel can be used to select the final configuration.

3.3.2 Variant Compositions and Configuration Consistency

As the components of a software system vary for variant configurations, so does the overall structure of the system. The central issues are control over different compositions of a system, and tracking of the relationships between the system's components.

In language sensitive systems such as Gandalf, the environment's SCM tools can take advantage of the components' interface specifications to derive the dependency structure [Hab86]. Gandalf's System Version Control Environment (SVCE) introduced a number of language constructs for configuration management purposes. The *Composition* construct is used to specify the way in which components within a system are combined to form viable configurations of the system [Hab81a]. The language oriented approach not only permits a precise definition of variant system compositions, but also enables the environment to determine whether a requested variant configuration is consistent with respect to the static semantics of the programming language. Haberman and Perry elaborate on this issue in their concept of well-formed compositions [Hab81b]. The ideas of SVCE were picked up and carried further by Perry, with the development of the Inscape environment [Per87]. The concept of well-formedness of compositions is augmented by component relationships such as compatibility and consistency of component versions.

Although SVCE is basically a system modeling facility, its scope is restricted to the language oriented Gandalf environments. The general concept of system modeling for capturing different configurations is not limited to language based environments, however. A *system model* is an external description of the components that make up a system, and the relationships between them. The term system model was coined by the authors of the Cedar system [Lam83], but popularized by Apollo's Domain Software Engineering Environment (DSEE) [Leb84]. Although system modeling does not provide the same degree of semantic integration that is known from language based environments, system modeling is the approach of choice in many practical configuration management systems because of its simplicity and flexibility. Systems like DSEE, ShapeTools, and Adele [Est85, Est92] are based on system modeling.

While the first two tool systems store system models as separate documents that explicitly list a system's components and relationships, Adele exploits the potential of its underlying object management system. The component versions in Adele's database are annotated with descriptive attributes and explicit relationships to other components. In Adele, system models define an initial set of desired global characteristics (initial constraints). Based on this set of constraints, components are selected that impose further constraints. These are added to the set of constraints for the proceeding configuration selection, and so on. Nicklin describes a similar variant management facility that uses *contexts* to select appropriate components for a configuration [Nic91]. Contexts are boolean expressions that are matched against descriptive attributes attached to the components stored in the database.

A very powerful and simple concept for modeling variant system compositions is found in ClearCase. The ClearCase repository uses an extended file system approach (*multi-version file system, MFS*) for the representation of revisions and variants. The full set of version control functions for regular files are also available for directories. Thus, the composition of a complex (sub-)system can be directly represented by a directory. Structural variants are simply represented as branches in the version tree of a directory. The variant branches of directories list only those components that are part of a specific configuration.

ClearCase's virtual file system technology also provides dynamic tracking of component dependencies—a major problem for all system model based SCM systems. When, during system build, the compiler makes a system request to open an include file, this request is dispatched to ClearCase's MFS file-open handler, making the system aware of the dependency. Thus, the SCM system dynamically keeps track of which objects are needed in order to build a derived object.

3.3.3 Variant Builds and Derived Object Management

In her analysis of the software manufacturing process, Borison pointed out that in addition to precise selection of component versions, a reliable software manufacturing facility must provide means of describing the steps that must be performed by the manufacturing process in order to build a software artifact. In addition to these mechanisms it is incumbent on the manufacturing facility to provide a record of the system as built. The record serves to identify a given instantiation of the system and to distinguish it from all other instantiations [Bor86]. Borison developed a general concept of *difference predicates* that determine whether two components are to be treated equivalent according to certain criteria. Thus, significance of variation in the source context, or manufacturing process can be flexibly defined according to the rationale of a software product's development process.

Classical build tools, such as *make* [Fel79] offer only insufficient support for reliable production of different software product variants: only the file modification times of source and derived objects are used as difference predicates in the decision whether a component needs to be rebuilt. If a second variant of a software system is to be build, for example by specifying different compiler options, the build directory must be cleared from previous build results. Several more recent implementations of the make facility, such as *nmake* [Fow85], try to eliminate this deficiency by recording the command that was used to produce each derived object.

A more powerful approach to driving software builds is found in Odin [Cle90]. Odin is a tool integration system designed to deduce the necessary, potentially complex sequence of tool activations upon sets of source and derived objects, in order to build a requested object. The centerpiece is a derivation graph, in which the edges correspond to the tools that Odin integrates while the nodes correspond to types of objects. Different configurations of a software product are treated as *objects*, just as source components and intermediate results. In Odin, software objects with varying properties are requested by the user through a simple request language. Thanks to the tool's complete control over the build process for any directly or indirectly requested object, the user need not worry about how an object is created.

One of the most important features of advanced build tools is the management of derived objects. Derived object management was introduced by DSEE [Leb84], and Odin [Cle84]. With this function, each of the—intermediately, or finally — derived objects is cached, and associated with a description of how it was built. This has several advantages. If any of the relevant build parameters changes, any affected derived object will be (re-)build as appropriate. For example, if a requested object with appropriate properties already exists, Odin will return a pointer to it instead of rebuilding it. If such an object does not exist, Odin searches its object store for any objects that represent some progress from the most elementary source objects toward what has been requested. Odin then applies the remaining transformations to the already existing objects to derive them into what has been requested. In DSEE's derived object management, not only the derivation parameters are stored for each derived object but also the the version information for all of a derivation's prerequisite objects. Derived object management not only supports more sophisticated difference predicates for source and derived objects, but also drastically improves build performance.

3.3.4 Variant Authoring

The authoring process for multi variant software systems shall preserve a maximal degree of source sharing between the variants while those parts that differ be clearly identified. Where redundancy cannot be avoided, the authoring process shall ensure that changes to redundant parts of a component instantiation are appropriately propagated to its siblings. In contrast to the other technical areas involved in variant management, there are only few basic techniques to support variant authoring. These shall be called *fragments-and-attributes*, and *modify-propagate*. The first is related to single source variation, the second to variant segregation.

The most widespread form of fragments-and-attributes authoring is the use of conditional compilation techniques along with conventional text editors. Maintaining source objects with many variants can become a particularly complex and error prone task, because many or all of the variants are edited—and visible—at the same time. Without the support of variant sensitive tools, the burden of structuring the meta source object, and keeping mutually exclusive variants consistently apart is left to the developer.

A first approach towards a dedicated multi-version editor was taken by Fraser and Myers [Fra87]. The described EH editor represents component revisions as lists of lines that are shared between different revisions as long as they are not altered. EH integrates the functions of a text editor, and classical revision control systems such as SCCS. There is no direct support for variants.

Kruskal developed an editor that combines the features of an editor with classical revision control, and conditional compilation [Kru84]. In P-Edit, multi-variant components are represented as collections of attributed source fragments that are tied together by variant specific *threads*. Threads are defined by attribute expressions that are used to select and sequence the fragments that make up a certain version. Sarnak et.al. describe an editor that evolved from P-Edit [Sar88]. Like P-Edit, their Multi-Version Personal Editor (MVPE) enables the user to edit a specified set of variants, the edit-set, simultaneously. Views are used to present to the user unambiguous, variant specific instantiations of the edited variants. MVPE's user interface employs color to distinguish those parts common to all variants in the edit set from variant specific parts. If a modification is made in a part marked as common, the modification applies to all variants. Similarly, modifications to variant specific parts are inserted as variant specific. A new variant can be created at any time by explicitly declaring it.

Narayanaswamy describes a text based representation for program variants that uses a similar approach [Nar89]. He proposes a hypertext structure for the representation of single source variants that can be edited with a standard EMACS-style editor. The developer maintains program fragments that are attributed with *contexts* in which these are activated.

If variant segregation is used to keep component variants separate, there is no need for special support during the immediate writing of a component. Rather, any applicable changes need to be propagated to the siblings of a modified, variant specific component instance, as soon as the basic change is complete. In most SCM systems there is no dedicated support for a *modify-propagate* authoring process. Although *merge* functions are generally available in source control systems, these are mostly tuned for support of the optimistic change control model (*copy-modify-merge*). In this model, concurrent changes are stored as separate branches in the version tree that are to be merged back into the main branch. Use of branching for optimistic change control has nothing to do with variant management, and merging should not be confused with change dissemination to variant siblings. SCM tools that concentrate on the provision of mechanism rather than methodology, such as ClearCase, can be used for modify-propagate variant authoring, if applied carefully. As Feiler pointed out, SCM tools that are focused at a certain change control methodology, e.g. the transaction model, often cannot be used for this process [Fei91].

A completely different approach to variant authoring is taken by change oriented source management systems, such as EPOS or Aide-de-Camp (see discussion above). However, similar to change dissemination across segregated variants, there is the problem of consistent automatic incorporation of these changes. The problems that are involved here are subtle and hard to tackle. Research on the integration of non-interfering changes is still in the early stages. A thorough description of the relevant work is beyond the scope of this article. For a discussion of the issue, and a first approach to a solution, see [Hor89, Rep89]. For a discussion of structure oriented merging in syntax oriented development environments, see [Wes91].

3.4 VARIANT MANAGEMENT WITH SHAPE

Existing configuration management tools tend to either impose their own, built-in concept of variants, thereby limiting the developers' flexibility, or they provide a portfolio of basic techniques upon which to build a coherent variant management concept is left to the user. The intricacies of variant management, even for moderately complex software products, are so abundant that many development organizations are forced to craft their own, more or less ingenious, custom solutions that suit their needs (often based on stock SCM tools). The resulting, potentially complex and delicate web of representation techniques is often unwieldy. What is needed is an abstraction that maps *logical variants* to the appropriate technical representation(s), and the corresponding instantiation process when a certain variant (or a consistent combination of variant properties) of a component or product is requested. *Shape* is a software configuration management tool that provides such an abstraction mechanism in a simple way.

Shape is the build driver of the *ShapeTools* software configuration management toolkit. It combines the capabilities of classical build programs, such as *make*, with those of conventional source control systems, such as *RCS*. It is straightforward to think of shape as a *make* program that works with versions of files stored in a source control archive, rather than plain files. Similar to make, shape relies on a description file that contains all the structural information about the managed product. When invoked, shape builds aggregates (this is more general than just "programs") from their constituent components. Before shape delegates any processing to other tools, for example a compiler, it makes sure that the proper versions of all components are found by those tools. Similar to DSEE's configuration threads [Leb84], shape selects source versions according to selection rules that can be dynamically associated with any target object. Just like DSEE and Odin, shape stores derived objects, along with a description of how these were exactly derived, in a derived object cache. These basic concepts of shape have been described in greater detail in [Mah88a], and [Mah88b]. ShapeTools' repository for source- and derived objects is discussed in [Lam88], and [Lam94]. This section describes shape's variant control mechanism, a feature that has not been covered thoroughly in previous publications.

The distinctive characteristic of shape's variant control approach is its concept of *variant definition*. Overall, variant definitions are a *mechanism to control mechanisms*. A variant definition associates a logical name to a set of more primitive definitions that in turn control various aspects of variant related functions, e.g. component selection strategies, preprocessor directives, compiler switches, tool selections, and so on. During build runs, variants can be dynamically activated and deactivated as necessary on a target by target basis.

Shape is not built on any particular concept of variant. It rather applies the techniques for maintaining variants that were discussed in the previous sections, in a well coordinated manner. Independently from particular semantics that might be associated with the variant notion, there exists a small number of techniques to implement software variation on a technical level. These techniques are variant segregation, single source variation, aggregate variation, and derivation variation. Depending on the particular needs of a project, all of these techniques may be in simultaneous use, and can occur intermixed as appropriate. Shape's approach makes it possible to request variants (and compatible variant combinations) simply by name. For the user, there is no need to worry about the potentially complex blend of mechanisms that is employed to realize them.

3.4.1 Variant Definitions

Much of the information in Shapefiles (just as is the case with Makefiles) is defined in variables. Use of variables is not just a matter of good style, but the essential technique that introduces the versatility into shape's control information that is key for managing variants. Shape variant definitions are simply groups of variable definitions that take effect when the variant is requested in a build. A variant definition has the following format:

variant-name : + *[variant-name]*

variable-name1 = *[Value]*

When a variable is defined during a variant activation, any previous definition of the variable that was made in the description file but outside of a variant definition is eclipsed by the new definition. If a variable is defined in multiple variants that are activated simultaneously, the respective values are concatenated. A set of shape variants that are used to define different varieties of the compilation process for C source modules is shown in the example below. A variant definition starts with the name of the variant (printed in **boldface**), and continues with a series of indented variable definitions. The variant definition is terminated by a blank line.

```
vclass compiler ::= (gnu, proprietary)

gnu:+
        CC = gcc
        OPTIMIZE = -O2 -inline-functions
        STDC = -ansi -Wall
        OLDSTYLE = -traditional
```

```
proprietary:+
        CC = cc
        OPTIMIZE = +O3
        STDC = -Aa

optimize:+
        VARCFLAGS = $(OPTIMIZE)

vclass c_style ::= (ansi, traditional)

ansi:+
        VARCFLAGS = $(STDC)

traditional:+
        VARCFLAGS = $(OLDSTYLE)

production:+ proprietary ansi optimize
gnu_ansi:+ gnu ansi
gnu_kr:+ gnu traditional

CFLAGS += $(VARCFLAGS)
```

The first two variants, gnu and proprietary, define *compiler profiles*, i.e. the way in which compilers are invoked, and the specific switches used to determine the compilers' input and output disposition. The remaining variants define more or less complex sets of constraints that can be imposed selectively. production, gnu_ansi, and gnu_kr exemplify variant definitions with dependent variants. If, for example, the user requests a build for the production variant, the variants proprietary, ansi, and optimize are implicitly activated. The last line of the example does not belong to any of the variant definitions, but is part of the global description file. It has the effect that the current value of the VARCFLAGS variable will be appended to the static value of the variable CFLAGS, whenever CFLAGS is referenced. Because variable references are evaluated as late as possible, values defined by one variant are dynamically used in other variants that reference the variable.

3.4.2 Variant Combinations and Variant Classes

The *vclass* construct tells shape that the listed variants are *incompatible*, i.e. if a user requests a build which activates more than one variant of a given class at the same time, shape will complain. Variant classes can be interpreted as the independent *dimensions* in which the described product may vary. Shape variant class definitions have the following format:

vclass *variant-class-name* ::= (*var1, var2*)

The same variant can be member of multiple variant classes. If a combination of variants is requested with any two variants that are member of the same variant class, an error is raised. While it is impossible for shape to determine whether a given combination of variant properties will lead to a consistent configuration, variant classes provide a simple means to prevent builds of obviously inconsistent configurations.

3.4.3 Activation of Variants

Variants are activated at build time. When a user requests a build for a specific target object, she can set the desired variants from the command line (there is no graphical user interface for shape, yet). In addition, variants can be activated individually for each target in shape's description file.

3.4.4 Derivation Variants

The flexibility of variant specific variable settings, and the potential effect that may be achieved with them can only be appreciated if shape's generic transformation rules are considered[4]. The example below shows a rule that shape uses to derive objects, that contain relocatable object code, from C source code objects.

```
%.o : %.c : +(CC) +(CFLAGS)
        $(CC) -c $(CFLAGS) %.c
```

The `CC` and `CFLAGS` variable references in the second line are substituted and used to construct a command line that invokes a particular compiler with the appropriate set of switches. Although the given example is very simple, the combination of variant specific variable settings, and shape's transformation rules is powerful enough to describe a wide range of variability in derivation processes. ShapeTools' repository provides a derived object cache that facilitates storage of multiple versions (and variants) of derived objects, along with a description of how these objects were produced, the *derivation key*. Equivalence of derivation keys is the difference predicate that shape uses to determine whether a requested object needs to be rebuilt. The derivation key is a distinguishing characteristic of the entire derivation process (which can be a complex chain of elementary derivations) for a given target.

Technically, a derivation key is an attribute that contains unique IDs for all prerequisites from which a given object is derived. Also, all relevant parameters of the derivation process are stored in the derivation key. It is user definable, which parameters shall be considered "relevant". In the transformation rule example, the variables `CC` and `CFLAGS` are declared *ingredients* of the transformation by the enclosing "`+(`*variable-name*`)`" expression. The current values of all ingredient variables are recorded in the derivation key when a transformation rule fires. This feature provides for flexible management of derived object variants, because it is easy to make an object dependent on the tools, tool invocations, tool versions, etc., that were used to derive it.

3.4.5 Locating Physically Separate Variant Source Objects

Shape provides a special variable, `vpath` that is intended to be used in variant definitions. The `vpath` variable defines shape's search precedence when source archives are located in ShapeTools' repository. If `vpath` is non-empty, shape tries to find any referenced source object in the locations pointed to by `vpath` first. If more than one active variant defines `vpath`, the variant search path is concatenated, with the most recently activated variant taking precedence. Only if a referenced source component cannot be found in any of the `vpath` locations, the build directory is searched.

---

[4] Generic transformation rules are by no means specific to shape. All implementations of the make utility provide some notion of generic transformation rule.

The *variant path* search strategy in shape is different from the VPATH search in most implementations of make. The reasoning behind shape's strategy is that physically separate copies of variant source objects are organized such that the build directory, which is searched last, holds the default variant (if any). If a variant is requested for a build, it is obvious that variant specific copies of a component should be preferred over the default. This search rationale corresponds to the *inverted branching* approach to represent segregated variants.

A problem with this technique occurs if variant specific copies of the same component exist for multiple variants that are activated simultaneously. In this case, only one instantiation of a multi-variant component is selected, thereby eclipsing properties of other instantiations that should also be present in the requested configuration. This problem relates to a general drawback of variant segregation which allows a component to vary only in one dimension. A practical solution to this apparent dilemma is the application of change oriented techniques à la Aide-de-Camp. A generic base version of the component is stored in the main directory, while variant specific change sets are stored in the appropriate vpath locations. In the description file, the base version is declared dependent to all variant specific change sets. Thus, before a component variant is subject of further processing, it is derived from its base version and the applicable change sets. With shape, the definition of derivation rules that take care of the described situation, is straightforward.

```
%.c: %.c.base $(VARCSETS)
        mv %.c.base %.c;
        patch %.c < $(VARCSETS)
```

For this exemplary derivation rule to work as described, it is assumed that those variant definitions that reference specific instantiations of the same component, provide a suitable definition of the variable VARCSETS. Although the sketched approach proved useful, it is vulnerable to difficulties that arise if different change sets are in conflict with each other, i.e. they attempt to modify the same text locations in the source. This is a systematic weakness of the change set approach for variant management, however. The problems are the same as with *merging* of conflicting versions in revision control.

3.4.6 Aggregate Variation

With shape's variant definition concept, no special support for handling variant system compositions is necessary. Two issues need to be considered for variant compositions: the component list(s), and the component dependencies. Variation of component lists is facilitated by using variables for holding them. The example below shows a shape description file fragment that controls configurations of a generic, multi-variant software product.

```
(1)     SOURCES = g_applic.c g_main.c g_dialog.c
(2)     DEPENDENCIES = g_Dependencies
(3)     OBJECTS = $(SOURCES:.c=.o)

(4)     SOURCES += $(VARSOURCES)
(5)     DEPENDENCIES += $(VARDEPENDENCIES)

(6)     whs_mgr: $(OBJECTS)
(7)             $(LOAD) -o whs_mgr $(OBJECTS)

(8)     include $(DEPENDENCIES)
```

Static variables are used to hold the list of those components that are part of all possible configurations (1, 2). Components that are part of the configuration only upon request of a certain variant, are listed in variant variables (the variant definitions have been omitted for brevity). By convention, variant variables are named after the corresponding static variables with the prefix "VAR". Whenever either of the static variables `SOURCES` or `DEPENDENCIES` is referenced, the list of components is dynamically extended by the current value of the variant variables (4, 5). In the example, the list of source objects is referenced indirectly through the variable `OBJECTS` that is applied in the build rule (6, 7). The value of `OBJECTS` is the current evaluation of `SOURCES` with all ".c" suffixes replaced by ".o".

While those components that are shared by all variants provide a body of fixed dependency relationships, the addition of variant specific components will inevitably introduce new dependencies. With shape, this fact may be taken into account by keeping mere dependency information in separate documents. Dependencies that are invariably present in all configurations are stored in a file that is invariably included into the description file (2, 8). Additional dependency files are appended to the list of included files if corresponding variants are requested in a build.

3.4.7 Variants in Shape—An Abstraction from Mechanisms

Shape's variant definitions provide a simple and very flexible approach to control most of the variant representation techniques. discussed in this article, during configuration identification, and system build. Variant definitions are a *meta-mechanism* that helps to employ sets of different elementary variant control mechanisms under the umbrella of an informally defined, logical variant. Logical variants of this sort are used with the *shape* utility, a version sensitive build- and system management tool. Once a framework of logical variants is defined (and perhaps made available for an entire project team), developers can comfortably request builds for different variants, or combinations of variants on a high level. For the build of product configurations there is no need to mind the tricks of the trade used to represent the variations technically.

Meta-mechanisms such as shape's variant definitions provide the missing link between the technical possibilities offered by modern software configuration management systems, and a high-level variant management concept that is tailored to the specific needs of individual projects. With logical variants, this can be achieved without invoking the inflexibilities that often come with turnkey solutions that pretend to have the ultimate concept for all configuration management needs.

3.5 CONCLUSION

Variant management is still one of the prime causes for severe headaches among software development managers. Despite its practical relevance, it has not gained an adequate level of attention in the software engineering community. The diversity of concepts and terminology introduced by various software configuration management tools can even aggravate the problems. A common understanding of the nature of this software management problem would be a great step forward.

Variant management in the software development process is often regarded as a specific instance of the version control problem. This perception is misleading, if not plain wrong. Since change control is a concern that pervasively affects all aspects of the software development process, variant- and version control are closely intertwined. Both disciplines serve completely different purposes, though. While change control provides a framework for managing the *temporal evolution* of a long lived software product, variant control is concerned with the inherent flexibility of the product structure, in order to make it as widely applicable (and sellable) as possible. An in-depth analysis of the principal mechanisms for software variant management reveals a close resemblance to the techniques found in software reuse frameworks. It is believed that both, the software reuse- and the software configuration management communities could benefit substantially if they combined their research efforts.

The discussion of variant management approaches pointed out the distinction of techniques for program variation in the large (PVITL), and program variation in the small (PVITS). From an abstract point of view, this distinction appears arbitrary and founded in technical concerns only. The conceptual essence of variant configuration management is *consistent aggregation of software artifacts from attributed, reusable software fragments according to specified constraints* (the relation to the basic software reuse paradigm is obvious). Although there exist a number of advanced SCM environments that are based on this insight, these are only rewarded with limited success. The reason appears to be that real world software development has the nasty habit of producing ever new, unanticipated quirks in the development process that demand custom solutions that cannot be foreseen by turnkey development environments.

Besides the inadequate (anticipatory) attention that is paid by many project managers to variant management issues, real projects face the problems imposed by real operating systems, real file systems, real tools, real (i.e. legacy) products, and real budgets that prohibit acquisition of the grand solution plus conversion of existing projects. Thus, the distinction between PVITS and PVITL, although arbitrary from a conceptual viewpoint, is justified because the abstract concept needs to be projected onto existing operating platforms. As has been described, current configuration management tools and environments offer a wealth of techniques and mechanisms for PVITL and PVITS. There is little support, however, for devising clear projections that map desired properties of variant product configurations to the adequate blend of PVITL and PVITS techniques, used to represent software variation. One result are popular misconceptions, such as thoughtless equalization of variants and branches in version control systems.

The shape utility, described above, provides an approach for projecting a logical conception for product variation onto the set of mechanisms that is most appropriate to represent variance and its dimensions. Shape's variant definitions support the development of a problem oriented, high level variant management concept without locking the project team into any particular variant representation scheme.

With few exceptions and despite its obvious drawbacks, *variant segregation* appears to be the component variation scheme of choice for most SCM tools. Techniques for program variation in the small are completely left to user discretion. The prime reason should be the avoidance of additional complexity introduced by the necessary support for the variant authoring process. Massive use of single source variation is either hampered by the close relation of such mechanisms to specific document types (e.g. conditional compilation, and generic constructs), or by its dependence on sophisticated special purpose tools. Shape is somewhere in between here. It does not provide any special support for the authoring process, but encourages systematic use of document type specific techniques that can be accessed at build time under a unified variant notion.

Other than general change control, variant management in the software development process is a field that still lacks a profound understanding. Today, there is no tool or concept available that would be flexible or complete enough to address all of the practical needs that are generated by real world projects. Although there is a bunch of appropriate techniques and powerful tools, none of them is sufficient for solving all involved problems. Flexibility is a must. As the experience with shape's variant definitions shows, mappings from logical variants to a range of basic variation techniques help to reduce the complexity of identifying and building different product variants from a common repository. The bad news is that the authoring process for variant software products remains particularly cumbersome. It is subject of further research, if and how abstract variant definitions can improve this segment of software development technology.

3.6 SHAPETOOLS STATUS

The ShapeTools software is freely available and is distributed via anonymous ftp. The master ftp site for ShapeTools is *ftp.cs.tu-berlin.de* (file */pub/local/shapeTools/shapeTools-*.tar.Z)*. Other sites that usually carry up-to-date versions of ShapeTools are *gatekeeper.dec.com, std.world.com*, and *ftp.th-darmstadt.de*.

3.6.1 Acknowledgment

The development of ShapeTools was supported by the Bundesministerium für Forschung und Technologie (BMFT, Federal Ministry for Research and Technology of Germany) under grants number ITS-8308, and ITS-8902E8.

References

[Atr92] Atria Software, Inc. *ClearCase Concepts Manual.* Document Number 3000-002-A. Atria Software, Inc. Natick, Massachusetts 01760. (1992).

[Bor86] Ellen Borison. *A Model of Software Manufacture.* Proceedings of the Workshop on Advanced Programming Environments, Trondheim, Norway. Lecture Notes on Computer Science, 244, Springer Verlag, (June, 1986).

[Cle84] Geoffrey M. Clemm. *ODIN - An Extensible Software Environment.* Technical Report, CU-CS-262-84). Department of Computer Science, (1984).

[Cle90] Geoffrey M. Clemm and Leon J. Osterweil. *A Mechanism for Environment Integration.* ACM Transactions on Programming Languages and Systems, 12, 1, pages 1–25. (January, 1990).

[Dar90] Susan Dart. *Spectrum of Functionality in Configuration Management Systems.* Technical Report CMU/SEI-90-TR-11 ESD-90-TR-212. Carnegie Mellon University, Software Engineering Institute, Pittsburgh, Pennsylvania. (December 1990).

[DeR76] Frank DeRemer and Hans H. Kron. *Programming-in-the-Large Versus Programming-in-the-Small.* IEEE Transactions on Software Engineering, SE-2, 2. (June, 1976).

[Est85] J. Estublier. *A Configuration Manager: The Adele Database of Programs.* Proceedings of the Workshop on Software Engineering Environments for Programming-in-the-Large, pages 140–147. GTE Laboratories, Harwichport, Massachusets. (June 1985).

[Est92] Jacky Estublier. *The Adele Configuration Manager.* IMAG Technical Report. Grenoble, France. (February, 1992). available via anonymous ftp from ftp.imag.fr.

[Fei91] Peter H. Feiler. *Configuration Management Models in Commercial Environments.* Technical Report CMU/SEI-91-TR-7 ESD-9-TR-7. Carnegie Mellon University, Software Engineering Institute, Pittsburgh, Pennsylvania. (March 1991).

[Fel79] Stuart I. Feldman. *MAKE - A Program for Maintaining Computer Programs.* Software - Practice and Experience, 9,3, pages 255–265. (March 1979).

[Fow85] Glenn S. Fowler. *A Fourth Generation Make.* Proceedings of the USENIX Summer Conference, pages 159–174. USENIX asc., Portland, Or. (June 1985).

[Fra87] Christopher W. Fraser and Eugene W. Myers. *An Editor for Revision Control.* ACM Transactions on Programming Languages and Systems, 9, 2, pages 277–295. (April, 1987).

[Gen89] W. Morven Gentleman, Stephan A. MacKay, Darlene A. Stewart, and Marceli Wein *Commercial Realtime Software Needs Different Configuration Management.* Proceedings of the 2nd International Workshop on Software Configuration Management, pages 152–161. Princeton, NJ. ACM Press, ISBN 0-89791-334-5. (October 1989).

[Hab81a] A. Nico Haberman and Dewayne Perry. *System Composition and Version Control for Ada.* In H. Hünke, editor, *Software Engineering Environments.* North Holland Publishing Company. (1981).

[Hab81b] A. Nico Haberman and Dewayne Perry. *Well-Formed System Compositions.* Technical Report CMU-CS-80-117. Carnegie Mellon University, Computer Science Department, Pittsburgh, Pennsylvania. (April 1981).

[Hab86] A. Nico Haberman and David Notkin. *Gandalf: Software Development Environments.* IEEE Transactions on Software Engineering, SE-12, 12, pages 1117–1128. (December 1986).

[Hor89] Susan Horwitz, Jan Prins, and Thomas Reps. *Integrating Non-Interfering Versions of Programs.* ACM Transactions on Programming Languages and Systems, 11, 3. (July 1989).

[Kro93] Maren Krone and Gregor Snelting. *On the Inference of Configuration Structures from Source Code.* Technical Report 93-06. Technische Universität Braunschweig, Institut für Programmiersprachen und Informationssysteme. Braunschweig, Germany. (August 1993).

[Kru84] V. Kruskal. *Managing Multi-Version Programs with an Editor.* IBM Journal of Research and Development, 28, 1, pages 74–81. (January, 1984).

[Lam88] Andreas Lampen and Axel Mahler. *An Object Base for Attributed Software Objects.* Proceedings of the Fall 1988 EUUG Conference, pages 95–106. European Unix systems User Group. Lisbon, Portugal. (October 1988).

[Lam93] Andreas Lampen and Axel Mahler. *Getting Started with ShapeTools.* STONE System Documentation, ISSN 0944-3037. Technische Universität Berlin, Fachbereich Informatik. (1993).

[Lam94] Andreas Lampen. *Attributierte Softwareobjekte als Basis zur Datenmodellierung in Software Entwicklungsumgebungen.* Technische Universität Berlin. Berlin, Germany. Dissertation. (Juni 1994).

[Lam83] B. Lampson and E. Schmidt. *Organizing Software in a Distributed Environment.* Proceedings of the SIGPLAN 83 Symposium on Programming Language Issues in Software Systems. ACM SIGPLAN Notices 18, 6, pages 1–13. San Francisco, CA. (June 1983).

[Leb84] David B. Leblang and Robert P. Chase. *Computer-Aided Software Engineering in a Distributed Workstation Environment.* ACM SIGPLAN Notices, 19, 5, pages 104–113. (April 1984).

[Lie89] Anund Lie, Reidar Conradi, Tor M. Didriksen, Even-Andre Karlsson, Svein O. Hallsteinsen, and Per Holager. *Change Oriented Versioning in a Software Engineering Database.* Proceedings of the 2nd International Workshop on Software Configuration Management, pages 56–65. ACM Press, ISBN 0-89791-334-5. Princeton, NJ. (October 1989).

[Mah88a] Axel Mahler and Andreas Lampen. *shape - A Software Configuration Management Tool.* Proceedings of the International Workshop on Software Version and Configuration Control, pages 228–243. B.G. Teubner, ISBN 3-519-02671-6. Grassau, West-Germany. (January 1988).

[Mah88b] Axel Mahler and Andreas Lampen. *An Integrated Toolset for Engineering Software Configurations.* ACM Software Engineering Notes, Vol. 13, No. 5, pages 191–200. (November 1988).

[Mil89] David B. Miller, Robert G. Stockton, and Charles W. Krueger. *An Inverted Approach to Configuration Management.* Proceedings of the 2nd International Workshop on Software

Configuration Management, pages 1–4. ACM Press. Princeton, NJ. (October 1989).

[Mor88] Thomas M. Morgan. *Configuration Management and Version Control in the Rational Programming Environment.* Proceedings of the Ada-Europe International Conference, Munich 1988, pages 17–28. Cambridge University Press. Cambridge, England. (June 1988).

[Nar89] K. Narayanaswami. *A Text-Based Representation for Program Variants.* Proceedings of the 2nd International Workshop on Software Configuration Management, pages 30–32. ACM Press, ISBN 0-89791-334-5. Princeton, NJ. (October 1989).

[Nic91] Peter J. Nicklin. *Managing Multi-Variant Software Configurations.* Proceedings of the 3rd International Workshop on Software Configuration Management, pages 53–57. ACM Press, ISBN 0-89791-429-5. Trondheim, Norway. (June, 1991).

[Per87] Dewayne E. Perry. *Version Control in the Inscape Environment.* Proceedings of the 9th International Conference on Software Engineering, pages 142–149. IEEE. Monterey, CA. (March 1987).

[Rei89] Christoph Reichenberger. *Orthogonal Version Management.* Proceedings of the 2nd International Workshop on Software Configuration Management, pages 137–140. ACM Press, ISBN 0-89791-334-5. Princeton, NJ. (October 1989).

[Rei93] Christoph Reichenberger. *Voodoo: A Tool for Orthogonal Version Management.* Proceedings of the Fourth International Workshop on Software Configuration Management (PREPRINTS), pages 203–219. Baltimore, MD. (May, 1993).

[Rep89] Thomas Reps and Thomas Bricker. *Illustrating Interference in Interfering Versions of Programs.* Proceedings of the 2nd International Workshop on Software Configuration Management, pages 46–55. ACM Press, ISBN 0-89791-334-5. Princeton, NJ. (October 1989).

[Roc75] Marc J. Rochkind. *The Source Code Control System.* IEEE Transactions on Software Engineering, SE-1, pages 364–370. (1975).

[Sar88] N. Sarnak, R. Bernstein, and V. Kruskal. *Creation and Maintenance of Multiple Versions.* Proceedings of the International Workshop on Software Version and Configuration Control, pages 264–275. B.G. Teubner, ISBN 3-519-02671-6. Grassau, West-Germany. (January 1988).

[SMD92] Software Maintenance and Development Systems, Inc. *Aide-De-Camp Software Management System Product Overview.* Software Maintenance and Development Systems, Inc., Concord, Massachusetts (1992).

[Tic85] Walter F. Tichy. *RCS—A System for Version Control.* Software - Practice and Experience, 15,7, pages 637–654. (July 1985).

[Tic88a] Walter F. Tichy. *Tools for Software Configuration Management.* Proceedings of the International Workshop on Software Version and Configuration Control, pages 1–20. B.G. Teubner, ISBN 3-519-02671-6. Grassau, West-Germany. (January 1988).

[Tic88b] Walter F. Tichy. *Summary of Plenary Discussion: What is a Configuration ?.* Proceedings of the International Workshop on Software Version and Configuration Control, pages 169–171. B.G. Teubner, ISBN 3-519-02671-6. Grassau, West-Germany. (January 1988).

[Wes91] Bernhard Westfechtel. *Structure-Oriented Merging of Revisions of Software Documents.* Proceedings of the 3rd International Workshop on Software Configuration Management, pages 68–79. ACM Press, ISBN 0-89791-429-5. Trondheim, Norway (June, 1991).

[Whi91] David Whitgift. *Methods and Tools for Software Configuration Management.* John Wiley & Sons. Chichester, England. (1991).

[Win88] Jürgen F.H. Winkler. *Program Variations in the Small.* Proceedings of the International Workshop on Software Version and Configuration Control, pages 175–196. B.G. Teubner, ISBN 3-519-02671-6. Grassau, West-Germany. (January 1988).

[Zel94] Andreas Zeller. *Configuration Management with Feature Logics.* Technical Report 94-01. Technische Universität Braunschweig,Institut für Programmiersprachen und Informationssysteme. (March 1994).

4

The Adele Configuration Manager

Jacky Estublier and Rubby Casallas
L.G.I. IMAG France.

ABSTRACT

This article proposes an overview of the Adele system and also discusses other approaches and other systems. While most of our work on Configuration Management is covered, we have deliberately chosen to discuss in greater depth the Work Space aspect and the relationship between the Repository Space and the WSs.
It is argued here that an SCM system must satisfy conflicting requirements. There is the need for a powerful and dedicated OMS with high modelling power (and thus complexity), and the need for files and directories which are simple concepts, but with low modelling power. We show how different systems have met these requirements.
This article shows how different aspects of the Adele system contribute to meeting these requirements and how this provides a highly customizable and extensible system with services for complex data management, tool integration, inter-tool cooperation, process support and configuration management.

4.1 INTRODUCTION

Software, and especially software quality, can no longer be understood without taking into account the Process Model, i.e., all the actors, activities, methods, tools and procedures used throughout development, from the specification of requirements up and including maintenance. Quality cannot be added during the testing phase! This has only become apparent recently, and the goal of "process technology" is now to provide formalism methods and tools for defining, enacting (i.e. executing) and tailoring software processes.

The main difficulty in achieving this goal is a consequence of the duality between the two spaces manipulated in an SCM: the Repository Space and the Work Space. The first is intended to store the software objects and their versions according to a given conceptual

Configuration Management, Edited by Tichy

product model. The second is the place where users and tools create, access and modify these software objects, usually unversioned files and directories.

Until now all SCM tools have been characterized by shortcomings in one, at least, of these two areas. At one extreme we have SCM systems which offer good services for Repository Space management, i.e., a good Object Manager System (OMS), but little control over the corresponding files; at the other extreme are WS managers supporting only files and directories as product model (i.e., a file system model).

We propose an approach that reconciles the various aspects of SCM for providing simultaneously powerful models and management for RS, WS and Processes. But, more importantly, an approach, provides a way of making these aspects cooperate harmoniously. Each object used in the WS has a corresponding object in the RS. Activities are controlled and supported by Processes whether they are in the WS or in the RS.

This paper is organized as follows: in section 4.2 we present the different RSs and show how versions and products can be modelled; section 4.3 deals with the relationship between the WS and the RS; in section 4.4 we discuss more Process Management related issues and finally we present a global evaluation of Adele and our conclusions.

4.2 MODELLING PRODUCTS AND CONFIGURATIONS

When modelling products and configurations, two issues are of primary importance. Firstly, there is the problem of coping with object evolution, i.e., versions, and, secondly: there is the problem of representing products and configurations, i.e., complex objects.

Both issues have been looked at by, at least three different communities, namely, the Software Engineering Environment (SEE), the Computer-Aided-Design (CAD) databases and the Historical Databases. In this section, we first show how these communities solved these issues and how they evolved towards a data rich model in which complex objects and versions are explicitly defined. We then discuss Adele System evolution in relation to these issues and the new requirements.

4.2.1 Versioning Modes: an Overview

In SEEs and CAD there were several proposals for clearly distinguishing the version, revision, and variant concepts. However, these concepts are still subject to much confusion. The main reason is the intertwining of different problems and different needs such as the versioning graph, parallel work, object evolution and historical information.

Almost all current commercial Configuration Managers have poor data models: they propose *file management* where *software management* is needed, i.e., the models do not allow complex software objects to be modelled and, as a consequence, it is impossible to define an adequate and customized Product Model. The versioning problem is reduced to the evolution of a single file, regardless of its content. This makes for flexibility but, on the other hand, little control is possible.

CAD systems use more complex data models because they are based on database technology. They use extensions to entity-relation, relational and, more recently, object-oriented models.

In the following paragraphs we present a brief overview of the different approaches.

4.2.1.1 VERSIONING IN SEE

In the early seventies, the SCCS system [Roc75] proposed a solution for the management of a single file regardless of its content. An object (file) is a sequence of *revisions*, one for each change to the object.

The RCS system [Tic82] is an extension of SCCS and solves the multiple development problem. It considers that evolution is not a simple sequence of revisions but forms a tree where each branch (or variant), follows its own evolution as a succession of revisions.

Almost all commercial version managers retain the solutions proposed by SCCS and RCS for multi-user control, history management and space consumption using the delta mechanism. The distinction between variant and revision is not always clear. In practice the only common property between all versions is that they share a large number of lines!

All tools based on RCS/SCCS feature a very weak data model (revision/variant). To support enhanced versioned models we need a data model in which the concept of version is explicitly supported. Few practical systems currently have this.

Aide De Camp is one of the few commercial systems based on the Change Set Model (section 4.4.4.1). A change set is a complex object containing the changes (i.e. file fragments) performed in all files for a given logical change. A version here is a change set, and arbitrary change-set composition is allowed. Unfortunately, in ADC, the data model is restrictive; there is no way to model complex objects explicitly. It is possible to associate attributes with entities, but the abstraction level is low.

Damokles [Dit89] was one the first prototypes to use database technology for SEEs. The Damokles data model allows complex and arbitrary objects to be modelled and enables objects be as the union of a set of (unversioned) attributes with a set of versioned attributes to explicitly defined. This idea formed the basis for most subsequent database approaches to versioning.

[Wie93] proposes an object oriented data model with an extension for modelling version families. This involves the use of partial objects, i.e., objects with attributes of known and unknown value. A given class may define different partial objects; all instances of that class whose attributes have the same values as the bounded attributes of a partial object pertain to that partial object family.

In PCTE [Tho89] the data model is an Entity-Relation-Attribute one; complex objects are built using links of the predefined "composition" category. Special commands are required to manage complex objects like "revise", "snapshot", "copy" which most often duplicate links and components, and rapidly lead to a very complex graph. Here, files and attributes are versioned.

4.2.1.2 VERSIONING IN CAD

In CAD systems the emphasis has been on the structure of Composite Objects and their versioning from a database perspective. A Design Object is a coherent aggregation of components, managed as a single unit. All three major database data models have been used, i.e., Relational, Entity-Relationship and Object Oriented Models. The relational model [HL82] was first extended to represent Composite Objects as a hierarchical collection of tuples, allowing long fields to contain data of unlimited length. The E-R model uses explicit relationships, with a predefined semantics, to manage aggregates and derivation graphs (*derived-from, is-part-of, etc.*). A survey of these systems is found in [Kat90].

In recent work on Object-Oriented Models the aim has been to separate the *physical* and *conceptual* levels of versioning. The physical level is concerned with the management and storage of derivation graphs (space saving). All SCCS type systems only support physical versioning.

At the conceptual level, a version is independent from storage representation. An object is a set of versions; the system must provide mechanisms with which to structure and control this set. Almost all models are based on the Generic Object concept. A generic object has two parts: a set of attributes (shared attributes) and versions (version group). An instance of a generic object is the union of the shared attributes and one of the versions pertaining to the version group. The semantics of the version group is defined and maintained by the applications.

[Sci91] has put forward a theoretical object-oriented data model for powerful versions management. Here a versioned object is composed of a single generic type and a set of version types, thus allowing multidimensional versioning. The logical versioning model allows the application to give the semantics to versions, by means of parameterized selection predicates.

4.2.1.3 VERSIONING IN TEMPORAL DATABASES

Temporal databases deal with the problem of entity evolution in time. This is a logical versioning since versions are related to time, and the semantics of time is known by the system. It allows queries to be made at a high level, for instance using time intervals.

The main requirement in temporal databases is for queries information concerning entities in the past; and for the retrieval of time slices. Configuration Management is not a relevant problem. Usually, the data models are relational models where the time dimension has been added. Most of these models distinguish between *valid time* and *transaction time* dimensions. The former represents the time as a fact observed in reality, while the latter indicates when the fact was recorded in the database. The temporal query language TQuel [Sno93] is an example of one that supports these two dimensions.

In Software Engineering, since most entities are directly managed in the system , valid time and transaction time are identical (most software artifacts are directly controlled files). Furthermore, since all times are taken from the machine, we may assume a complete ordering of events. These two properties, along with specific SEE needs like traceability explain why temporal databases have never been used in SEE. Whatever the case may be, the control of the temporal dimension is an SEE need which is usually underestimated.

4.3 COMPLEX OBJECTS AND CONFIGURATION MODELS

In Historical Databases the configuration problem is not relevant at all. In CAD systems the problem is slightly different. The principal difference between CAD configurations and SEE configurations is the fact that, usually, the structure of a "Design Object" is known beforehand; components are stable and clearly defined; there are no derived objects. The problem is limited to the selection of the appropriate version for each one of the versioned components (this is the dereferencing problem).

It is in an SEE context that configuration management appears in all its complexity; this is due to the extremely "soft" nature of the components, their "unlimited" refinement, the fact that components are really managed by the computer (whereas a circuit is not), and the existence of tools for object derivation.

In an SEE context we find the System Model (SM) concept. It describes the structure of software, the set of components and their relationships in a generic way. Each configuration manager uses a System Model as input. System Models can be found in different forms: we have the "system model" in DSEE [LC84], [LCM85], [LCS88], the "component" of NSE [Mic88], the "makefile" in Make [Fel79], the "structure model" in [Wat89]. Modules Interconnection Languages also provide System Models [RPD86], [Per87]. See [Tic88], [Est88], [Dar91] for a survey of configuration management.

What all these systems have in common is that the SM must be provided directly by the user. To build a System Model manually requires extensive work and its consistency is very difficult to ensure: the SM must be updated when software changes. In a large software product this is an error-prone process since the SM is large and it person who changes the software is not usually the one who updates the SM.

4.3.1 The Adele Version and Product Model

We present here the commercial Adele Data/Version model and the current Configuration Manager.

4.3.1.1 THE BASIC MODEL

The Adele data model is object-oriented. The model extends this formalism with relationships, objects and relationships being treated in almost a homogeneous way.

Objects can represent files, activities and functions as well as simple values like strings or dates. Relationships are independent entities (external to objects) because they model associations with different semantics such as derivation, dependency and composition. A relationship is set up from an *origin* object to a *destination* object.

A Type describes the common structure and the behavior of the instances of that type[1]. The structure corresponds to a set of *attributes* modelling properties of the instance. Relation Types have additional information related to the *domain* of the relation, i.e., constraints defining between which object types the relationship can be established. The behavior is encapsulated into operations (*methods*) and extended by means of triggers (see 4.5.1)

External names must be assigned to objects at creation time; a relationship is also identified by a unique name. This name comes from the concatenation of the Origin object name (O), the Relation type name (R) and the Destination object name (D) to give the string, O|R|D.

Attributes model the properties of the instances. An attribute is defined by a name, its domain type (integer, date, boolean, string, enumeration) and other information such as the default value, the initial value, whether the attribute can be multi-valued or not, whether or not its value is dynamically computed, etc.

Types are organized in a type hierarchy corresponding to specialization. A type can have one or more super types (i.e multiple inheritance).The subtype relationship is a relation of inclusion between corresponding extensions.

Methods are used to model the behavior of the instances. They are defined by a name, a signature and a body or implementation. Methods and triggers are inherited down through the type hierarchy but unlike methods, triggers can not be overloaded.

---

1. When confusion does not arise, we use the term "instance" to refer either to an object or an association and "type" to refer either to an object type or a relation type.

The Adele Version Model is based on the *branch* concept. A branch models the evolution of a file and its attributes. It is a sequence of *revisions* where each revision contains a snapshot of the object.

In this Adele version, Composite Objects are not explicit in the model; the attribute domain cannot be an object type.

Different kinds of derivation graphs can be defined, establishing explicit relationships between branches; version groups can thus be easily defined. The Adele kernel provides the generic object concept (a branch is an object) and a mechanism for sharing attributes. Arbitrary versions and composite objects are created and managed using explicit relationships between the different components.

However, version groups, versioned objects and composite objects are not explicit in the model, their semantics and building are left to the application.

4.3.1.2 CONFIGURATION PRODUCT MODEL

The Adele Configuration Manager relied on a predefined product model. This model was designed to represent modular software products and automatically compute software configurations.

This model borrowed the *module* concept from programming languages: the association of an *interface* with a body or *realization*. The distinction between interface and realization is interesting for numerous reasons, and has been widely recognized [Par72], [Sha84], [Kam87]. This Product Model has three basic object types, viz. Family, Interface and Realization. The *Family* object maps the *module* concept. Families allow Interfaces to be grouped together. It gathers together all the objects and all their variants and revisions related to a module. A Family contains a set of interfaces [EF89].

Interfaces associated with a Family define the features (procedures, types, etc.) exported by that family. An interface contains realizations [HN86]. Realizations are functionally equivalent but differ in some other (non-functional) characteristics. None is better than the others, and none is the main variant; each one is of interest and needs to be maintained in parallel.

An *is_realized* relationship is defined between an interface and each one of its realizations. The dependency relation is also predefined. X and Y being variants, X *depends_on* Y means that X needs Y directly (usually to be compiled). Often it simply mimics the #include directive found in programs.

4.3.1.3 THE CONFIGURATION MODEL

Building a configuration in Adele involves selecting a complete and consistent collection of objects. The collection is complete with respect to the structure of a software system defined by the dependency graph closure and consistent with selection rules. The dependency relation being defined over variants, a system model contains variants; it is a generic configuration [BE86].

The *depends_on* relationship is an AND relation (all destination objects must be selected) while the *is_realized* relationship is an OR relation (only one destination must be selected). The dependency relation is an acyclic graph.

To be consistent, a system model must satisfy (at least) the following rules:

R1 = Only one interface per family is allowed.
R2 = Nodes must satisfy the constraints defined by the SM.
R3 = Nodes must satisfy the constraints set by all node ancestors in the graph.

Point 1 ensures that functionalities will not be provided twice. Point 2 ensures that all components are in compliance with the characteristics required by the model. In Adele, the characteristics required by the model are expressed in a first order logic language (and, or, not connective) constraining component properties. Examples of such constraints can be *recovery=Yes and system=unix and messages=English* [Est85].

Point 3 ensures that all components are able to work together. All compatibility constraints between components are associated with the component ancestor in the graph. Such constraints in Adele use the same language and can for example be *if (arguments=sorted) then (system=unix_4.3) or (recovery=no).*

4.3.1.4 CONFIGURATION INSTANCE.

An instance of a generic configuration, also called a bound configuration is a set of revisions, one for each variant of the generic configuration. The instance is defined by the constraints to be applied in order to select the convenient revision for each variant. This selection is made in Adele on the basis of the revision properties, using the same first order logic language. An example of this sort of expression could be

```
((reserved=john) or (author=john) or (state=official)) and (date>18_02_89).
```

In Adele, a configuration is a standard realization: its interface is the root of the graph, its source text contains the constraints, its components are the destinations of the relation *composed_of* and its revisions are its instances. As a consequence a configuration also evolves as variants and revisions in the usual way.

Evolution can be seen as a twin speed process. Firstly, we have fast evolution, when a configuration process is used as baseline. This is every day evolution; it covers bug fixes, minor enhancements and development, in other words all changes leading to new revisions. Slow evolution is when a new configuration must be built. This is only necessary if new variants are to be incorporated in the model: new functionalities are needed, non-functional characteristics are desired or new internal constraints have been set.

The *current value* at time T of a configuration is its instance built at time T without constraints. Changes performed, in a configuration, by user *john* can be captured using attributes *reserved_by* or *author.* This is similar to DSEE [LC84], [LCS88] and ClearCase [Leb93]. Any configuration can be built at any time by setting a cut-off date using *date<T* as a constraint and it is easy to reuse old revisions of the SM. A special configuration instance can be built using other revision attributes: *state=official and date<88_08_23* retrieves the official instance (if it exists) of this configuration as it was on August 23rd 1988.

4.3.2 Evaluation

This configuration builder and its associated product model were released in 1984, and have been used intensively by many customers. The experience gained brought out some drawbacks:

- The default product model does not match all software easily. In particular old products being designed with other structures in mind have problems in finding an interface/realization association.
- The version definition and evolution constraints are often too rigid.
- Other constraints for building software configuration could be defined, using roughly the same process.
- The default product model does not easily support objects other than software programs.

These considerations led us to open up the data model, based on a general model for complex object management, a general versioning model including extended history, and general process support.

4.3.3 Extensions to the Adele Data and Version Model

We concentrate here on static characteristics, i.e., how objects are built UP, and how they are versioned. The Data Model has been extended to allow:

- Composite Object definitions of any kind.
- General Versioning and history
- Automatically built objects, including configurations.

We shall briefly cover each of these points.

4.3.3.1 COMPOSITE OBJECTS

An Object Type is a set of attribute definitions whose type can be *simple* (integer, boolean, string, data, or file) or *complex*, i.e., any other object type. The attribute value is a reference to another object. In both cases, the attribute can be multi-valued (set-of). For example:

```
OBJTYPE Module IS cobj;
        responsible     :   STRING;
        spec            :   FrameDoc;
        interfaces      :   Int_Type;
        test            :   set_ of files;
END Module;
```

Complex attributes are a special case of composition relationship. To each complex attribute name there corresponds a relation type with the same name.

```
RELTYPE spec IS...;
....
END spec;
OBJTYPE FrameDoc IS Document;
...
END FrameDoc;
```

The composition semantics is defined by the behavior of the corresponding composition relationship; i.e., by the relationship methods and triggers (see section 4.5.1). Using the subtyping mechanism the relationship behavior can be inherited and refined; predefined relation types like the *Has* relationships have a semantics recognized by the kernel. Using triggers it is possible to express, for example, that the components are shared or not, that a *copy* of an object produces a *copy* of its components; etc. Once a relationship is established between two objects, the behavior of both objects is automatically modified; this is what we have called *contextual behavior* [BM93].

Query Language

Objects and the relationships between them can be seen as graphs: objects are the nodes and relationships are the arcs. The query language uses this fact to reach the instances by navigation through graphs. It also offers a filtering mechanism for selecting the instances on which the operations will be applied.

Querying the database is takes place using *path expressions.* These are defined by a *navigation* and a *selection*:

```
path          ::= navigation
              |   navigation path
navigation    ::= nodes -> arcs [ (selection) ]
              |   nodes <- arcs [ (selection) ]
```

Navigation. Navigation allows instances to be reached starting from a set of instances and following a path through the graph. A navigation expression defines a multiple path on a graph. As associations are directed, navigation can take place from the origin object to the destination object (noted **->**) and in the other direction, from destination to origin (noted **<-**). *Nodes.* This term denotes the set of objects from which the navigation starts while *arcs* refers to the set of relationships to be crossed. This means that navigation take place along various paths at the same time. For example:

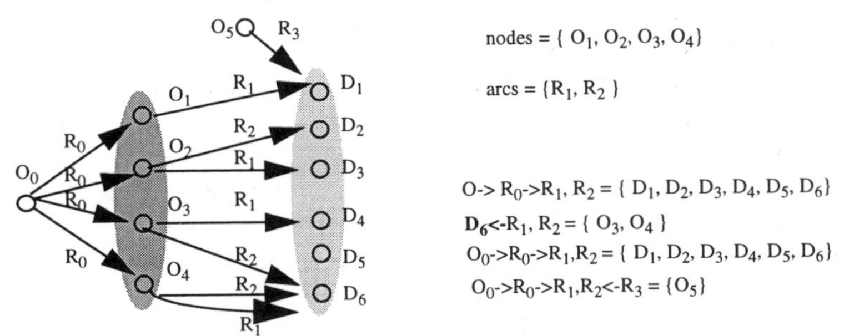

Figure 4.1 Navigation.

Selection. A selection allows the set of instances reached by the navigation to be filtered. It is a logical expression wherein the variables are instance attributes. The expression is evaluated for each instance in the set returned by the navigation. The result of this evaluation is the instances for which the expression is true. If there is no selection expression, the initial set is returned.

```
foo->dep (state=stable and language = english)
```

This returns from all the objects *foo* depends on, those satisfying the condition (*state=stable and language = english*).

Substitution allows the values of instances attributes to be accessed. The syntax is:

```
~instance%attribute
```

where *instance* is a set of objects or associations and *attribute* is an attribute name. The result of a substitution expression is a set of instance names. Note that substitutions can be used in any term of a *path*.

4.3.3.2 GENERAL VERSIONING

We identified three classes or versioning:

- **Temporal**. There is a great need for *traceability* in an SEE database. Historic objects, control of activities and far reaching consequences of actions must be retrievable found, even much later.
- **Logical**. Objects exist in multiple *variants* or representations.
- **Dynamic**. Multiple and concurrent *activities* are taking place in an SEE database. An SEE database must support software processes.

These three dimensions are completely orthogonal. The first is the time dimension, designed for history and traceability reasons; The second arises from the need to support logical versioning, i.e., *real* versioning. The third dimension is related only to the support of processes and so called long transactions, i.e., dynamic versioning.

Temporal Versioning

Our experience and involvement with process modelling showed that one aspect has been underestimated in all systems, we are referring to traceability. We need a generalized history mechanism intended to answer questions involving multiple objects (some being currently deleted) over a long period of time. Given a change request CR, we must be able to answer the following questions: "what are all the actions performed as consequences of this CR", "who decided to accept this CR", "which changes in which objects have been performed to include that CR"; "in which configuration are they present", "for how long is it required", "who was involved and when", "how expensive was it "?.

Our temporal versioning was designed with these requirements in mind. An object is a set of attributes, including files and other objects. Any attribute may have *immutability* characteristics which means that any attempts to change its value automatically produces a new "state" (i.e., revision) of the object. Note that in most systems, a single and implicit immutable attribute is assumed: the file. Remember that, in our system, files are attributes.

An object *State* is defined as the attribute values of that object at a given point of time. Between two successive states there is at least one attribute whose value has changed. A *generic object* is the set of all its successive states, from creation until now.

```
OBJTYPE Module IS cobj;
        responsible   IMM   :  STRING;
        spec          IMM   :  FrameDoc;
        interfaces          :  Int_Type;
        test                :  set of files;
END Module;
```

In this example, the *responsible* and *spec* attributes are immutable. It means that each time these attributes are modified, the system keeps the previous object state and creates a new current state. The value of a complex attribute, such as *spec*, is a reference to another object, we must indicate whether it refers to an object state or to the generic object.

Using the navigational notation, we can access directly past states and we can make queries involving past information, we refer to this as historical navigation. Note that, in this model, revisions constitute a special case.

A generic object is identified by its name and an object state by its generic object name followed by the "@" sign and a selection clause. For example, if *ctrlmem* is the name of a module we can write

```
1       ctrlmem@now
2       ctrmem@(responsible = john)
3       ctrlmem@ti->interfaces
```

Expression 1 returns the current state of object *ctrlmem*; expression 2 returns all *ctrlmem* states for which *john* is *responsible*, and expression 3 returns the *ctrlmem interfaces* as they were at time *ti*.

For traceability purposes, states are not the only concern. They are also arbitrary facts and events occurring in or out of the database. Adele allows history types and history instances to be recorded, when an arbitrary event happens. A history object is similar to any other object but cannot contain complex attributes. Tool executions, time events, coordination events, logs, object creation/destruction, side effects, relationships between entities can be recorded and historic relationship paths followed at any time later on.

Complex expressions can be written using historical navigation. As a special case, if no state is given in the expression, navigation is entirely on the DB "surface", as in any other DBMS.

Logical Versioning

From a conceptual point of view, an object is a generic entity, i.e., the sequence of all its states from its creation until now, X = seq {X@1, X@2,....X@now}. At a given point in time there exists a single current state for a given object. The evolution of the object is linear. In the following the word object means generic object; its historic dimension will not be taken into account.

From a logical point of view an object can evolve simultaneously in different ways. Thus, at a given point in time, there are different current states of the same object, and thus different generic objects. These different generic objects are versions or variants of the same object.

If a complex attribute has *versioned* characteristics, its value is a *version group*, i.e., a reference to a set of objects that are versions. A *versioned object* is an object containing at least one version group.

By construction, at the relevant level of abstraction, a versioned object is perceived as a single object (unversioned). An *instance* of a versioned object is that object restricted to a single value for each one of its version groups.

In our data model, version groups are defined by the key word VERSION. In our example:

```
OBJTYPE Module IS cobj;
```

```
    responsible     IMM :  STRING;
    spec            IMM :  FrameDoc;
    interfaces          :  VERSION Int_Type;
    test                :  set of files;
END Module;
```

The interface attribute refers to a version group.

Dynamic Versioning

If different processes share the same data, conflicts will arise. Traditionally this is solved by the locking mechanism; a single activity may change an object. However, for process support, we need a higher level mechanism for controlling overlapping activities.

We need both to give each process the illusion of working alone on "its" object, and the ability to define, control and enforce user-defined collaboration and synchronization protocols. These aspects are described later.

The former aspect is supported by *dynamic versioning,* i.e. the dynamic and transparent (for users) creation of object copies as part of the protocol to solve the concurrence control problem. They are temporary versions, automatically created during process execution and automatically removed when that process terminates. When a process accesses an object, its private copy is automatically assumed. This dynamic versioning is the basic mechanism on which Adele work space manager is built (see section 4.4.2).

We think that synchronization and collaboration protocols must be explicitly defined in the Process Model.

4.3.3.3 BUILT OBJECTS

Configurations are now generic; they are a special case of built objects. Built objects are those complex objects whose components can be found by an automatic computation directed by generic build constraints. Generic build constraints can be expressed at type level. These express the process to be followed when any object of that type is to be built, including consistency constraints. For a configuration this process is roughly defined by

```
starting_object -> (dep->is_realized(unique))+
```

which expresses that any configuration is built from the transitive closure "(path)+" of the *dep* and *is_realized* relationships. All *dep* relationships must be followed, but a unique *is_realized* relationship must be followed (*unique*). Generic consistency constraints can be specified in build constraints, for example, rules in section 4.3.1.3. can be expressed as follows:

```
R1 = IF !selected!famname = !famnanme THEN ERROR ;
R2= EVAL (%select).
```

The R1 constraint states that a single interface per family is allowed. R1 must be checked when reaching interfaces, thus after traversing *dep* relationships. R2 states that constraints expressed in the *select* attribute of the configuration instance being built must be verified. Thus a more realistic generic configuration builder can be expressed by

```
-> (dep(R1)-> is_realized(R2, unique))+
```

The selection constraint specified in a select attribute can be for example:

```
select = "recovery = yes and system = unix and message = english"
```

Unique is a built-in function returning a single one of the objects satisfying rule R2 at each navigation step.

This work is under way, but first experiments have shown that the current configuration manager is definable in 1/2 page of process definition.

4.4 WORK SPACE CONTROL

In the previous section we presented the data and version models proposed by currently available CM tools. These models are intended to define the content of the *Repository Space* (RS), i.e. which objects can be stored, and how they are versioned. It is the task of the Object Manager System of each CM tool to manage the Repository Space, i.e., to represent, optimize, access, enforce protection and internal consistency of the RS. However, this is only the static aspect of CM. Storing and representations are not sufficient.

The dynamic aspect of configuration is performed in *Work Spaces* (WS). A WS is the place where the usual Software Engineering tools are executed. The objects that can be found in a WS depend on each system, but must include files and directories, since they are the only entities known by standard tools (editors, compilers, etc.). We can say the product model governing WS includes the File System (FS) model, i.e., file, directory and link types.

Normally, a single version of files is present in a given WS, since standard tools do not recognize version concepts. It means that the RS, wherein all objects and their versions are stored, is different from the WS. The product model governing an RS is highly variable, but potentially high modelling power is allowed. Almost any concept, any kind of abstract and/ or complex object, any version model, any software and team definition and structure and history dimension can be defined. This contrasts with the simple model governing WSs.

It is clear for us that software engineering can only really be supported if WSs, RSs and Processes are closely controlled and managed, and *if they work in symbiosis.*

We shall first present the relationships between WS and RS, i.e., how they communicate and what correspondences exist between entities managed in the RS and the WS. Secondly, we will present the relationships between WSs and configurations, i.e., how activities in WSs and in the RS can be controlled and synchronized. Finally, the Adele proposition for solving the various problems caused by the duality of these two spaces is presented.

4.4.1 Work Space and Repository Space Relationships

Some of the entities stored in the RS are also present in WSs when they are needed to perform activities.

We have to satisfy two opposing requirements here: The WS model must be as close as possible to a bare File System (FS), in order for users and tools not to be disturbed. The learning curve for most users should be steep, and ideally almost vertical. On the other hand, the modelling power of the RS should be as high as possible, in order to easily represent software artifacts, tools, users, teams, schedules and processes, to allow different versioning models, to support process management, to provide team leaders with adequate of information, to help responsible for configuration with services and so on. The “ideal” RS product model is not simple!

Software CM systems are responsible for securing correspondence and consistency between the two worlds. It is interesting to see how different CM tools solve these conflicting requirements. We present here an overview of how the various CM systems have solved these conflicting requirements.

4.4.1.1 BASIC TOOLS

In basic tools, like RCS and SCCS the RS model is implicit, embedded in the CM and limited to revisions and variants for a single file (there are no configuration or aggregate concepts). The WS model is the bare FS. Two basic operations are provided Check-In (CI) and Check-Out (CO)

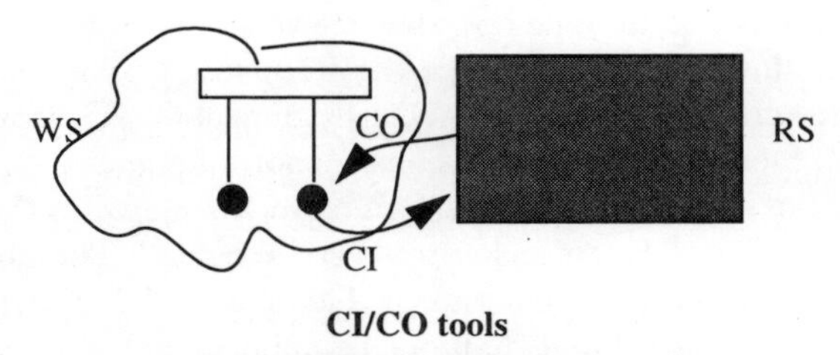

CI/CO tools

Figure 4.2 Chech-in check-out paradigm

Pros:

- WS Model = FS, thus no learning overhead!
- RS Model is simple. Easy to learn.
- Can be used for any file.

Cons:

- Very low level RS Model. No configuration or aggregate concept.
- The CM has almost no knowledge.
- Cooperative work: no support out of locks.

These simple tools oblige users to establish their own rules and conventions. All consistency control is left to users. On the other hand, they are free and necessitate little training. These tools are not CM systems but basic version managers.

4.4.1.2 EXPLICIT MAPPING BY COPIES.

In this class of tools, the mapping between the WS and the RS is explicitly managed by the CM; files are explicitly copied back and forth between both spaces.

This approach extends the previous one in a number of ways; CI/CO is global, a (hopefully) consistent set of files is simultaneously checked in/out and the CM has some knowledge of the WSs. It can usually manage different WS simultaneously.

The majority of CM tools belong to this class, even if many differences can be found. Different WS management strategies can be developed in this class. The power of the CM tool depends essentially on the possibilities of the RS Model and the functionalities of the WS manager

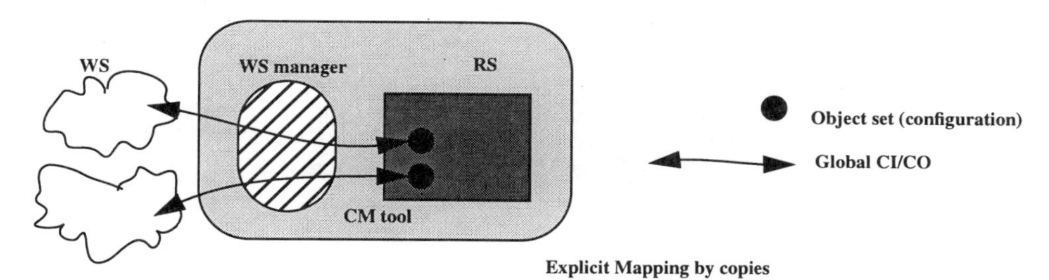

Figure 4.3 Mapping by copy.

WSs can be controlled if all file access operations are encapsulated into WS manager commands. This is the solution most CM tools use. Even in this case the WS is a bare File System; a single file is present in a WS and no WS local versioning is available. For that reason, this approach has difficulties in managing the interactions between the different WSs and cooperative work cannot be easily supported. NSE [Mic88] was one of the few systems to propose implicit local versioning, but conversely imposes a specific cooperative policy. Most often these systems use a static locking mechanism; an object (file) can be modified in a WS only.

Pros:

- The WS Model is the FS Model. No overheads.
- WSs can be managed simultaneously, built globally and controlled.
- The RS Model can be powerful.

Cons:

- The WS model is very low level (the FS Model)
- No (conceptual) mapping between RS Model and WS Model.
- Collaboration between WSs is ill supported.

4.4.1.3 SUB-DATABASES.

The database community, for different reasons have tried to solve some of the problems of the previous approach. Versioning in databases led to the interesting concept of Sub-databases.

A sub-database (sub-database) is a sub-set of the central database instances. Each sub-database is isolated; a change to an object is visible only in the current sub-database. A sub-database is often seen as a (long) transaction, changes are propagated to the central database only when "committed". This is similar to the usual WS, replacing *object* by *file*, but does open up interesting new possibilities.

The RS Model can be very rich as not only files can be managed. Usual DB services like (short) transactions, associative queries, distribution, protection, and so on can be used. Complex and precise protocols can be defined between the central DB and its sub-databases;

transparent versioning can be provided, and concurrent modification of the same objects can be supported..

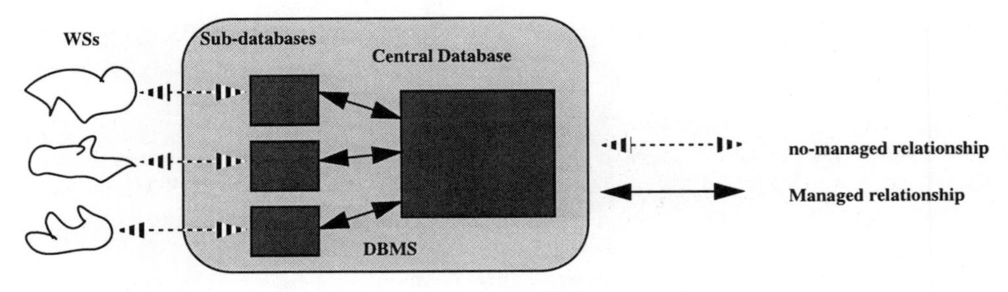

Figure 4.4 The database approach.

The main drawback is that a sub-database is not a WS. In these approaches there is no WS support, no control of activities performed there, and, consequently, little potential for process support. This is a new and difficult domain; current implementations provide only partial solutions. In Orion [KBGW91] there is no direct communication between sub-databases, and a single level of sub DB is possible. In Damokles [Dit89], explicit versioning and simple sub-databases are provided.

Pros:

- Cooperation protocols can be defined and concurrent activities supported.
- A powerful RS Model can be supported.
- Database services can be used.

Cons:

- No WS support.
- No activity control, poor Process support potential.
- Not a mature technology.

4.4.1.4 WS = (VIRTUAL) FS = RS

Some tools decided to solve the mapping problem between WS and RS by behaving as if the RS WERE the WS. Of course, some "tricks" are needed (if only to solve the multiple version problem). Either the FS supporting the WS must be "adapted", or tools must be encapsulated

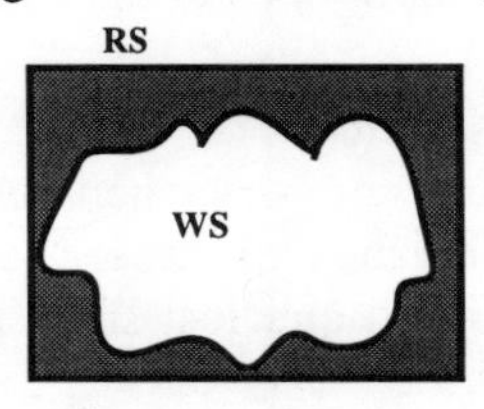

Figure 4.5 A File System in the database.

Adapting the FS

Different lines of approach have been followed to "extend" a file system in order to support this approach. The first attempts involves "cheating" with NFS. The FS supporting the WS is mounted by NFS, and the NFS driver, on the machine supporting the physical FS, is replaced by another one which decides dynamically, when opening a file, which version should be provided [AS93].

A more delicate approach, followed by ClearCase [Leb93], is to write a specific Unix FS driver. Any access to a file in this Virtual File System (VFS) is interpreted by this driver which decides dynamically on the file version to provide. A more powerful RS Model can also be provided. Transparency is provided at the cost of efficiency; all accesses to files are interpreted.

The same kind of trick can be done by replacing the open/close functions in the libraries by a program which selects the real file to open. A tool like 3D, COLA [KK90] does this kind of work, and should be available on most Unix machines [BK93]. It assumes that all tools use dynamic links with I/O libraries.

Encapsulating Tools

CaseWear [CW93] prefers to let users access the CM repository directly, but to solve the versioning problem, all tools have to be encapsulated.

In PCTE [Tho89], the user must be logged under PCTE, which first interprets any command and file access. It is a totalitarian approach (complete encapsulation). Furthermore PCTE is not a CM tool and no version selection is automatic; tools need to be encapsulated if versions are used.

In any case, it must be borne in mind that, tools can be encapsulated whilst users can not..

Pros:

- The WS Model is extended by the RS Model.
- Implicit and transparent version selection.
- Easy adaptation for users.

Cons:

- The RS Model must be an extension of the FS Model.
- The FS must be changed, or tools encapsulated.
- Single RS/WS mapping is possible. The software structure is rigid.

4.4.1.5 WS = SUB-DATABASE = RS

Most drawbacks disappear if it is possible to directly map a WS to a sub-database.

In this solution, the WS is a sub-database. It means that all the DBMS services are available in each WS (local versioning, queries, short transactions, protection, and interfaces). It is the availability of all these services, along with the fact the DBMS knows the various WSs well, i.e., where they are, who created them, when, for what purpose, and so on, which explains why the concept of sub-database makes it possible to define the relationships between WSs, as well as the relationships with the central data base.

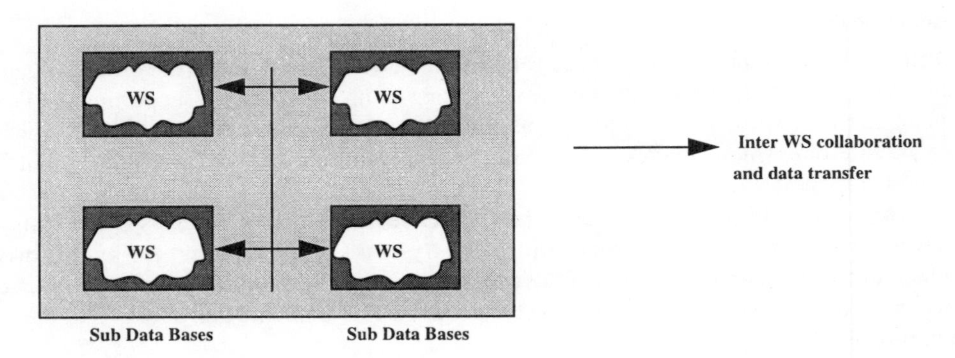

Figure 4.6 Multiple File systems as DB Work Spaces.

It should be noted that each sub-database (WS) may have a different "view" of the same objects, both structurally (the directory/file sub tree may be different), semantically (the attribute and relationship may be different for the same object) and behaviorally (the constraints and methods for a given type may be different). The WS management policy may also be different (a different process can control each WS).

Note also that a direct consequence of the sub-database concept is that each individual user has the illusion of working alone on his objects. Here, we have both simplicity for end users and considerable modelling and control power.

Pros:

- The WS is enriched with RS concepts and DBMS services.
- Collaboration and cooperation patterns can be defined and controlled.
- Each WS defines and supports different structures, processes and properties.

Cons:

- Complex immature technology.
- Numerous open issues.

This solution opens up some interesting doors. Since the structure of each WS can be different, checking out the same configuration may end up in very different WSs. It can be envisioned that a WS is actually the internal storage for another platform or tool (PCTE or VMCS for example). In this case each platform or tool works in a different sub database, on a well defined configuration. The central tool is in charge of controlling the inter cooperation protocols and the versioning dimension.

This solution is the one used for our project and forms the basis for the Adele Work Space manager presented below.

4.4.2 The Adele Work Space Manager

Following the previous approach, the system has to solve two apparently incompatible classes of problems:

- The isolation problem between WSs (sub-database concept),
- The coordination problem between WSs.

4.4.3 Isolation and Sub-databases

A WS can only be a full sub-database if it is isolated, i.e., if it has the usual ACID properties of transactions: Atomicity, Consistency, Isolation and Durability. However, ACID, in the framework of short transactions, and ACID, in the framework of long transactions, have a slightly different meaning.

The fundamental difference is that in short transactions isolation is provided to ensure consistency by an enforcement of sequentialization, whereas, in long transactions, isolation is provided to ensure consistency when parallelism is allowed. The isolation of the new and modified data is performed using dynamic versions, and by applying a visibility mechanism so that a transaction does not "see" the objects produced/modified by other transactions.

Setting a lock becomes the transparent creation of a copy (dynamic versioning) and releasing locks becomes the merging of the dynamic copies.

4.4.3.1 COORDINATION CONTROL.

Coordination is related to the management of concurrent changes to shared artifacts. We need the ability to define when a modified component must be propagated (notified, made visible, copied, merged, etc.) to the other WSs containing (copies of) this component.

The fundamental reason for coordination is that object merging is not a perfect mechanism. Inconsistencies may arise from an object merger; the probability of problematic mergers rapidly increases with the number of changes performed in both copies. Were mergers to be performed only at transaction commit, most of them would not be successfully performed. Frequent mergers, at some well defined points, are needed to maintain two cooperating WSs in synch.

Of course, if the coordination mechanism is used, work under way in a WS is made visible to other WSs while they are operating. A WS can then no longer, be considered in any aspect, an ACID transaction. This is why the word transaction in this document only applies to short transactions

Coordination control will be presented using the following example: A *Release* WS contains a Design document (*D*) and a configuration (*C*); it has sub WS *Design*, where the design is developed, and a *development* WS containing both. Development WS exists in two instances.

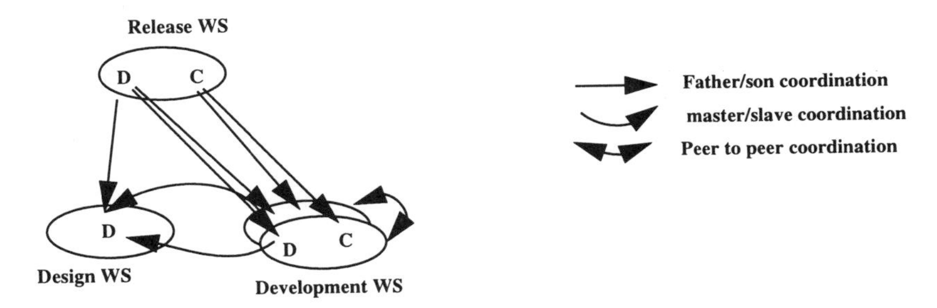

Figure 4.7 Coordination between Work Spaces.

Classically, the father/son relationship is identified, it links a WS (the son) with the WS wherefrom its objects are issued (the father). If a WS contains more than one object, a potentially different father/son coordination applies to each original/copy pair.

In our example the two design WSs must coordinate their work using a coordination policy different from the release/design coordination (peer to peer coordination). Similarly, design and development may coordinate their work (when a design is changed), with still another coordination policy (master slave coordination).

In actual fact, all these coordinations are identical as far as we are concerned; peer to peer is the same coordination type instantiated in both directions; a father/son is just a special case of master/slave. All coordination operations rely on the following operations:

- **promote**. The modified or created object components in the WS become visible for its parent WS (and eventually merged);
- **resynch**. The components updated in the master WS are copied from the master to the slave WS (and eventually merged).

Coordination is *Asymmetric* since only the slave can execute operation resynch. The different coordination policies are implemented, in our system, depending on the way copies are created and resynchronized, on the moment of synchronization and so on. For purposes of illustration there follow the most popular predefined coordination policies.

Private coordination: This is an explicit coordination; at the user's request coordination (through the resynch operation) is performed. This is the default father / son relationship.

Controlled coordination. The resynch operation is automatically performed when a user defined condition, defined on the slave or the master components, is satisfied. (see an example in section 4.4.3.1).

4.4.3.2 FILE SYSTEM VS. DATABASE REPRESENTATION

For activities executed by people such as like the project leader or the configuration administrator, there is a need for high level and abstract concepts. The team leader would manage users, schedules, teams, etc.; the configuration manager has to deal with complex objects, queries, consistency, transaction and so on. These users need a substantial modelling power, and thus an advanced database representation.

Conversely, most Software Engineering activities manage files and use tools for managing files. this is the case with all production activities such as designing, developing, testing, validating etc., and tools such as editors, compilers, linkers and debuggers. Clearly these activities need a file system representation. It follows that at least two representations are of concern, namely, the database (DB) and the file system (FS) representations.

At first glance, these requirements conflict. How can a WS containing a FS representation (called a File system Work Space: FS_WS) be built which meets all the above requirements? The guiding principle for such architecture is described in section Figure 4.8 .

The characteristics of this solution are that a WS, with an FS representation, is in fact a pair: a WS in the DB (called DB_WS), and a part of an FS system (called FS_WS) containing copies of the files present in the DB_WS. In this solution, the FS is a real operating system FS.

This implementation meets requirements for openness, transparency and efficiency but raises a very difficult problem. The FS supporting the WS is not controlled by the data base. There is an inherent shift between the FS and the DB WS[2]. If the FS_WS is a bare FS,

2. . The DB_WS is designed to support process enaction, and the FS_WS to support (parts of) process performance. Not surprisingly, there is exactly the same difference between DB_WS and FS_WS as between enaction and performance.

requirements for cooperation control, high level modelling, and DB services cannot be met. Such an implementation can work only if the system can enforce consistency between the FS_WS and its corresponding DB_WS.

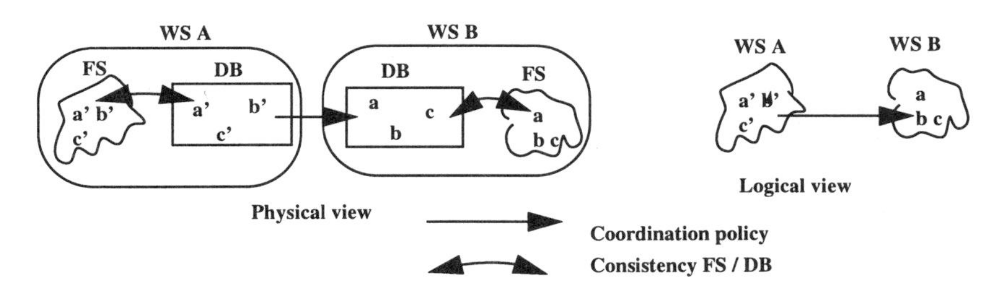

Figure 4.8 Double representations: File System and Database.

The *file mapper* is an essential basic component. It is responsible for determining the place and name (directory, files name, links, etc.) where an Adele object is (must be) located in the FS. Conversely, given a file in an FS, the file mapper knows which Adele object (if any) it is the image. As a consequence, and because all Adele commands can be called directly from shell level, users can request for attributes and relationships of files, by simply providing file names. Examples are request for files which a given user has created or the dependencies of a file.

In the future, we envisage similar, simultaneous management. WSs supported by different operating system (e.g. Unix, VMS, DOS, etc.), supported by foreign platforms (Other CM tools, other DBM, PCTE), and in general any other object manager. This evolution would appear to be mandatory in future heterogeneous PCEs (Process Centered Environments) where various large-scale tools, each containing its own data management system, will have to collaborate. Our ambition is not to centralize and manage all the data of the environment, but to manage the WSs in which the data is managed, and to define and enforce the coordination between WSs. Great difficulties remain to be overcome. We feel that research direction (through WS support and coordination) is a useful approach to the problem.

4.4.4 Work Space Management and Configurations

In the previous chapters we saw which kind of relationships can exist between Work Spaces and the Reference Space. This was a static view. We should like now to discuss the relationship between the activities performed in WSs and the configurations (which are in the RS).

4.4.4.1 PREVIOUS APPROACHES

All CM managers have a concept of WS and configuration, even if ill defined. Following Feiler and Dart [Dar91], [Fei91], the following classes of work space management strategies have been identified.

CI/CO.

There is no real WS management strategy here. The only service provided is a locking mechanism that ensures changes on individual components are sequentialized. Users must define and enforce rules and conventions themselves.

Composition

In the composition approach, configurations are entities understood by the system (they are part of the product model), and a WS is created from a configuration. The system controls which components are in each WS, such that it is possible to know how derived objects have been built and thus to reuse them later.

Change Set

In the Change Set approach, configurations are also objects which are checked-out in a WS, but here the changes performed in a WS are known (at least their name) by the system as a logical change, and themselves stored as an object. A logical change applies to all modified files of the WS and bears a name. For a given configuration, the system is then able, to compose known logical changes to provide a new configuration incorporating all the changes performed in the various WS wherein this configuration was checked-out. Aide De Camp is the only commercial system that implements this approach; a more academic one is presented in [Mun93].

Transaction

In the transaction approach, the work performed in a WS is seen as a transaction. Sub transactions can be defined. In this approach, relationships between a transaction and its sub-transactions are explicit, and managed by the CM tool. This can be compared with the sub database approach (section 4.4.1.3).

4.4.4.2 A PRIORI VS. A POSTERIORI CONFIGURATION BUILDING

It is interesting to note that two main approaches are in use for building configurations.

A Priori Configurations

Under this philosophy, a WS is built containing (normally) a configuration, with the explicit goal of building another configuration. For instance checking out V2.3 (a WS) configuration to build V2.4. The goal is known from the outset; file changes may occur and components may be added or deleted in the WS. At the end of the activity, the fact that version (V2.4) is valid is taken for granted and check-in builds version V2.4.

This philosophy underlies most CM tools: the user is in charge of defining the components and making sure the configuration is consistent; the CM tool does not provide any help in this process.

A Posteriori Configuration

Under this philosophy, the system provides some support to try and work out how to build a configuration, given some of its characteristics. This is not unlike a DBMS approach in which the content of the database and the components that could be used to constitute a configuration are known. It is an approach that privileges the reuse of existing components, whereas a priori configurations lead all too often to duplicate components.

In theory, almost anything can be checked-out in the WS, and components are checked-in along with their semantic properties. Configurations are built using only the CM system.

A posteriori configuration follows the composition approach if component selection is supported (and not just revision selection). Given the properties a new configuration must have, the CM searches for all components that could constitute the configuration. Completeness and consistency control are checked in the process. To a lesser extent the Change Set approach is in this class, since the system is able to "invent" component versions providing an original configuration (a baseline) and a set of change names are known.

Adele, in an earlier version, was a "pure" a posteriori approach: only the Adele configuration manager was allowed to build configurations. We soon realized that it was often too academic. Currently, both approaches are supported and complement each other. For instance, a WS can be built from an existing configuration or from a computed configuration. It is possible to check-in either components with their semantics, or indicate to the system that the WS now IS configuration X. Configuration X is created and contains the WS components. However, it is always possible to ask whether the X configuration is complete and consistent, and provide the semantics of the changed components, to help in computing later configurations reusing these components. The Adele WS Manager naturally supports this feature.

4.4.4.3 EVALUATION

Various strategies have been used for controlling activities and providing users with WSs; they all have their strengths and weaknesses. It is noticeable that all the previous classes of approaches involve an implicitly WS concept. The current state of the art is characterized by the following weaknesses at least:

- Either the RS or the WS has taken precedence; their relationship and consistency is frequently unsatisfactory.
- WS management strategies are predefined by the SCM systems, they are often inflexible.
- Coordination and cooperation are ill supported. Parallel work is either prohibited or unsupported.

We believe our WS manager subsumes all current approaches, in generality and flexibility. It has been designed by successively refining from previous ad-hoc WS management policies implemented on clients' requests. Predefined policies such as private, parallel, shared, exclusive) are provided in a library, in the form of predefined generic relationship types (see example in section 4.5.1.3). They can easily be adapted, customized, refined and combined (private, exclusive for example).

4.5 PROCESS SUPPORT

A constraint which customers would often like to integrate is that "a configuration is valid only when all tests have been successfully executed". While this is quite understandable, supporting this type constraint requires in-depth knowledge of the activities to be carried out, the place where they are executed (WS) and the nature of the collaboration between team members (tests may be shared out among various people). Good configuration management needs powerful process support.

However, process support imposes extremely varied requirements on the system. It means that all actors, artifacts, activities, methods tools and procedures used throughout software development must be modelled, from requirement specification up to (and including) maintenance. The way in which activities are defined, enacted and controlled, services for global visualization of all activities and so on all need to be carefully thought through.

Process support, in Adele, takes place through a layer of services. The basic level is the process engine which is based on triggers. Overlying that comes the Work Space Manager, discussed earlier, and, finally, we have high level process support.

4.5.1 The Process Engine

Our Process Engine relies on Event/Condition/Action (ECA) rules or triggers. The general expression for these rules is as follows:

```
"ON Event WHEN Condition DO Action".
```

We have modified these rules slightly. Triggers are defined within types and they are inherited along the type hierarchy.

Figure 4.9 Triggers on objects.

In relation type definition there are two additional definitions: triggers related to events arising in the relationship origin object and triggers related to events occurring in the relationship destination object.

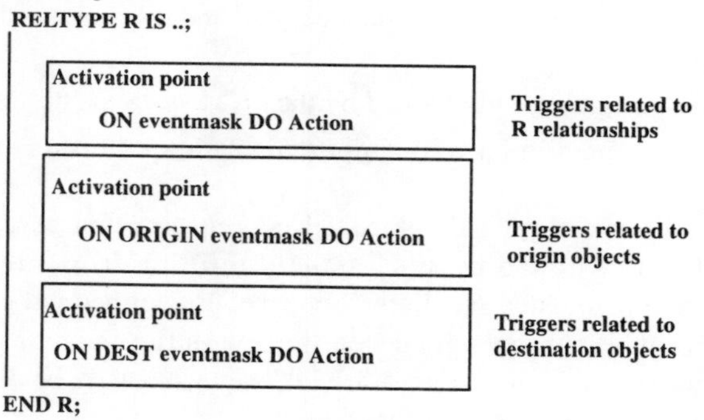

Figure 4.10 Triggers on relationships.

Activation point. When a method is called, the system opens a transaction to execute it. Method execution always generates events at certain specific points within its associated transaction:

PRE triggers are activated immediately after opening the transaction, before method execution. They enable the system to check objects and the system state before operation execution, to extend the method by prologues and so on.

POST triggers are executed immediately before the commit of the corresponding transaction. Their aim is to analyze the database results, to assert the new state of the data base, to undo (rollback) the modifications performed by the operation, to add more computation, to chain with further actions and so on.

AFTER triggers are executed after the validation of the transaction. They can be used to notify the validated operation and to take historical information, to chain with further actions and so on.
ERROR triggers are executed if the transaction is aborted, as an exception mechanism. They allow alternative action to be taken.
Eventmask. This is a condition defining when events are to be taken into account. Eventmasks are first-order logical expressions. A priority level is an integer which determines the execution order when multiple triggers are simultaneously fired.

```
EVENT eventmask = Condition, PRIORITY nn;
```

An *Action* is any program in the Adele Language.

4.5.1.1 THE TRIGGER EXECUTION MODEL

When an event occurs, the system executes the triggers whose eventmask is true. The instance on which a method is invoked is called the *reference instance*. This instance plays a central role because the triggers to be activated are found in its type definition. The reference instance can be either a relationship or an object.

If the reference instance is an object, the triggers to be executed are found in that object type definition, and also in the *relation type* definitions associated with that object. If the object instance O is the origin of $O|R_1|O_1$, and the destination of $O_2|R_2|O$. for any method on O the triggers will be found in the:

- definition of the O object type (ON clause),
- definition of the relation type R_1 (ORIGIN clause)
- and, definition of the relation type R_2 (DEST clause)

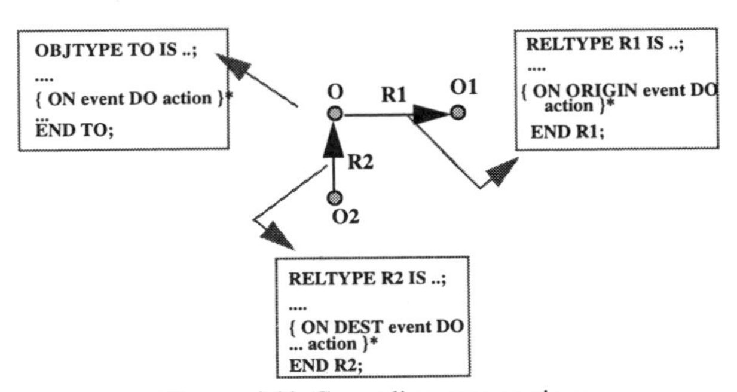

Figure 4.11 Controling propagations.

This mechanism is used to propagate events along potentially complex graphs. The execution of a trigger or a method can create new sub-transactions because other triggers can be activated in reaction to new events. These new sub-transactions are nested in the initial one.

4.5.1.2 AN EXAMPLE OF CONSISTENCY CONTROL

Assume that *AdlConf3* is a configuration and that its type is called *TConf. TConf* has, among its attributes, a *state* attribute which indicates the configuration state, e.g., stable, in-development, in-test, in-documentation. If the configuration is stable (state = stable), its components cannot be modified. Its components are objects (instances of heterogeneous types, e.g., programs, binaries, documentation, etc.) and are related to *AdlConf3* via associations, instances of *compconf* relation type.

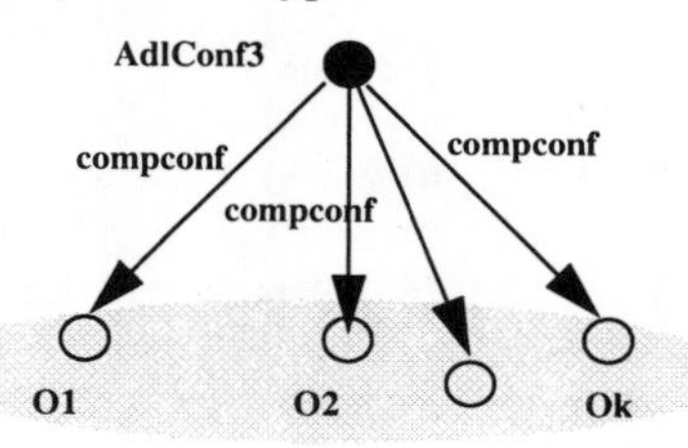

Figure 4.12 Consistency for complex objects.

Triggers can be used to prohibit modifications on the configuration components. We can use the *compconf* relation type to define a trigger related to the destination objects, i.e., the configuration components. The transaction will be aborted if there is a modification attempt:.

```
RELTYPE compconf IS ...;
      DOMAIN !type = TConf --> !type = Object
      POST ON DEST modified DO {
          IF (~!O%status == stable) THEN ABORT;
END compconf ;
```

4.5.1.3 COORDINATION PROTOCOL

Assume that WS1 and WS2 are coordinated by a *controlled* policy (see section 4.4.3.1), with condition "the master object get status = valid", and that X is a shared object

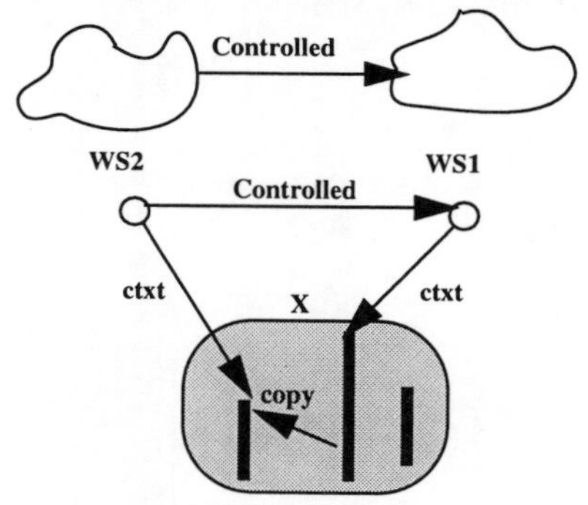

Figure 4.13 Implementing coordination policies.

```
RELTYPE ctxt ;
1       DEST ON modified DO updated (!O -d !D !cmdline) ;
END ctxt ;
RELTYPE controlled ;
2       EVENT to_resynch = updated and ~!d%state = valid ;
3       DEST ON to_resynch DO
            copy (!d, ~!O->ctxt (!name = !d)) ;
END controlled ;
```

The meaning of Line 1 is that each time a component is modified (it is the destination of a *ctxt* relationship), the method *updated* is propagated to the origin (the WS itself); here!D = X and !O = WS1. Thus, the *controlled* relationship is alerted by the *updated* event on its destination; event *to_resynch* (line 2) becomes true if the state of the modified object (now called !d as being option -d of the *updated* method) has also state = valid. If that is the case, line 3, a copy (and possibly a merger) is performed on the WS2 object having the same name as the modified object. ~O->ctxt returns all WS2 components, and (!name = !d) select those (unique here) whose name is X (!d).

The WS manager was implemented using just a few pages of triggers.

4.5.1.4 CM BASIC SERVICES.

It has been repeatedly argued that CM basic services include reporting, auditing, change report, accounting and so on. Our process engine has been designed to implement these services quite easily.

For purposes of illustration, the Work Space Manager was programmed in a few pages of triggers, our generic change control in 2 pages and 3 days' work, and the change set approach (inspired by ADC) in 3 pages. A state transition diagram defining the successive state of an artifact typically corresponds to one page of programming.

4.5.1.5 EVALUATION

The Adele Process Engine has been designed to be able to support almost any specialized process formalisms. For example, simple state machines such as those in CaseWare, petri nets like those in ProcessWeaver [Fer93]; notifications such as those in DSEE [LCS88] and command encapsulation of the ClearCase type are easily supported. Goal-oriented approaches like those in Marvel [KBS90] can also be implemented but more arduously.

The use of our triggering mechanism shows that it is possible to model and automate a wide range of software management strategies. Consequently, the system is highly adaptable and can be customized to specific users' needs.

4.5.2 High Level Process Support

It has been found that triggers are powerful but that they fragment of the process into a large number of tiny definition types, making it difficult to get a clear view of a complete process description. Trigger are not only, a process modeling formalism, but a process engine defined to support different process formalisms. A process modelling language should allow users to describe different software management policies in terms of concepts more abstract than objects, triggers and associations.

For the design of our high level process formalism, we identified the following requirements:

- coordination and cooperation are ill supported, although they involve the most work; they are also highly uncertain.
- The complete process is very complex; the support should present a simplified view to all human agents.

Consequently, we have defined a process formalism, called *Tempo*, based on the concepts of *role* (viewpoint) and *connection* (coordination control). This language is presented below.

4.5.2.1 THE ROLES AND VIEWPOINT APPROACH

Each agent class have different activities. Examples are a project manager's activities (project status control, planning), a configuration administrator's (selecting components for a given baseline), a software process engineer's (defining data models, process models, enaction control), a development engineer's (editing, compiling) and testers' (running test cases, writing problem reports). All have a very different perception of the same reality. Processes should respect and even reinforce these different perceptions, proposing suitable representations.

It would seem worthwhile to respect and even emphasize this fact; this is the goal of the role concept. A role gathers together all entities with the same static and dynamic definition in a given process. A role looks very much like a type: it is the description of the common characteristics of a set of objects, and is called its extent. The original point is that a role extent may contain objects of different types, and that objects of the same type may belong to different role extents in the same process.

The viewpoint approach features a number of conceptual properties.

- From the process engineer's standpoint:
  A new process can be defined almost regardless of previously existing processes. The size and complexity of a process definition is substantially reduced.
- From an agent's standpoint:
  A human agent, when engaged in a process, plays a role (human-agent) in this process. The process description is really the agent's view of the process, since it contains everything that is pertinent for executing that activity, and no more.
- From an evolutionary perspective:
  The modification or creation of a role is only propagated in the process definition where it appears. Any new process definition can be defined, modified or removed at any moment. Interested readers should refer to [BM93].

4.5.2.2 CONNECTIONS

We define a Work Environment (WE) as a process occurrence. It is a tuple:

```
WE =  (WS, PM, Tools, User)
```

where WS is a Work Space, i.e., the set of object instances the process will perform on, *PM* is the process model, *Tools* the tools that will be executed on the WS objects, and *User* the user(s) allowed to work in this Work Environment.

A WS has the properties presented before: by default any change performed in a WS is local to that WS (isolation property). The PM describes only what is done in the WS. This property makes it easier to define a PM.

Our ambition is to do this in such a way that:

- Synchronization is fully transparent (granted by default).
- Coordination between two processes is explicitly defined, at the model level, outside these two process descriptions. It is implemented in such a way that independence of process descriptions is (almost) respected.
- Cooperation is an intrinsic part of the process description. This will include the description of cooperation between sub processes.

Currently, most process formalisms provide support for only some of these dimensions; SCM systems usually only support synchronization and most process managers only propose cooperation. For example, Process Wise Integrator 'interactions' [Rob94], [SW94] implement an explicit client-server interface. This is only one kind of cooperation, Process Weaver only supports message passing which is another kind of cooperation; formalisms relying on a database only have explicit locking of objects, i.e., basic synchronization.

Synchronization being provided by the Adele kernel, we propose the concept of *connection* to implement both coordination and collaboration. A connection is a link between two roles allowing to communicate, either through data flow, status checking, notification or message passing.

To illustrate how role collaboration can be defined, let us imagine the following scenario from the example provided in Figure 4.7 When a new release of a given software product must be developed, a process, called *release* is created. An arbitrary number of *development* WE and a single *design* WE can collaborate in this release process. Each *development* WE can change configuration components (role *conf*) and have read access to the design objects (role *design_doc*).

The synchronization between *development* WEs is as follows: when a given module M receives the *ready* state in a *conf* role, M copies in each *conf* role of all other *development* WE must be merged, and their owner notified. If a design document D in a *design_doc* role is changed in a *design* WE, the new D version automatically replaces the previous one, and notification is sent to the WE user.

A module M receives the *available* state, in a release WE, only if all its copies have the *ready* state. When all modules have the *available* state, a *validation* WS can be created.

```
TYPEPROCESS release ;
      ROLE implement = development ;  -- Implement sub WEs.
      ROLE design = designing;        -- Design Sub WE
      ROLE valid = validation ;       -- Valid Sub WE .
      ROLE design_doc = document ;{ ..}-- Indicate the process for these documents.
      ROLE components = module ; {    -- Contains all conf modules of that WE.
1         EVENT ready = (implement.conf.*.state := ready) ;
          ON ready DO {
2             IF implement.conf.!name.state == ready THEN
3                 state := available ;
4             IF *.state == available THEN new valid ;}
      };
5     CONNECTION dev_conf IS notify, merge ;
6         CONNECT implement.conf WITH implement.conf ;
7         EVENT   notify_when  = ready ;
                  resynch_when = ready ;
      END ;
      CONNECTION md_design IS notify, resynch ;
8         CONNECT design.design_doc WITH implement.design_doc ;
          EVENT   notify_when  = ready ;
                  merge_when   = ready ;
      END ;
END release ;
```

- Line 1 stipulates that when, in any implementation WE (role conf), any object (*) enters the *ready* state, the event *ready* occurs.
- The line 2 sentence *implement.conf.!name.state* evaluates the set of values of the attribute *state* of the object that produced the *ready* event, as found in the *conf* roles of all impelment processes. Operator "==" means set equality. Line 2 means that each copies of the object *name,* in all development WE have the *ready* state.
- Line 3 says that the M copy, as found in the release WE must take the *available* state.
- The line 4 expression **.state* returns all state values of all objects in the component role in the release process. Line 4 means that when all module get the *available* state, a *valid* role (i.e., a validation WE) must be created.

Some basic behavior is provided in a standard library, for example *notify, resynch* and *merge* in this case. Using standard inheritance mechanisms, each connection can reuse these process fragments (line 5), and redefine, for instance, the events for which some behavior must be executed. Line 7 means that notification and resynch must happen when the object becomes *ready* . The CONNECT clause expresses which pair of roles must be coordinated. Line 6 means that, for a given release process, the *conf* roles between each pair of *development* WEs are connected by a *dev_conf* connection (peer to peer connection). Line 8 stipulates that each *design* WE (role design_doc) are to be coordinated with each *development* WE (role design_doc) by an *md_design* connection (master/slave connection). The father/son connections in Figure 4.7 (SELF.component with implement.conf; design with design.design_doc and SELF.design with implement.design_doc) are defined in the same way.

Thus, depending on the connections, the activity performed inside a WE may or may not interfere with other activities carried out in parallel during the software process.

4.5.3 Current State

The translation between Tempo and Adele is quite clear. A process model is associated with a WS type and a specific schema. The PM is defined in this schema as the behavior of the WS. The connection concept is directly mapped to Adele coordination relationships (controlled). Roles are implemented using complex objects, a multiple schema approach, and semantic relationships. However, this does not yet correspond to full implementation of the role concept.

Tempo has not been experimented with yet. More research is needed before an implementation can be made available. Efforts have been made instead to design and implement the process engine and in a commercial level WS manager, since it was felt that these are the major components needed for implementing any process support environment.

4.6 EVALUATION

The Adele project has now been running for ten years. Its earliest commercial versions were distributed, directly by our university, to large companies from 1984 onwards (notably Sextant and Bull, the former for the development of embedded systems, including the Airbus series and the Ariane rockets; the later for the support of its proprietary operating systems). They have been heavily used ever since. Major SEEs have been developed on top of the Adele system. Examples are afforded by Palas (Sextant), Emma (Bull), SDE (Matra), CajMarie (Ericsson). Currently hundreds of licences are in daily use. Since 1993, Adele has been distributed and developed by the Logiscope/Verilog company. Sales may therefore be expected to increase in the near future[3].

Throughout this period the practical problems encountered in the setting up and use of SCMs in critical environments have been studied in collaboration with our clients. Roughly speaking, the customer's requirements may be said to be as follows:

1. Efficiency, efficiency, efficiency,
2. Transparent, open, evolutive, non-intrusive.
3. Better product modelling, versioning facilities.
4. A custom-built SEE is too expensive. Even its design is beyond our capability. Please help us.

Seen from a technology provider's standpoint, these requirements are interpreted as follows:

(1) Efficiency becomes truly critical as soon as large-scale development is under way. Selecting the platform to start with is critical.

(2) The SEE to be built must not be constrained by the underlying SCM tool. Naming conventions, data model constraints and so on should be invisible from the outside. WS policy definition and implementation were found to be very costly in most SEEs. Process support, when lacking, means that huge amounts of code have to be written in order to implement the desired process. One ends up with a very expensive and inflexible environment, and one which is difficult to maintain and evolve.

(3) There is a need for a better description of product structures, for controlling them and for defining product evolution constraints. Versioning capabilities are currently too primitive.

(4) The last point is totally at odds with the others. Most users need an immediate start-up solution, with the insurance they will be able to make it evolve as soon as they understand their own process better. In this respect, a good SCM should be seen as a way to gradually understand, define, improve and adopt processes in an evolutive way.

Most of our customers, until recently, have been large companies, with critical software. They have used Adele as a kernel, building dedicated SEEs on top. Generally, customers liked the great flexibility and power of the tool, its capabilites for modelling complex products, integrating and interfacing with tools and methods, and its programming facility for implementing specific interfaces. They disliked the strict product model, the overly constraining automatic configuration selection, and the lack of associated services. We, on the other hand, have been disappointed to note that automatic configuration selection was not used as much as expected.

These remarks, and others, have provided the incentive to make the product evolve as an efficient and highly customizable kernel. Process capabilities are currently the major focus of our research, as well as more general and powerful data models (points 1, 2, 3).

More recently, with wider marketing of the product, emphasis has been placed on predefined high level services (point 4), such as a generic graphical interface, the WS manager, and the design of a few predefined SEEs dedicated to certain types of customers. Indeed, it has been found that the cost lies much more in defining the services to be provided and their interconnection, than in their implementation. In this respect, our process support

---

3. Adele is distributed by Logiscope Technology 3010 LBJ freeway, suite 900 Dallas, Texas U.S.A. Verilog SA 52 av. Aristide. Brian 92220 Bagneux France

has proved to be highly effective, with most implementations being a matter of just a few pages of program. The WS manager itself is fully implemented in 4 pages of triggers. This may be compared with the thousands of lines of code customers have had to write to realize a single specific WS implementation.

4.7 CONCLUSION

We have tried to show that an SCM system should rely on three major components: an object manager controlling the Repository Space (RS) where software artifacts and their versions are stored, a Work Space manager controlling the content and activities performed in the Work Spaces (WSs), and finally a Process Manager controlling the tasks and activities performed in both the WSs and the RS.

We think there is a need for:

- a powerful data model including an explicit versioning model, controlling the RS.
- a WS model, which is much more powerful than a bare file system.
- explicit mapping between RS and WS including inter-WS collaboration.
- an explicit Process Model, controlling both the RS, the WS and their relationships.

We have presented an approach based on an advanced database, supporting a specific data model, sub databases, WS control and process control. Commercial SCMs first used the bare file system with no data model at all. Currently, advanced SCMs use databases and offer some data and process modelling capabilities. But much progress needs to be made in both directions. Adele is specifically designed for the support of a specific data model and full process support, but the ideal has not yet been reached.

We claim that future configuration managers will have to start from more specialized databases, providing high-level data modelling, full process support and the specific services needed by configuration management. We expect our work on Adele to provide both a practical database and deeper insight into the class of database we shall need in the future.

REFERENCES

[AS93] Paul Adams and Marvin Solomon. An overview of the CAPITL software development environment. Technical Report TR 1143, Computer Science Department, University of Wisconsin-Madison, April 1993.

[BE86] N. Belkhatir and J. Estublier. Experience with a data base of programs. In *Proceedings of the ACM SIGSOFT/SIGPLAN Software Engineering Symposium on Practical Software Development Environments*, pages 84–91, Palo Alto, California, December 1986.

[BK93] N.S. Barghouti B. Krishnamurthy. Provence: A process visualization enactement environment. *ESEC93, 4th European Software Engineering Conference.Garmish, Germany. Springer Verlag.*, Septembre 1993.

[BM93] N. Belkhatir and W. Melo. Supporting software maintenance in tempo. In *Proceedings of the Conference on Software Maintenance*, Montreal Canada, 1993.

[CW93] M. Cagan and A. Wright. Untangling configuration management: Mechanism and methodoloy in cm systems. In *Proc, 4th International workshop on Software Configuration Management*, Baltimore, May 1993.

[Dar91] Susan Dart. Concepts in configuration management systems. In Springer Verlag Peter H. Feiler, editor, *International Workshop on Software Configuration Management SCM3*, pages 1–18, Trondheim, Norway, June 1991.

[Dit89] K.R. Dittrich. The Damokles database system for design applications: its past, its present, and its future. In K. H. Bennett, editor, *Software Engineering Environments: Research and Practice*, pages 151–171. Ellis Horwood Books, Durhan, UK, 1989.

[EF89] Jacky Estublier and Jean-Marie Favre. Structuring large versioned software products. In *Proceedings of IEEE COMPSAC 89*, pages 404–411, Orlando, Florida, September 1989.

[Est85] J. Estublier. A configuration manager: The Adele data base of programs. In *Workshop on Software Engineering Environments for Programming-in-the-Large*, pages 140–147, Harwichport, Massachusetts, June 1985.

[Est88] Jacky Estublier. Configuration management: The notion and the tools. In Springer Verlag, editor, *Proc. of the Int'l Workshop on Software Version and Configuration Control*, pages 38–61, Grassau, Germany, january 1988.

[Fei91] P. Feiler. Configuration management models in commercial environment. Technical Report CMU/SEI-91-TR-7 ADA235782, Software Engineering Institute (Carnegie Mellon University), 1991.

[Fel79] S. I. Feldman. Make: a program for maintaining computer programs. *Software–Practice and Experience*, 9(4):255–265, April 1979.

[Fer93] C. Fernstrom. Process weaver: adding process support to unix. In *Proceedings of Second Intl. Conference on the Software Process ICSP2*, pages 12–26, Berlin, Germany, 1993.

[HL82] R. L. Haskin and R. A. Lorie. On extending the functions of a relational database system. In M. Schkolnick, editor, *sigmod*, pages 207–212, Orlando, FL, June 1982. acm.

[HN86] A. N. Habermann and D. Notkin. Gandalf: Software development environments. *Transactions on Software Engineering*, SE-12(12):1117–1127, December 1986.

[Kam87] R.F. Kamel. Effect of modularity on system evolution. *IEEE Software*, January 1987.

[Kat90] R. H. Katz. Toward a unified framework for version modeling in engineering databases. *ACM Computing Surveys*, 22(4):375–408, [12] 1990.

[KBGW91] Won Kim, Nat Ballou, Jorge F. Garza, and Darrell Woelk. A distributed object-oriented database system supporting shared and private databases. *ACM Transactions on Information Systems*, 9(1):31–51, 1991.

[KBS90] G. E. Kaiser, N. S. Barghouti, and M. H. Sokolsky. Preliminary experience with process modeling in the Marvel software development environment kernel. In *Proc. of the 23th Annual Hawaii Int'l Conf. on System Sciences*, pages 131–140, Kona, HI, January 1990.

[KK90] David G. Korn and Eduardo Krell. A new dimension for the unix file system. *Software—Practice and Experience*, 20(S1):19–34, June 1990.

[LC84] D. B. Leblang and Jr. Chase, R.P. Computer-aided software engineering in a distributed workstation environment. In P. Henderson, editor, *Proceedings of the ACM SIGSOFT/SIGPLAN Software Engineering Symposium on Practical Software*

Development Environments, pages 104–112, Pittsburgh, PA, may 1984. acm, acm.

[LCM85] D. B. Leblang, Jr. Chase, R.P., and Jr. McLean, G.D. The DOMAIN software engineering environment for large scale software development efforts. In *Proceedings of the 1st International Conference on Computer Workstations*, pages 266–280, San Jose, CA, November 1985. IEEE Computer Society.

[LCS88] David B. Leblang, Robert P. Chase, and Howard Spilke. Increasing productivity with a parallel configuration manager. In Springer Verlag, editor, *Proc. of the Int'l Workshop on Software Version and Configuration Control*, pages 21–37, Grassau, Germany, january 1988.

[Leb93] C. Leblang. Clearcase. In *Proc. of the 4th International Workshop on Software Configuration Management*, Baltimore, Maryland, may 1993.

[Mic88] Sun Microsystems, editor. *Introduction to the NSE.* Network Software Environment: Reference Manual. Sun Microsystems, Inc., 2550 Garcia Avenue, Mountain View, CA 94043, USA, part no: 800- 2095, march 1988.

[Mun93] B. P. Munch. Uniform versioning: The change-oriented model. In *Proc. of the 4th International Workshop on Software Configuration Management*, pages 232–240, Baltimore, Maryland, may 1993.

[Par72] D. L. Parnas. On the criteria to be used in decomposing systems into modules. *Communications of the ACM*, 15(12):1053–1058, December 1972.

[Per87] Dewayne E. Perry. Version control in the Inscape environment. In *Proceedings of the 9th International Conference on Software Engineering*, pages 142–149, Monterey, CA, March 1987.

[Rob94] I. Robertson. An implementation of the ispw-6 process example. In *Third European Workshop On Software Process Technology EWSPT94*, february 1994.

[Roc75] M. Rockhind. The source code control system. *IEEE Trans on Soft. Eng.*, SE-1(4):364–370, Dec 1975.

[RPD86] J.M. Neighbors R. Prieto-Diaz. Modules interconnection languages. *The journal of systems and software*, pages 307–334, 1986.

[Sci91] E. Sciore. Multidimensional versioning for object-oriented databases. *Proc. Second International Conf. on Deductive and Object-Oriented Databases*, December 1991.

[Sha84] M. Shaw. Abstraction techniques in modern programming languages. *IEEE Software.*, pages 10–26, October 1984.

[Sno93] R. T. Snodgrass. *An Overview of TQuel*, chapter 6, pages 141–182. Benjamin/Cummings, 1993.

[SW94] Jin Sa and B. Warboys. Modelling processes using a stepwise refinement technique. In *Third European Workshop On Software Process Technology EWSPT94*, february 1994.

[Tho89] I. Thomas. Pcte interfaces: Supporting tools in software engineering environments. *IEEE Software*, November 1989.

[Tic82] Walter F Tichy. Design implementation and evaluation of a revision control system. In *Proc.6th Int. Conf. Software Eng., Tokyo*, septembre 1982.

[Tic88] Walter F. Tichy. Tools for software configuration management. In *Proc. of the Int. Workshop on Software Version and Configuration Control*, pages 1–20, Grassau, january 1988.

[Wat89] Richard. C. Water. Automated software management based on structural models. *Software Practice and experience*, 1989.

[Wie93] D. Wiebe. Object-oriented software configuration management. In *Proc 4th Software Configuration Management workshop*, Baltimore, May 1993.

5

n-DFS: The Multiple Dimensional File System

Glenn Fowler, David Korn, and Herman Rao
AT&T Bell Laboratories

ABSTRACT

n-DFS, the Multiple Dimensional File System, is a logical file system that allows new services to be added to underlying file systems, without any modification of applications and the kernel. *n*-DFS was motivated by the need to tailor traditional UNIX-like file systems for configuration management. We have demonstrated the extensibility and generality of *n*-DFS by introducing six novel services to UNIX-like file systems, including viewpathing, versioning, event notification, process monitoring, file tree replications, and synchronized replication. Compared with other systems, *n*-DFS is unique in that it is implemented as a library, which is linked by an application and run in the application's address space. Portability is a major advantage of this library approach. Performance of *n*-DFS shows 23% overhead when compared with the UNIX file system in the Andrew Benchmark.

5.1 INTRODUCTION

The Multiple Dimensional File System (*n*-DFS) is a logical file system being developed by the Software Engineering Research Department in AT&T Bell Laboratories. Inspired by its predecessor, the Three Dimensional File System (3DFS) [Korn90], Bell Labs' Plan 9 [Pike90], and the Jade File System [Rao93], the goal of *n*-DFS is to tailor traditional UNIX-like file systems to meet the needs of configuration management in software development environments. Layered on top of a UNIX-like file system, *n*-DFS allows new services to be added to the underlying file system. Examples of services include naming services (e.g., viewpathing [Korn90], semantic naming [Giff91], and attribute-based naming [Pete88]); monitoring file systems operations and communication [Krel92]; replicating critical files in underlying file systems to remote backup file systems [Fowl93]; accessing Internet-wide file

Configuration Management, Edited by Tichy

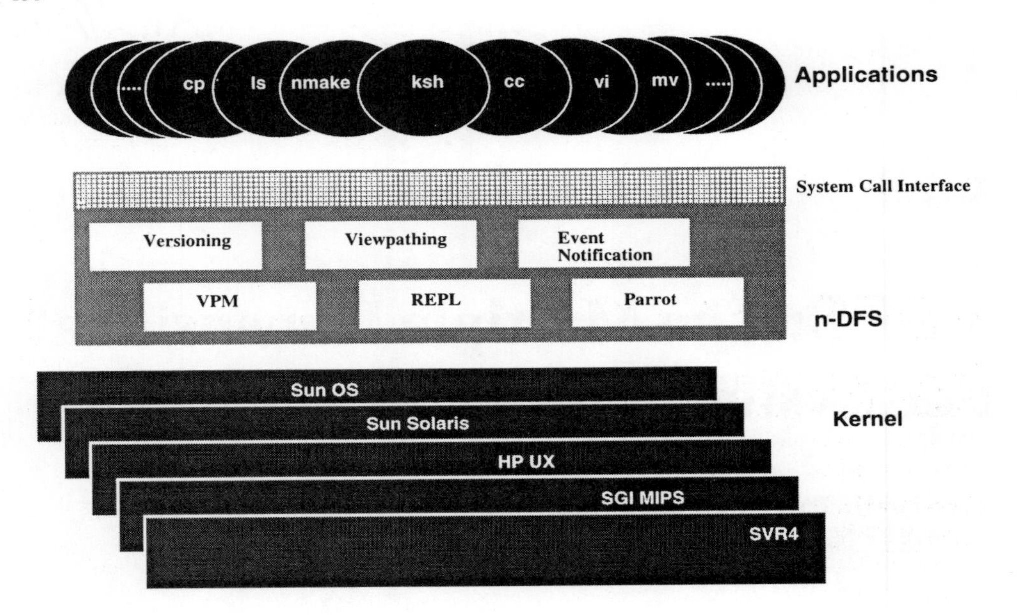

Figure 5.1 The Multiple Dimensional File System

systems [Rao93, Summ94]; and providing versioning of files [Lebl85, Korn90]. 3DFS was named the Three Dimensional File system because it introduced a third *physical* dimension (i.e., viewpathing) to the UNIX file system. Conceptually, we view each new service in *n*-DFS as a new *virtual* dimension to the file system, and thus we call *n*-DFS the Multiple Dimensional File System. The versioning service, for example, is analogous to a *time* dimension to file systems.

The design philosophy of this project is that overloading file system semantics can improve software reusability and customer acceptability, when compared with the alternative of creating a new interface that is incompatible with existing applications. For example, UNIX tools such as nmake [Fowl90] and build [Eric84] have demonstrated the usefulness and power of viewpathing in configuration management. This notion has been implemented by adding extra code to each of these tools. *n*-DFS, however, embeds viewpathing into the file system so that not only do all tools (e.g., UNIX system commands ls, vi, etc.) take advantage of viewpathing without any modification, but they also share the same view of the underlying file system. As another example, by implementing a versioning service as the front-end of a source code control system (e.g., SCCS [Allm86] and RCS [Tich85]), *n*-DFS introduces to UNIX-like file systems a new repository that supports versioning of files. Hence, users are able to reuse the ls command to browse different versions of a file.

Rather than considering individual functionality separately, our focus is to provide a generic and extensible architecture that allows new functionality to be added. Conceptually, *n*-DFS introduces a *logical layer* between the operating system and user applications, as illustrated in Figure 5.1. This layer presents applications with the same interface that the underlying system provides. However, it also allows users to *mount* services on nodes (i.e., directories or files) in the name space by maintaining a per-process name space. *n*-DFS intercepts system calls from applications, and then passes them to the mounted services. For example, consider the viewpathing service that allows a virtual directory to refer to a sequence of physical directories.

Users define a directory as a virtual directory by attaching the viewpathing services to the directory. When the system call open is invoked by an application (e.g., vi) to access a file under this directory, *n*-DFS translates the pathname into the corresponding physical pathname by invoking the viewpathing service, and then calls the real system call open on the physical pathname.

n-DFS's services are implemented as built-in functions resident in the *n*-DFS layer, or as external user-level server processes. As illustrated in Figure 5.1, we have designed and implemented the following services:

- **Viewpathing Service**
  Allows a logical directory to refer to a sequence of physical directories/trees, the virtual content being an ordered union of files in the physical directories [Korn90].
- **Versioning Service**
  Supports a repository that provides multiple versions of files [Korn90].
- **Event Notification Service**
  Collects file access events and notifies remote event-action servers (e.g., yeast [Kris91]).
- **Visual Process Manager (VPM)**
  Monitors interaction among a group of processes by collecting system calls invoked by them, and displays the result graphically in real time.
- **Tree Replication Service (REPL)**
  Replicates files under *replicated trees* in underlying file systems to a backup file system whenever their context/attributes are changed [Fowl93].
- **Parrot Service**
  Presents users with a coherent, single-copy view of two loosely-connected replicated physical file systems [Rao94].

These services demonstrate the extensibility and generality of *n*-DFS. Indeed, *n*-DFS has been used as a research vehicle, enabling us to explore a variety of new services not provided by traditional UNIX-like systems.

n-DFS is unique in that the logical layer is realized as a library which is linked by applications and run in the application's address space. For systems, such as Sun OS 4.1 [Sun88], that provide the concept of dynamic linking of shared libraries, we are able to replace the standard C shared library with *n*-DFS's library, and applications with dynamic linking may access *n*-DFS without any change. For systems without dynamic linking of shared libraries or applications with static linking, we need to re-link applications with *n*-DFS's library. In either case, *n*-DFS is transparent to the kernel and applications; no modification of the kernel or applications is required, and the syntax and semantics of system calls are preserved. Built-in services are accessed by local function calls without requiring any context-switch overhead.

With the library approach, *n*-DFS is more portable than the approach of modifying the kernel (e.g., semantic file system [Giff91] and watchdogs [Brer88]) and adding new drivers (e.g., Pseudo Devices [Welc89]). Furthermore, *n*-DFS runs in the client side. It uses standard UNIX system calls to access the underlying file system, regardless of what access protocols are provided by file servers. Hence, heterogeneity is another advantage. The drawback to the library approach, however, is that it requires all commands to be linked with the library in order for everything to work correctly. Fortunately, most systems use dynamic linking; and nearly all the standard utilities are dynamically linked to the system call library. In most cases, we have been able to get third party software vendors to provide dynamically linked versions of their software.

As shown in Figure 5.1, we have an implementation of *n*-DFS running on Sun OS 4.1, Sun Solaris, HP-UX, SGI MIPS, and SVR4, all of which support dynamic linking of shared libraries. The implementation includes the services described above. Most UNIX tools and commands, such as vi, nmake, and ls, are able to run on *n*-DFS without any modification, and without re-linking for systems supporting dynamic shared libraries. *n*-DFS and its predecessor, 3DFS, have been used as a software development environment in our department and other AT&T organizations for several years by hundreds of active users.

In this paper, we describe the design and implementation of *n*-DFS, and overview configuration management services supported by *n*-DFS. The rest of this chapter is organized as follows. Section 5.2 describes *n*-DFS services and gives an overview of the system from the users' aspect. Section 5.3 presents *n*-DFS's architecture, focusing on its per-process name space and a mechanism of attaching services on the name space. Section 5.4 describes implementation of the current system. Section 5.5 evaluates the system by measuring overhead of the logical layer and costs of two services: viewpathing and replication. Section 5.6 offers further discussion of *n*-DFS in comparison to related projects, and Section 7 provides a summary conclusion.

5.2 *n*-DFS's SERVICES

n-DFS's services are implemented as built-in functions in the *n*-DFS layer, or as external user-level server processes. These services can be classified into three categories: naming services, file services, and monitoring services. Naming services map a given name to a physical handle (e.g., a file descriptor) used by the underlying file system. Subsequent accesses to the desired file use this handle. Naming services add overhead only during name resolution. Once the desired file is opened, applications directly access data using the file descriptor. File services support functionality other than regular file operations. Examples of file services include file replication, data compression, and accessing wide-area file systems. Monitoring services provide file access and process control information to external servers. Configuration management systems, for example, can trigger some actions.

Originally, *n*-DFS was motivated by the need to tailor traditional UNIX-like file systems for configuration management in software development environments. However, in addition to services for configuration management, we have also implemented services for replication and monitoring.

5.2.1 Configuration Management Services

Two ingredients for the success of the UNIX system for software development are its process model and its file system. The process model makes it easy to connect simple tools together to perform complex tasks. The file system is simple to understand, has relatively few limitations, and encourages sharing of information. This has led to the creation of a rich set of software development tools.

The hierarchical nature of the file system has several advantages. It is easy to create separate directories to keep source files, header files, and libraries. It leads quite naturally to hierarchical decomposition of software into subsystems. The sharing of include files and libraries is accomplished by using shared naming conventions.

However, using the UNIX file system for source code has several drawbacks. One drawback

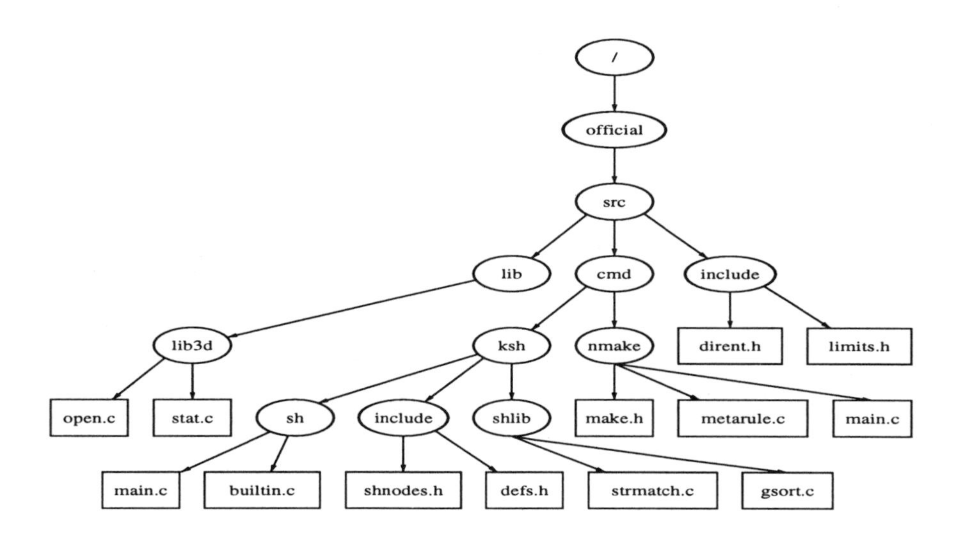

Figure 5.2 Official source

is that there are no intrinsic capabilities for storing multiple versions of the same code. This has led to the creation of software database management systems such as SCCS [Allm86] and RCS [Tich85] to store variants of each module by encoding the changes into a file. Because SCCS and RCS are not integral parts of the file system, commands are needed to first extract the information from the database before using it.

The second drawback is that the UNIX file system fails to provide adequate mechanisms for file synchronization. In a development environment, several developers are likely to be making changes to a software system concurrently. While it is unlikely that two developers will update the same file at the same time, there is the potential for serious problems if this were to happen. SCCS and RCS provide for locking portions of the source database to prevent the same module from being changed by different developers at the same time.

The third drawback is the lack of an event notification mechanism. Building large complex software systems involves coordination and correct sequencing. It is often necessary to know when someone else on a project is making changes to software, and to notify others or trigger other actions when certain changes have taken place.

Our approach has been to augment the UNIX file system to make it easy to store multiple versions of the same files under the same name, and to make it easy to operate on several configurations simultaneously, sharing files whenever possible. The augmented UNIX file system is used to store the many program variants instead of using SCCS or RCS databases.

This approach does not eliminate the need for software configuration tools. It still requires make or its derivatives to rebuild object code when changes to the source code have been made. It also requires a change management system to keep track of changes to the source, and to manage configuration threads for the software releases. However, it does eliminate the

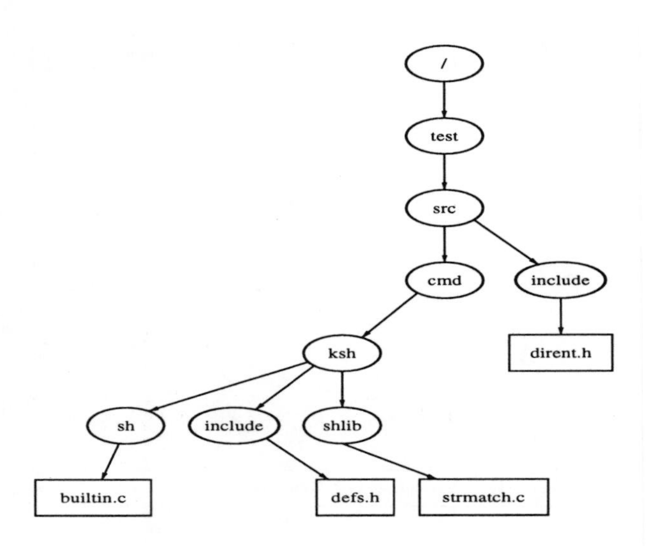

Figure 5.3 Tester's source

need to store the source files in the change management system itself and allows the use of the UNIX file system for this purpose.

5.2.1.1 VIEWPATHING SERVICE

A user view is created by mounting one file tree onto another. The result is that the top file tree now virtually contains the union of files from both trees. It is as though each file in the bottom tree that was not in the top tree was copied to the top tree. The user can now work in this merged top file tree. Only the top layer is writable; All other layers are read-only. Consequently, when the user modifies a file located below on the top layer, the desired file is copied to the top layer before it is accessed. Files from the bottom tree that have the same name relative to the root of the tree as a file on the top tree are obscured. However, files on the underneath layer can be referenced with the special file name "... ". The effect of "... " is to remove the top layer, exposing files that are covered.

Unlike ordinary mounts, these mounts are visible only to the current process and its descendants. Trees are mounted pair-wise. It is possible to mount **a** on **b**, and **b** on **c**, to get viewpathing effect equivalent to setting the **VPATH** environment variable to **a:b:c**, a technique introduced by build.

For example, consider a software project where the released source files reside in an official area (see Figure 5.2). After software bugs are found and fixed, but before another release, the changed files are left in a separate directory tree controlled by system testers (see Figure 5.3). To add a new feature or fix a bug, a user creates a *working area* to modify files as illustrated in Figure 5.4. The user may construct his/her own view of the project by viewpathing the private

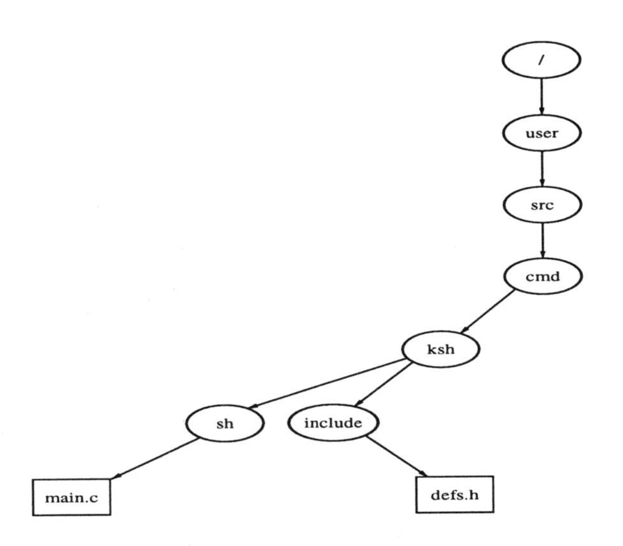

Figure 5.4 User's workspace

working area on top of the system tester area, which is in turn viewpathing on top of the official area; Figure 5.5 shows the three dimensional view of the system through the user's working area. The user can then modify and build the system using conventional tools. However, only the top layer—the user's working area—is writable. And when the user modifies a file located below on the top layer, the desired file is copied to the top layer before it is accessed. After finishing modification, the user can copy modified files to the system tester area.

5.2.1.2 VERSIONING SERVICE

A version file is a new type of file used to support multiple *instances* of a file, all under the same name. It is organized like a directory, with instances as entries. It is possible to browse instances using regular directory commands, such as ls. Unlike regular directories, however, when a version file is referenced, the system returns a reference to one of its instances rather than to the version file itself; it may actually invoke actions to check out the desired instance from the version file. Each instance is named by one or more version names, and users are able to specify search paths of instances on a per-directory basis. We employ a byte-oriented, block-move algorithm, similar to Tichy's algorithm [Tich84], to compute the delta of an instance related to a common base and to store the delta in the version file. A central server is used to handle checking out (in) instances from (to) the version file using the corresponding delta.

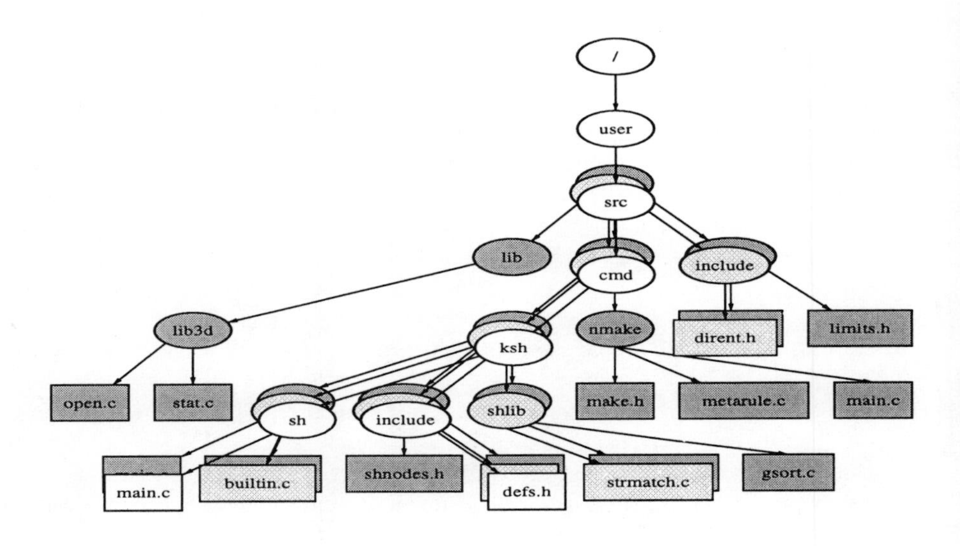

Figure 5.5 Three-dimensional view

5.2.1.3 EVENT NOTIFICATION SERVICE

Many aspects of configuration management can be modeled as the occurrence of events that require additional actions. For example, the upgrade of a library module is an event whose occurrence triggers several actions, e.g., rebuilding all systems of which the library is a component. The usual way of collecting events is to have a daemon periodically polling the file system. *n*-DFS provides an alternative: event notification. Users are able to specify interesting events in the context of system calls. *n*-DFS catches events when they happen and notifies an external server, called Yeast [Kris91], which in turn triggers the proper actions.

5.2.2 Monitoring and Replication Services

5.2.2.1 VISUAL PROCESS MANAGER (VPM)

VPM displays and monitors the relationship of, and communications among, a group of processes running in a distributed environment. The system is designed for debugging distributed applications. The front-end of VPM, implemented as a monitoring service, intercepts three kinds of system calls: process management system calls such as fork, exec, and exit; I/O channel management system calls such as open, close, dup, and pipe; and I/O operation system calls such as read and write. Messages of system calls are sent to a back-end server, which uses a graph viewer (called dotty [Kout94]) to display the relationship of, and communication among, these processes.

Since monitoring may open a potential security hole, it is disabled when the process real uid is different from the process effective uid, unless the real uid is root.

5.2.2.2 TREE REPLICATION SERVICE (REPL)

REPL increases the availability and reliability of physical file systems by replicating files located on one physical file system—the primary file system—onto another physical file system—the backup file system. REPL is designed for a dual-system architecture, where applications are accessing the primary file system. The purpose of this replication is to maintain the state of the backup file system immediately after the crash of the primary file system, to be the same as that of the primary file system after rebooting from the crash. Hence, when the primary file system fails, applications can quickly recover by switching over to the host of the backup file system rather than waiting for recovery of the primary file system. REPL uses *n*-DFS to intercept system calls from applications that modify files/directories (e.g., creat, write, chmod, etc.) and propagates these calls to a remote server, which in turn performs them on a backup physical file system.

In conjunction with a process watch mechanism called Watchd Daemon [Huan93], REPL is capable of recovering from a single failure. Failure and recovery are transparent to applications, in that a failure does not force operations in progress to terminate. An on-line recovery mechanism synchronizes the backup file system with the primary file system without interrupting running applications.

5.2.2.3 PARROT SERVICE

Parrot is a successor to REPL. Like REPL, Parrot replicates files on the underlying file system onto another physical file system. Parrot advances REPL in that it supports sequential write sharing. File access under Parrot has exactly the same semantics as if all of the processes on both hosts were executing on a single time-sharing system. Thus, processes on different hosts accessing the same file see changes made to the file at the granularity of the read and write system calls. The Sun Network File System (NFS), on the other hand, handles cache consistency using a simple heuristic: file data is assumed to be valid for 3 seconds after it is fetched from a server; directory data is assumed to be valid for 30 seconds after its arrival [Sand85]. Distributed applications (like parallel make [Fowl90]) are much easier to build on a file system with coherent replica/caching, such as Parrot, than on a file system with incoherent caching, such as NFS [Mann93].

Parrot implements a read-one write-all synchronization protocol. It guarantees consistency at the granularity of read and write operations on the files that it replicates, and it supports transactional synchronization for sequences of read and write operations on the same file. This is done through a consistency control mechanism within Parrot that maintains and issues read and write tokens on a per-file basis. The process requests the proper token before reading or writing the file and releases it after the read/write operation. The token mechanism takes advantage of the local file-locking mechanism provided by the kernel to handle busy-waiting, scheduling, and semantics-based locking [Skar93].

5.3 ARCHITECTURE

Layered between an application and the operating system, *n*-DFS is an attempt to extend the functionality of the underlying file system by providing additional services. Basically, *n*-DFS maintains a per-process name space that allows a service to be *mounted* on a subtree in the

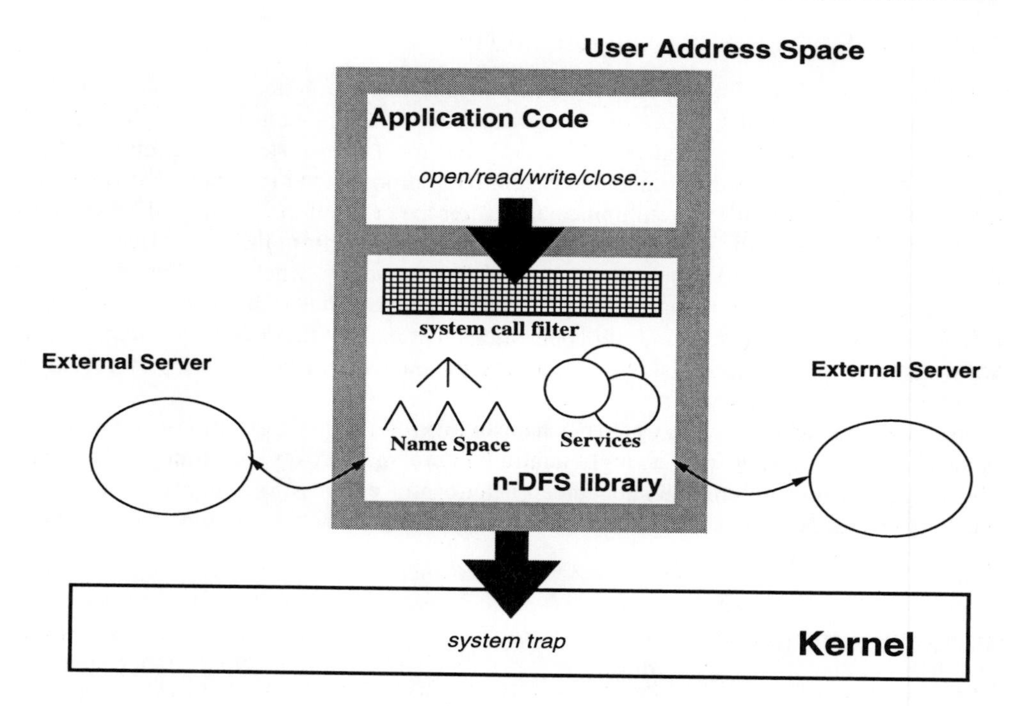

Figure 5.6 System architecture

name space. Whenever a system call is made by an application for a file that lies in the subtree where the service is mounted (we say that the service is *mounted* on the file), *n*-DFS invokes the service to handle the request.

As a replacement of the system call library (i.e., libc), *n*-DFS is linked to the application code, and run at the same address space as the application code. Figure 5.6 illustrates its architecture, including a system call filter, a name space, built-in services, and an interface for interacting with external servers. The system call filter catches system calls from the application code, e.g., open, read, write, close, and fcntl. It then locates and calls the mounted service. If no services are mounted on files referred by the system call, *n*-DFS simply passes the call to the kernel.

n-DFS provides a set of built-in services, which are implemented as regular function calls and reside in the application's address space. No context switch is required to access these services. The viewpathing service, for example, is implemented as a built-in service. In addition to these built-in services, *n*-DFS also provides an infrastructure to implement external services supported by external servers, which run in different address spaces or even on different machines. The infrastructure includes a naming mechanism to name servers, a library to implement servers (called libcs), and a message protocol for communicating between *n*-DFS and each server.

In *n*-DFS, each running server has a unique, global name in a distributed environment, as follows:

/**dev**/*proto*/*host*/*service*[/*options*]

where *proto* is fdp for local streams, and tcp or udp for remote streams; *host* is either a host name (local names the local host), or an IP *n.n.n.n* address. The special host name share names one service that all hosts share on the local network. Otherwise the service may run one per host. *service* is either a service name (for new services), or an integer port number (for old Internet services). The *options* are "/" separated and further qualify the connect stream: user[=*uid*] restricts the service to the current [*uid*] user; group[=*gid*] restricts the service to the current [*gid*] group; other (default) specifies no user or group service restrictions. Other options are service dependent and are used to name different instantiations of the same service; different connect streams name different services. For example, "/dev/fdp/local/coshell/user" and "/dev/fdp/local/coshell/group=ship" both name different processes running the coshell daemon program. It is also possible to interact with the running server at the shell level. For example,

```
$ echo  "I did it" >  /dev/tcp/share/logger
```

sends the message "I did it" to the shared server logger.

A service is defined by *mounting* a server on the service's pathname, as follows:

```
$ mount  /#fs/service_name  /dev/proto/host/server_name
```

"/#fs/*service_name*" is the service pathname, and the second argument "/dev/*proto/host/server_name*" refers to the name of the running server that provides the service. Users may choose different pathnames for the same service. The binding of a service and its server may change dynamically. It is possible to turn on/off services temporarily.

The mapping from a pathname and its mounted service is maintained by a name space. Like Plan 9, *n*-DFS maintains a per-process name space. Unlike Plan 9, the per-process name space resides inside the user address space rather than in the kernel. The name space is modifiable on a per-process level. It is, however, inherited across the system call fork in that the child process would have the same name space as its parent after fork. Users construct their own private name spaces using two system-wide, global name spaces: a name space supported by the underlying operating system and a name space of naming servers provided by *n*-DFS. At the beginning, the per-process name space contains only these two global name spaces. Users then are able to *attach* services onto their per-process name spaces.

Services supported by *n*-DFS can be classified into three categories: naming services, file services, and monitoring services. *n*-DFS intercepts system calls and then invokes the corresponding services. A service defines which calls it wants to intercept. Usually, naming services are invoked only to resolve pathnames in system calls, while file services may be called from all system calls that are related to file operations. Users can specify the system calls that are to be monitored by the monitoring services.

5.4 IMPLEMENTATION

The original version of 3DFS was implemented by modifying the function of mapping names to i-nodes in the kernel. It proved too hard to maintain this version, since it relied on specific UNIX kernel implementations. *n*-DFS has been implemented as a user level library that contains versions many of the UNIX system calls. This library can either be merged with libc, or can be kept separately. Systems that do not have dynamic shared libraries require that programs be relinked in order to get the *n*-DFS extensions.

With the *n*-DFS library installed, each system call that *n*-DFS needs to know about is intercepted and interpreted. As necessary, zero or more system calls are made by *n*-DFS to carry out a given action.

Because *n*-DFS runs in the user address space, it is not possible to guarantee that it will not affect an application that uses it. If the application writes into a random location that happens to lie in its address space, it could overwrite data that is critical to one or more *n*-DFS services. However, *n*-DFS was designed to be as unobtrusive as possible so that it could be used with existing programs. For example, since the vi editor uses the sbrk call to obtain heap memory and expects consecutive calls to sbrk to return contiguous memory, we could not use malloc to get heap memory needed for *n*-DFS. Instead, *n*-DFS maintains a static data area along with a 4K buffer to handle dynamic information. This space is more than adequate to handle the relatively compact per-process information.

The mount system call is used to communicate with *n*-DFS itself. We chose to extend the mount call rather than adding another call, so that any program that needs to use *n*-DFS services directly will not have an unsatisfied external reference when run without the *n*-DFS library. The arguments to mount are chosen so that mount will return an error code if *n*-DFS is not involved.

Each process using *n*-DFS requires tables of information relating to each of its dimensions, and this table needs to be inherited by each child process. With 3DFS, the execve system call inserts an environment variable named "__" to the front of the environment list to pass down these tables. The first system call intercepted by 3DFS reads the environment, extracts this information, and then deletes this environment entry. This creates two problems. One problem is that it is possible for a user program to modify the environment before making any system calls, so that the correct information would not be present. The second problem is that programs that are close to the **ARG_MAX** limit of the size of the argument list plus environment, are pushed over this limit with the additional 3DFS data. To circumvent this problem, *n*-DFS passes down this information in an open file. Since *n*-DFS intercepts the close system call, there is no way that the user program can delete or modify this information before it is read by *n*-DFS. To save the time of creating and unlinking a file, *n*-DFS uses a UNIX pipe whenever the amount of information that is necessary is less then the **PIPE_MAX**, the number of bytes that can safely be written on a pipe without blocking. A second optimization is done when a process that has not made any mount calls executes an exec call, the *n*-DFS table that was passed to this process can be re-used to pass to the child process.

5.4.1 Connect Stream Library (libcs)

n-DFS supports a library, called libcs, to implement external servers. libcs places service names in the file system namespace. At the same time it provides a common interface based on either BSD sockets [Leff83] or System V TLI [ATT89]. (Porting to Microsoft Windows NT is under way.) A *connect stream* is a path name that names a service. Connect stream files allow unrelated processes to rendezvous. A server first creates a connect stream, then each client open of the connect stream received by the server presents a unique bi-directional pipe connection between the client and server. Connect streams may be either *local* or *remote*. Local connections support file descriptor exchange, while remote streams support pipe or datagram semantics.

Most servers reside in the directory "**lib/cs/***proto/service*." *service* is the name of the server executable in this directory. For remote connect streams, the file *hosts* lists the hosts on which the service can be automatically started. If not specified then the file "lib/cs/share" is used. If *hosts* is empty, then the service must be started manually. Otherwise, the service is started by the first user open of the service. Service maintenance is trivial: no modifications to the kernel *init* sequence or *rc* files are necessary.

libcs also supports calls to pack and unpack system call messages that may be sent over stream (socket) pipes. All system calls intercepted by *n*-DFS are supported, and the message format is independent of byte order and word size. System call messages are used to monitor processes, as well as to provide alternate system services.

A glaring omission in the UNIX IP address-port IPC interface is client authentication. In a modern computing environment, services must be able to identify clients, or service integrity may be compromised. Authentication traditionally requires some form of encrypted key exchange between client and server, but such an intrusive mechanism would shatter the file-based illusion of libcs connect streams.

An libcs server enables client authentication when it creates the connect stream. Each client initiates the authentication protocol and handshakes with the server. Rather than invent a new authentication scheme, and in the interest of doing as much work in user space as possible, libcs relies on standard UNIX file access mechanisms for client authentication. The libcs method is based on challenge-response. A client requests a *challenge* sequence from the server. In response, the server sends back two 32-bit numbers in ASCII format. The client then creates a file, visible to all hosts on the local network, with the access time set to the first challenge number and the modify time set to the second challenge number (using the utime(2) system call). In addition, the set-uid, set-gid, user-read and user-write permission bits must be set and all other permission bits must be cleared; on UNIX only the file owner (or root) could create such a file. The client sends the full path name back to the server and the server authenticates the client by stat(2)ing the file and verifying the challenge numbers. The server then uses the file owner as the client user identity. If the file doesn't verify, then the connection is dropped. Otherwise the server sends back an OK acknowledgement and accepts the connection. The client then deletes the authentication file and continues.

Client authentication between server and client hosts that do not share a file system is slightly more complicated. In this case the client uses rsh to run an authentication agent command on the server host. The client and server handshake just as above, but the agent does the file create and delete. In this case remote client authentication is as strong as (or as weak as) rsh authentication.

The main advantage of the libcs authentication is that no new privileged service is required; it is based on mechanisms already present on all UNIX systems.

5.4.2 Shell Interface

At the shell level, the vpath command controls the *n*-DFS namespace. Like other commands that control per-process system information (e.g., cd and umask), vpath is a shell builtin. vpath uses the mount(2) system call, intercepted by *n*-DFS, to specify relationships between pairs of pathnames:

```
$ vpath  path1  path2
```

If *path1* and *path2* are directories, any reference to the directory hierarchy under path1 will be mapped to the ordered union of the *path1* and *path2* hierarchies, where files under *path1* take precedence over files under *path2*. *path2* of the form "/#*" controls the *n*-DFS internal state.

For this case, a *path1* of "-" can serve as a placeholder to preserve the vpath argument pairs. For example,

$ vpath - /#option/debug=5

sets the *n*-DFS debug trace output level to 5.

$ vpath - /#option/trace

prints the intercepted *n*-DFS systems calls on standard error for all child processes.

Replication is specified by first defining the replication service

$ vpath /dev/tcp/share/rpl/user /#fs/rpl/monitor/regular/write/call=open,close,write/ack=write

where "*/dev/tcp/share/rpl/user*" is the pathname of a per-user replication server that is shared among all hosts in the local network. "*/dev/tcp/host/rpl*" names a specific server running on *host*. "/#fs" defines a new file system service. The replication service is a file service that has the name rpl (usage described below), with the following attributes:

- **monitor**
  Intercepted calls are run locally but also passed on to the service.
- **regular**
  Monitors regular files (no directories, special devices, etc.).
- **write**
  Monitors only files open for write.
- **call=...**
  Monitors only these intercepted calls
- **ack=...**
  Blocks for server acknowledgment for these calls

Replication hierarchies are then specified by mounting directories on the replication service:

$ vpath dir1 /#fs/rpl dir2 /#fs/rpl

where rpl is the name from the "/#fs" mount above. The service can be switched off by

$ vpath - /#fs/rpl/off

and on by

$ vpath - /#fs/rpl/on

without breaking the service connection.

Finally, the command vpath with one argument prints out the physical path associated with the input logical path. vpath without arguments lists a complete configuration mapping. This can be saved into a file and used to restore an *n*-DFS configuration some time in the future.

5.5 EVALUATION

To evaluate the performance of *n*-DFS, we measured the overhead of the logical layer introduced by *n*-DFS, and the costs of two services: viewpathing and replications.

5.5.1 Viewpathing Service

We measured the overhead of the logical layer and the performance of the viewpathing service using the Andrew Benchmark [Howa88]. The input to the benchmark is a read-only source subtree consisting of about 70 files. These files are the source codes of an application program and total about 200 kilobytes in size. The benchmark includes five distinct phases as listed in Table 5.1.

MakeDir	Constructs a target subtree that is identical in structure to the source subtree.
Copy	Copies every file from the source subtree to the target subtree.
ScanDir	Recursively traverses the target subtree and examines the status of every file in it. It does not actually read the contents of any file.
ReadAll	Scans every byte of every file in the target subtree once.
Make	Compiles and links all the files in the target subtree.

Table 5.1 Five phases in Andrew benchmark

The hardware for testing is a Solbourne 5/800, running Sun OS 4.1 with a local disk. We compared three cases. In the first case, applications directly access files located on the local disk; we call this a UNIX file system case. In both the second and third cases, applications run on *n*-DFS, which in turn is layered on top of a UNIX file system. There is no viewpathing service defined by users in the second case, while in the third case, applications run on an empty directory which is on top of the source directory. Table 5.2 shows the performance results. The numbers presented in this section were derived from 10 runs, with the average of those runs reported. Although we do not report the standard deviation of the experiments, they were observed to be small.

		n-DFS	
	UNIX File System	No Layer	One Layer
MakeDir	5 sec	5 sec	-
Copy	15 sec	17 sec	-
ScanDir	18 sec	24 sec	25 sec
ReadAll	26 sec	36 sec	39 sec
Make	41 sec	48 sec	49 sec
Total	105 sec	130 sec	-

Table 5.2 Performance results

The second case (i.e., *n*-DFS/No-Layer) shows the overhead of the logical layer introduced by *n*-DFS. Most of this overhead comes from pathname resolution done in *n*-DFS in order to locate mounted services. Basically, *n*-DFS needs to translate a relative pathname to an absolute pathname and then to look up the mapping table for mounted services. In the phases ScanDir and ReadAll, which access individual files using their relative pathnames, this process costs 33%-38% compared with the UNIX case. However, this cost becomes less important when applications do more computation, as in the phase make. The third case, *n*-DFS/One-Layer, shows the overhead of the viewpathing service. As shown in Table 5.2, the overhead is less than 10%.

5.5.2 Replication Service

To understand the overhead of the logical layer, we measured the performance of the prototype using a variety of applications. The hardware for testing includes a Sun 4/75 named condor and a Solbourne 5/800 named gryphon, connected by a 10 Mbps Ethernet. Both machines are running Sun OS 4.1.

We evaluated three cases, each of which consisted of applications running on condor. In the first case, applications accessed files located on the local disk, i.e., on condor, with the standard library libc. In the second case, applications accessed files located on the remote file server, i.e., on gryphon, again with the standard library libc; the Sun Network File System was used to access remote files. In the third case, applications ran on *n*-DFS; the primary file system was located on the local disk and the backup file system on gryphon.

The majority of the overhead comes from the replication mechanism, which is proportional to the number of write calls invoked by the application. According to the number and size of write calls invoked, we have classified applications into three categories: *Light-Write Applications*, *Moderate-Write Applications*, and *Intensive-Write Applications*. The benchmark for testing includes three phases for different categories: in the Light-Write phase, we concatenate files using `cat`, scan every byte using `wc`, and output the result to a file; in the Moderate-Write phase, we compile a large source file using `cc`, and in the Intensive-Write phase, we unravel an archive file using `cpio`.

	UNIX FS	NFS	*n*-DFS
Light-Write	7.75 sec	7.80 sec	7.78 sec
Moderate-Write	13.01 sec	15.00 sec	14.08 sec
Intensive-Write	6.31 sec	12.70 sec	7.72 sec

Table 5.3 Performance results

As Table 5.3 shows, in the Light-Write category, the difference among the three cases was insignificant. In the Moderate-Write category, *n*-DFS exhibits an 8% slowdown compared to the UNIX File System case, but it has better performance than the NFS case. This is because *n*-DFS accesses files located on the local disk, and uses asynchronous communication to pass data to the backup file system. The NFS case, on the other hand, accesses files on the remote file server and synchronously writes data back to the remote file server. Finally, in the Intensive-Write category, the replication in *n*-DFS costs 23% overhead compared to the UNIX File System case. However, *n*-DFS is 40% faster than NFS.

5.6 DISCUSSION

There are many research efforts that share our philosophy of overloading file system semantics to improve system uniformity and utility, software reusability, and customer acceptability. Examples of the research include Watchdogs, Killian's process file system [Kill84], Pseudo Device Drivers, Semantic File System, and Automount daemon [Call89]. All these projects introduce new functionality by modifying the kernel or implementing new drivers. In fact, *n*-DFS's predecessor 3DFS was originally implemented by modifying the kernel. Because it relies on a specific UNIX kernel implementation, 3DFS proved too hard to maintain.

n-DFS, on the other hand, implements a logical layer using the library, which is running on the application's address space. As mentioned above, for systems providing dynamic linking of shared libraries, we are able to replace the standard C shared library with *n*-DFS's library, and applications with dynamic linking may access *n*-DFS without any change. For systems without dynamic linking of shared libraries or applications with static linking, we need to re-link applications with *n*-DFS's library. By porting the library to a variety of platforms, we have shown that the library approach is more portable than modifying kernels or implementing new drivers.

Indeed, most modern UNIX-like operating systems [Ging87, Nels93] support dynamic linking of shared libraries to reduce sizes of program images, and to improve page sharing between different programs running the same libraries. We take advantage of the dynamic linking feature to avoid re-linking applications with *n*-DFS's library.

Sun's Translucent File Service (TFS) [Hend90] embeds a viewpathing mechanism into file systems. Its first implementation used a user-level NFS server (called *tfsd*) that handles all file system operations to TFS files. The second implementation introduced a set of vnode operations in the SunOS kernel, and used *tfsd* only for pathname resolution. While the first implementation suffers I/O performance because all read and write operations to TFS files need to involve *tfsd*, the second implementation depends on a specific kernel architecture and is less portable. Another major difference compared with *n*-DFS is that TFS considers viewpathing information as system-wide, global data. *n*-DFS, on the other hand, considers viewpathing information private to the process, just like the current working directory. However, it is possible to implement an external server in *n*-DFS to handle shared views among multiple users.

Apollo's DOMAIN Software Engineering Environment (DSEE) [Lebl85] implements versioning files by storing all versions of a file in one file on disk. Digital's Vesta Repository [Chiu93] embeds the notion of versioning into file systems to support large-scale software development. DSEE and Vesta require kernel modification.

Systems like Bell Labs' Plan 9 [Pike90] and Sun's Spring [Khal93] provide an architecture for extensible file systems. Plan 9 supports a per-process name space and a message-oriented file system protocol. All services implement a file system-like interface. Users are able to attach new services to the per-process name spaces dynamically. Spring provides a general, global naming structure to name objects with interfaces not restricted to that of the file system. It also provides an architecture that enables the extending of file system functionality by *stacking* new services on top of existing file systems. Like Plan 9 and Spring, *n*-DFS supports an infrastructure that allows new functionality to be added into existing file systems. Unlike Plan 9 and Spring, however, this infrastructure runs in the user address space rather than in the kernel address space. Spring (and Ficus [Guy90]) also supports a *stackable layers* architecture to permit coexistence of multiple functionality.

Finally, for programs with static linking and no source codes available for re-build, we wrote a shell script, named vex, that processes each argument by replacing each virtual file name with a physical name, and then executes the original program. Statically linked programs that spawn child processes that are dynamically linked will inherit the *n*-DFS environment correctly. However, this approach doesn't handle the situation in which the program opens a file whose name is not given as an argument to the program. In addition, monitoring services are not severely curtailed for these processes.

5.7 CONCLUSION

n-DFS provides a generic framework that allows new functionality to be added without any modifications of the kernel or applications. By porting *n*-DFS to a variety of UNIX-like operating systems, we have shown that *n*-DFS is more portable than other systems. By implementing a set of novel services, we have also demonstrated the extensibility and generality of *n*-DFS.

3DFS, the predecessor of *n*-DFS, has been in production use for several years. It is used by several software development organizations at AT&T Bell Laboratories primarily because of the viewpathing capability. *n*-DFS has replaced 3DFS in day-to-day work, and other projects that currently use 3DFS are expected to migrate to *n*-DFS shortly. REPL is currently being used by two projects in AT&T.

Finally, we consider *n*-DFS both as a research target, enabling us to develop an environment for configuration management, and as a research vehicle, enabling us to explore a variety of new system services absent in UNIX-like systems. For example, we are working on the interaction and interface among *n*-DFS and configuration engines (e.g., nmake [Fowl90]) and software process managers (e.g., Provence [Kris93]) to support large scale software developments. We also intend to use *n*-DFS to implement services for different application domains, such as database and information retrieval, that require services with high functionality. Finally, we are interested in porting *n*-DFS to non UNIX-like systems such as Microsoft Windows NT.

REFERENCES

[Allm86] Allman, E. An introduction to the source code control system. In *UNIX Programmer's Manual Supplementary Documents Volume 1*. University of California at Berkeley, April 1986.

[ATT89] AT&T. *UNIX System V Release 3.2—Programming Reference Manual*, 1989.

[Brer88] Brershad, B. and Pinkerton, B. Watchdogs: Extending the UNIX file system. In *USENIX Association 1988 Winter Conference Proceedings*, February 1988.

[Call89] Callaghan, B. and Lyon, T. The Automounter. In *USENIX 1989 Winter Conference Proceedings*, 1989.

[Chiu93] Chiu, S.-Y. and Levin, R. The Vesta Repository: A file system extension for software development. Technical Report 106, Digital Systems Research Center, June 1993.

[Eric84] Erickson, B. and Pellegrin, J. Build - a software construction tool. *Bell System Technical Journal*, 63(6), July 1984.

[Fowl90] Fowler, G. A case for make. *Software—Practice and Experience*, 20(S1):S1/35 – S1/46, July 1990.

[Fowl93] Fowler, G., Huang, Y., Korn, D., and Rao, H. C. A User-level Replicated File System. In *Proceedings of Summer USENIX*, June 1993.

[Giff91] Gifford, D., Jouvelot, P., Sheldon, M., and OToole, J. Semantic File Systems. In *Proceedings of the Thirteenth ACM Symposium on Operating System Principles*, pages 16–25, October 1991.

[Ging87] Gingell, R. A., Lee, M., Dang, X. T., and Weeks, M. S. Shared Libraries in SunOS. In *Proceedings of Summer USENIX*, 1987.

[Guy90] Guy, R., Heidemann, J., Mak, W., Page, T., Popek, G., and Rothmeier, D. Implementation of the Ficus replicated file system. In *USENIX Conference Proceedings*, pages 63–71, June 1990.

[Hend90] Hendricks, D. A filesystem for software development. In *Proceedings of Summer USENIX*, June 1990.

[Howa88] Howard, J. H., Kazar, M. L., Menees, S. G., Nichols, D. A., Satyanarayanan, M., Sidebotham, R. N., and West, M. J. Scale and performance in a distributed file system. *ACM Transactions on Computer Systems*, 6(1):51–81, February 1988.

[Huan93] Huang, Y. and Kintala, C. Software Implemented Fault Tolerance. In *1993 Fault Tolerant Computing Symposium (FTCS23)*, June 1993.

[Khal93] Khalidi, Y. and Nelson, M. Extensible file systems in Spring. In *Proceedings of the Fourteenth ACM Symposium on Operating System Principles*, pages 1–14, December 1993.

[Kill84] Killian, T. Processes as files. In *Proceedings of Winter 1984 USENIX Conference*, June 1984.

[Korn90] Korn, D. and Krell, E. A New Dimension for the Unix File System. *Software—Practice and Experience*, 20(S1):S1/19 – S1/34, July 1990.

[Kout94] Koutsofios, E. and North, S. Applications of graph visualization. In *Proceedings of Graphics Interface 94*, May 1994.

[Krel92] Krell, E. and Krishnamurthy, B. COLA: Customized overlaying. In *Proceedings of the USENIX Winter 1992 Conference*, pages 3–7, 1992.

[Kris91] Krishnamurthy, B. and Rosenblum, D. S. An event-action model of computer-supported cooperative work: Design and implementation. In *Proceedings of the International Workshop on Computer Supported Cooperative Work*, pages 132–145. IFIP TC 6/WG C.5, 1991.

[Kris93] Krishnamurthy, B. and Barghouti, N. S. Provence: A Process Visualization and Enactment Environment. In *Fourth European Software Engineering Conference, ESEC '93*, pages 451–465, Garmisch-Partenkirschen Germany, September 1993. Springer-Verlag. Published as *Lecture Notes in Computer Science* no. 717.

[Lebl85] Leblang, D., Jr., R. C., and Jr., G. M. The DOMAIN software engineering environment for large-scale software development efforts. In *Proceedings of the First International Conference on Computer Workstations*, pages 226–280, November 1985.

[Leff83] Leffler, S. J., Joy, W. N., and Fabry, R. S. 4.2BSD networking implementation notes. In *Unix Programmer's Manual, Volume 2C*. University of California at Berkeley, July 1983.

[Mann93] Mann, T., Birrell, A., Hisgen, A., Jerian, C., and Swart, C. A coherent distributed file cache with directory write-behind. Technical Report 103, System Research Centers, Digital Equipment Corporation, June 1993.

[Nels93] Nelson, M. N. and Hamilton, G. High performance dynamic linking through caching. In *Proceedings of Summer USENIX*, June 1993.

[Pete88] Peterson, L. L. The Profile naming service. *ACM Transactions on Computer Systems*, 6(4):341–364, November 1988.

[Pike90] Pike, R., Presotto, D., Thompson, K., and Trickey, H. Plan 9 from Bell Labs. In *Proceedings of the United Kingdom Unix Users Group*, London, England, July 1990.

[Rao93] Rao, H. C. and Peterson, L. L. Accessing Files in an Internet: The Jade File System. *IEEE Transactions on Software Engineering*, pages 613–624, June 1993.

[Rao94] Rao, H. C. and Skarra, A. A Transparent Service for Synchronized Replication across Loosely-connected, Heterogeneous File Systems. Technical Report, Bell Laboratories, Murray Hill, NJ, 1994.

[Sand85] Sandberg, R., Goldberg, D., Kleiman, S., Walsh, D., and Lyon, B. Design and implementation of the Sun Network File System. In *Proceedings of Summer USENIX*, pages 119–130, June 1985.

[Skar93] Skarra, A. SLEVE: Semantic locking for EVEnt synchronization. In *Proceedings of Ninth International Conference on Data Engineering*, 1993.

[Summ94] Summit, S. Filesystem daemons as a unifying mechanism for network information access.

In *Proceedings of Winter USENIX*, January 1994.
[Sun88] Sun Microsystems, Inc., Mountain View, Calif. *Shared Libraries*, May 1988.
[Tich84] Tichy, W. F. The string-to-string correction problem with block moves. *ACM Transactions on Computer Systems*, 2(4), 1984.
[Tich85] Tichy, W. F. RCS—A System for Version Control. *Software—Practice and Experience*, 15(7):637–654, 1985.
[Welc89] Welch, B. B. and Ousterhout, J. K. Pseudo-File-Systems. Technical Report UCB/CSD 89/499, University of California Berkeley, Berkeley, Calif., 1989.

Trademarks

UNIX is a registered trademark of UNIX System Laboratories. Windows NT is a registered trademark of Microsoft Corporation. SunOs, Solaris, and NFS are trademarks of Sun Microsystems, Inc.

Index

Accueil de Logiciel Futur (ALF) 67
ACID 117
Activation point 123
Activity structure objects (AS-objects) 52–53
Activity Structures Language (ASL) 37–68
Activity Structures Managers (ASM) 57
Ada 79
ADC
  see Aide-de-Camp
Adele 65, 85, 99–133, 139–140
  see also Navigation
  Path expressions
  Query language
Adele configuration manager 99–133
Adele process engine 140, 144
AFTER triggers 125
Aggregate variation 81, 82
Aide-de-Camp 84
ALF
  see Accueil de Logiciel Futur
Andrew Benchmark 149
Apollo
  see DSEE
Apollo's Domain Software Engineering Environment
  see DSEE
APPL/A 67–68
Application, distributed 143
Arbitrary graph 14
  architecture 143
Articulator 64
ASL
  see Activity Structures Language
ASM
  see Activity Structures Manager
AS-objects
  see Activity structure objects
AT & T Bell Laboratories 135–152
Atomicity 43
Attributes 16
Auditing
  build 29
  dependency 30
Automation chaining 43
  rules 43, 65

Benchmark 39–41
Bi-level process modeling languages 37–68
Borison 86
Branch
  model 109
  symbolic 13
  variant 13
build 29, 136
Built objects 121
Business process reengineering 34

C 84, 89
CAD 101
CaseWare 144
Cedar system 85
CFLAGS 90, 91
Chaining 43
Challenge sequence 147
Change set 138
Change Set Model 101
  checked-out 26–27
CI/CO 138
Clearaudit 31
ClearCase 1–36, 83, 85, 144
  Multisite tool 11
  transparent access 7
Clearmake 32
CLF
  see Common Lisp Framework
Client authentication 147
Common Lisp Framework (CLF) 65

Compiler profiles 89
Component variation 82
Composition construct 85
Conditional compilation 79
condor 150
Configuration
  identification process 76
  instance 102
  management 1–36
  model 109
  specification 6
CONNECT 129
Connect stream library (libcs) 146
Consistency
  control 142
  rules 65
Constraint-oriented PMLs 65–66
Contexts 85
Coordination
  control 117, 136
  private 136
  protocol 125

Damokles 129
  data model 103
Dart's overview 83
Darwin's laws 66
DaSC
  see Database, sectors and Cels
Data
  binding 47
  constraints 38, 46–47
Data model, object-oriented 103
Database, sectors and Cels (DaSC) 83–84
Databases
  CAD 101
  historical 101
  temporal 101
Derivation variants 81, 91
Derived object management 86
Design modification 41
Difference predicates 86
Domain software engineering environment
  see DSEE
DOS 119
DSEE (Domain software engineering environment) 85, 86, 151
  enaction model 49–52
Dynamic versioning 121

Encapsulating tools 115
Environment, distributed 9
EPOS 84
ERROR triggers 123
Event notification service 137, 141
Eventmasks 123
Explicit derivation variants 81
Explicit mapping 125
Extended pathname 8

Family 109
Feature terms 84
File mapper 119
File service 148
File system Work Space 119
File systems 138
File trees 140
Fragments–and–attributes 87
Funsoft nets 64

Gandalf 85
Gandalf's System Version Control Environment (SCVE) 85
Generation 50, 51
Generatic Object 105
gryphon 150

Haberman 85
Heimbigner 66
HFSP
  see Hierarchical and Functional Software Process
Hierarchical and Functional Software Process (HFSP) 64
Hierarchical models 21

Implementation 56–61
Implicit derivation variants 81
Instantiation of variants 75
Intensive-Write application 150
Interface 109
International Workshop on Software Version and Configuration Control, 1988 74
Inverted branching 83
ISPW7 38

libcs
  see Connect stream library
Light-Write applications 150
Logical layer 136
Logical versioning 105, 109

make 86
MARVEL strategy language (MSL) 37–68
Melmac 64

Meta constructs 79
Meta program 79
Meta-mechanism 93
Minimal rebuilding 4
Model for Assisted Software Processes (MASP) 67
Models
  hierarchical 21
  repository 4
Moderate-Write applications 150
Modify-propagate 87
Monitoring service 142
Mount system 145
MSL
  see MARVEL strategy language
Multi-Dimensional File System 135–152
Multi-user implementation 38
Multi-variant software 74
Multiple variance 82

n-DFS 135–152
  architecture 143
  services 138
Namespace 17
Naming services 145
Navigation 107
NFS
  see Sun Network File System
nmake 86, 136
NORA environment 84
Notation 42, 45–46

Object Manager System 101, 111
Object types 19, 113
Object, derived 29, 33
Odin 86
Oikos 66
Orion 129
Orthogonal version 83

Parallel development 13
Parallel distributed building 33
Parallel versions 74
Parrot service 137, 143
Path expressions 107
PCEs 121
PCTE 101, 115
PDL
  see Process description language
Permanent variants 80
Perry 85
PML
  see Process modeling language

POST triggers 123
Posteriori configurations 121, 138–139
PRE triggers 125
Predicates 67–68
Priori configurations 123, 138–139
Process constrainers 66
Process description language (PDL) 64
Process management 55
Process modeling languages (PML) 37–68
Process support 140
Process Support Sytstem (PSS) 66
Process Wall 66
Process watch mechanism 143
ProcessWeaver 144
Program variation
  PVITL 76, 94
  PVITS 76, 94
PSS
  see Process Support System

Query language 107

RCS 127, 139
RCS system 101
Realization 109
Rebuilding 4
Recognition
  active 50, 51
  passive 50, 51
Redundancy 78, 79
Reference instance 125
Relation type 125
Release management 4
REPL
  see Tree replication service
Replication service 142, 147
Repository 4
  organisation 76
  space 99, 111
Riddle 39, 45–46, 55
Role collaboration 144–147
Role synchronization 55–56
Rule skeleton 48–49, 54

SCCS 101, 127, 139
SCM 94, 129, 131, 148
SCM systems 86, 101, 123
SCVE
  see Gandalf's System Version Control Environment
SEE 101, 103, 148
Selection 107
Selector files 84

Servers 144
Shape 88
Shape utility 73
Shapefiles 89
ShapeTools 81, 85, 88
Shared sections 79
Sharing data 74
Shell interface 147
Single source variation 79, 81
SNFS
  see Sun Network File System
Software enterprises 1–36
Software management 101
Software process modeling 37
Software variants 73, 74, 76
Standard repository (model) 4
Static variables 93
Strategy language 37–68
Sub-databases 111, 133
Sun Network File System (NFS) 143
Sun's Translucent File Service (TFS) 151
Synchronization 41
System call 143
System model 85, 86

Tasks 64
Tempo 144
Temporal evolution 94
Temporal versioning 119
Temporary variants 80
TFS
  see Sun's Translucent File Service
Tool constraints 47
Topology 38
Topology-oriented PMLs 61–65
TQuel 105
Transaction 138
Translucent File Service
  see Sun's Translucent File Service
Transparency 6
Tree replication service (REPL) 137, 142
Trigger execution model 125
Triggers 16, 35, 65, 140

UNIX 48, 121, 135, 136, 139, 140, 145, 149

VARCFLAGS 90
Variables 93
  see also Static variables
  Variant Variables

Variant
  authoring 87
  branches 77
  Builds 86
  change management 76
  combination 82
  definition 89
  management 73–95, 80
  path 92
  segregation 77–78, 94
  variables 93
Variants, instantiation 75
Version control 77
Version selection, rule-based 23, 25
Versioning service 137, 141
vex 133
Viewpathing service 136, 137, 140, 148–149
Visual process manager (VPM(137, 142
VMS 121
Voodoo system 83
VPATH 140, 147
VPM
  see Visual process manager

Watchd Daemon 143
WindowsMods 84
Work Environment 129
Work Space 99, 111, 138
  Workflow managers 34

Zeller 84